CISTERCIAN STUDIES SERIES:
NUMBER TWO HUNDRED EIGHTY

This Is My Body

Eucharistic Theology and Anthropology in the Writings of Gertrude the Great of Helfta

Ella Johnson

α

Cistercian Publications
www.cistercianpublications.org

LITURGICAL PRESS
Collegeville, Minnesota
www.litpress.org

A Cistercian Publications title published by Liturgical Press

Cistercian Publications
Editorial Offices
161 Grosvenor Street
Athens, Ohio 45701
www.cistercianpublications.org

1   2   3   4   5   6   7   8   9

Library of Congress Cataloging-in-Publication Data

Names: Johnson, Ella L., author.
Title: This is my body : Eucharistic theology and anthropology in the
    writings of Gertrude the great of Helfta / Ella Johnson.
Description: Collegeville, Minnesota : Cistercian Publications, 2020. |
    Series: Cistercian studies; number two hundred eighty | Includes
    bibliographical references. | Summary: "Examines how the writings of
    the thirteenth-century nun Gertrude the Great of Helfta articulate an
    innovative relationship between a person's eucharistic devotion and
    her body"—Provided by publisher.
Identifiers: LCCN 2019036576 (print) | LCCN 2019036577 (ebook) |
    ISBN 9780879072803 (paperback) | ISBN 9780879075804 (epub) |
    ISBN 9780879075804 (mobi) | ISBN 9780879075804 (pdf)
Subjects: LCSH: Gertrude, the Great, Saint, 1256–1302. | Lord's Supper |
    Human body—Religious aspects—Christianity.
Classification: LCC BX4700.G6 J64 2020 (print) | LCC BX4700.G6 (ebook)
    | DDC 234/.163092—dc23
LC record available at https://lccn.loc.gov/2019036576
LC ebook record available at https://lccn.loc.gov/2019036577

To my teachers

Contents

List of Abbreviations

Journals and Series

CCCM	Corpus Christianorum. Continuatio Mediaevalis
CCSL	Corpus Christianorum. Series Latina
CF	Cistercian Fathers series. Cistercian Publications
CS	Cistercian Studies series. Cistercian Publications
CSQ	*Cistercian Studies Quarterly*
PG	Patrologiæ cursus completus, series graeca. Ed. J.-P. Migne. 162 volumes. Paris, 1857–1866.
PL	Patrologiæ cursus completus, series latina. 221 volumes. Paris, 1844–1864.
RB	*Regula Benedicti*
SBOp	Sancti Bernardi opera. Ed. J. Leclercq, H. M. Rochais, C. H. Talbot. Rome: Editiones Cistercienses, 1957–1977.
SCh	Sources Chrétiennes. Les Éditions du Cerf

The Works of Gertrude the Great of Helfta

CF 35	Gertrud the Great of Helfta. *The Herald of God's Loving Kindness, Books One and Two*. Trans. Alexandra Barratt. Kalamazoo, MI: Cistercian Publications, 1991.
CF 49	Gertrud the Great of Helfta. *Spiritual Exercises*. Trans. Gertrud Jaron Lewis and Jack Lewis. Kalamazoo, MI: Cistercian Publications, 1989.

CF 63   Gertrud the Great of Helfta. *The Herald of God's Loving Kindness, Book Three.* Trans. Alexandra Barratt. Kalamazoo, MI: Cistercian Publications, 1999.

CF 85   Gertrud the Great of Helfta. *The Herald of God's Loving Kindness, Book Four.* Trans. Alexandra Barratt. Collegeville, MN: Cistercian Publications, 2018.

SCh 127   Gertrude d'Helfta. *Oeuvres spirituelles I: Les Exercices.* Trans. Jacques Hourlier and Albert Schmitt. Paris: Les Éditions du Cerf, 1967.

SCh 139   Gertrude d'Helfta. *Oeuvres spirituelles II: Le Héraut, Livres I et II.* Trans. Pierre Doyère. Paris: Les Éditions du Cerf, 1968.

SCh 143   Gertrude d'Helfta. *Oeuvres spirituelles III: Le Héraut, Livre III.* Trans. Pierre Doyère. Paris: Les Éditions du Cerf, 1968.

SCh 255   Gertrude d'Helfta. *Oeuvres spirituelles IV: Le Héraut, Livre IV.* Trans. Jean-Marie Clément, the nuns of Wisques, and Bernard de Vregille. Paris: Les Éditions du Cerf, 1978.

SCh 331   Gertrude d'Helfta. *Oeuvres spirituelles V: Le Héraut, Livre V.* Trans. Jean-Marie Clément, the nuns of Wisques, and Bernard de Vregille. Paris: Les Éditions du Cerf, 1986.

Other Works from Helfta

BSG   *Book of Special Grace.* Mechthild of Hackeborn. *The Booke of Gostlye Grace of Mechtild of Hackeborn.* Ed. Theresa A. Halligan. Toronto: Pontifical Institute of Mediaeval Studies, 1979.

FL   Mechthild of Magdeburg. *The Flowing Light of the Godhead.* Trans. Frank Tobin. New York/Mahwah, NJ: Paulist Press, 1998.

Licht   *The Flowing Light of the Godhead (Fliessende Licht der Gottheit).* Mechthild of Magdeburg. Ed. Hans Neumann

	and Gisela Vollmann-Profe. Munich: Artemis-Verlag, 1990, 1993.
LSG	*Liber Specialis Gratiae.* Mechthild of Hackeborn. Vol. 2 of *Revelationes Gertrudianae ac Mechtildianae.* Ed. Louis Paquelin. Paris: H. Oudin, 1877.

Augustine's Works

Civ Dei	De civitate Dei
Conf	Confessiones
De doc	De doctrina christiana
De Trin	De Trinitate
Div qu	De diversis quæstionibus
En in Ps	Enarratio in Psalmo
Ep(p	Epistola(e, letter(s
Gen lit	De Genesi ad litteram
Lib arb	De libero arbitrio
S(S	Sermo, sermones

Bernard's Works

Apo	Apologia ad Guillelmum abbatem
Asc	Sermo in ascensione domini
Conv	Sermo de conversione ad clericos
Csi	De consideratione
Dil	Liber de diligendo Deo
Div	Sermon de diversis
Ep(p	Epistola(e, letter(s
Hum	Liber de gradibus humilitatis et superbiæ
Nat	Sermo in nativitate domini
SC	Sermo super Cantica canticorum
Sent	Sententiae

Origen's Works

Cant   In Canticum Canticorum

Cels   Contra Celsum

Comm in Rom   Commentarii in epistulam ad Romanos

Hom 1–28 in Num   Homiliæ in Numeros

In Luc Fragm   Fragmenta in Lucam

Jo   Commentarii in evangelium Joannis

Princ   De principiis

Thomas Aquinas's Work

ST   Summa Theologiae

Acknowledgments

This book began, in its earliest form, in my doctoral dissertation, directed by Dr. Robert Sweetman, whose wise guidance has brought much depth and breadth to my fledgling academic interests and insights. This book and much of my scholarly development leading up to it is a result of his dedication, thoroughness, encouragement, enthusiasm, and instruction. Yet I would have not dreamed of writing such a book had it not been for the work of Caroline Walker Bynum and others following her, like Barbara Newman and Amy Hollywood, who wrote of medieval women in such eloquent ways.

Second, I must thank other teachers from whom I have had the pleasure to learn about medieval writers: Patricia Donohue first introduced me to this study; Gill Goulding, CJ, witnessed to me a study of these women with her own astute theological wisdom and personal integrity; and Ellen Leonard, CSJ, blazed new trails for women in theological scholarship and first led me and countless others to an understanding of God through the lens of feminism. Other colleagues at the University of Toronto deserve special mention. Reid B. Locklin has been a supportive friend and an inspiring mentor to me, both as a scholar and a teacher. Our writing group, including Reid Locklin, Iris J. Gildea, Caitriona Brennan, Michael O'Connor, Alison More, and Colleen Shantz, has given my work much needed peer editing and has provided me with lively discussion and encouragement for the journey.

Many thanks also go to my colleagues at St. Ambrose University and St. Bernard's School of Theology and Ministry for their support, especially Patricia Schoelles, SSJ, and Devadasan Premnath. In addition, I am grateful to the colleagues and friends I have met through the Wabash Center of Teaching Theology and Religion. Special thanks goes to Stephen G. Ray, Jr., Amy Oden, Paul Myhre, and Ruth Anne Reese, who affirmed my vocation to teaching and emboldened my pursuit of justice.

I also owe a great deal to the editor of this book, Marsha Dutton, who has provided me with fresh insights and new resources along the way. She has also convinced me of the dullness of metawriting. The general index for this book was produced by my St. Ambrose University student, Kayleigh Oleson. I am grateful for her careful and diligent work on this tedious task.

Palgrave Macmillan and *Viator* have graciously permitted me to reprint portions of my previously published work with them. I also owe a debt of gratitude to the anonymous readers of my work there, who have sharpened my thought.

I must especially thank the small but dedicated circle of Helfta scholars, especially Sr. Ann Marie Caron, Anna Harrison, Laura M. Grimes, Gertrud Jaron Lewis, and Else Marie Wiberg Pedersen. Through formal meetings at academic conferences and informal chats over email, I have learned much about our subject and have been refreshed with new scholarly energy and enthusiasm. Just as for the Helfta women themselves, I have found that our collaboration and conversation generates theology.

Finally, this book would not be possible without the love and support I have received from people not directly related to my studies. Kelly Bourke, Roslyn Karaban, Deepa Premnath, The Rev. Cheyanna Losey, Ari Anderson, and Sr. Nancy Charlesworth have been very special friends to me. The support, encouragement, and joy I have received from my spouse, Germano Noce, throughout the twists and turns of my academic career, have meant everything to me. I wrote this book during the time my daughter, Isa, was one-and-half to three-and-half years old. She has been my delight and, at the same time, has necessitated childcare to sustain my writing. Without my mother-in-law, Franca Noce, and my mother, Vicky Johnson, this book would have not been possible. For them I am truly grateful.

As Gertrude herself attested, writing can be a painful process. She suffered migraines and headaches and even once lost her pen! Through these times, I was reminded to persevere by her—and all others, especially today when it is just as much needed, who work for social justice and equality.

Preface

In the last few decades, a scholarly trend has emerged to re-appropriate the lives and writings of women in the history of Christian spirituality. Motivating this trend, what Elisabeth Schüssler Fiorenza termed a "hermeneutics of remembrance," is the desire to illumine the female half of the Christian tradition, which has been obscured by an almost exclusive focus on men.[1] The work of scholars heeding this call has led to the production of anthologies like *Her Story: Women in Christian Tradition*, and *Women & Christianity*.[2] As a result the standard canon of holy women in Christian history (at least what I was aware of as a young Christian girl), comprising Clare of Assisi, Catherine of Siena, Teresa of Avila, and Thérèse of Lisieux, has been broadened and extended to include women such as Hildegard of Bingen, Hadewijch of Antwerp, Mechthild of Magdeburg, Julian of Norwich, and Gertrude the Great of Helfta.

While reclaiming these women for Christian historical consciousness has been an important scholarly contribution, this work also has a problematic tendency to categorize them within the "female tradition," as if they were a homogenous group and isolated from the theological ideas and spiritual practices of their male contemporaries. As Grace Jantzen has shown, the recovery of women's lost history has tended to the essentialism of women and thus their further marginalization. This tendency is most

---

[1] Elisabeth Schüssler Fiorenza, *Bread Not Stone: The Challenge of Feminist Biblical Interpretation* (Boston: Beacon Press, 1984), 15–22.

[2] Barbara MacHaffie, *Her Story: Women in Christian Tradition* (Minneapolis: Fortress, 2006); Mary T. Malone, *Women & Christianity*, 3 vols. (Maryknoll, NY: Orbis Books, 2000).

evident in the false, yet sharp distinction that has been made between women who are categorized as "mystics" and male theologians and philosophers.[3] Of course, writings penned by men and women in Christian history differ. Medieval women, for instance, did not write in the scholastic mode of their male contemporaries, because they were denied the training; instead, they wrote in the only genre available to them, in visionary accounts and devotional instruction. But the difference in genre should not be understood as an essential one of gender, that is, arising from a false assumption that women did not have or write about theological ideas. Such a bias toward traditional genres of philosophy and theology serves only further to conceal rather than to reveal women's place in the history of Christianity.

A clearer and more accurate picture demands beginning to read the female-authored devotional texts that have begun to be recovered with a view to their theology.[4] The list of women writers in Christian history could then be celebrated rightly—not just for their holiness, but also for their scholarship, not just as mystics but also as theologians. Women would then receive the kind of theological authority accorded to traditional male authors in Christian history (e.g., Augustine, Aquinas, Bernard of Clairvaux). Illustrating the fact that much work needs to be done to achieve this ideal is that when Hildegard of Bingen was recognized recently as "Doctor of the Church," she became only the fourth woman on the list, alongside thirty-two men.

This study aims to contribute to the project of women's theological recovery by closely examining the theology in the devotional and visionary writings of Gertrude the Great of Helfta. Gertrude belonged to the thirteenth-century Cistercian convent of Helfta during its heyday of liturgical, contemplative, and scholarly activity, and like many other medieval women religious she taught and wrote within her community. Her two extant works— *Legatus memorialis abundantiae divinae pietatis* (*The Herald of the Memorial of the Abundance of Divine Love*), consisting of Gertrude's

---

[3] Grace Jantzen, *Power, Gender, and Christian Mysticism* (Cambridge: Cambridge University Press, 1995), 2–4.

[4] Margaret Ruth Miles, *Practicing Christianity: Critical Perspectives for an Embodied Spirituality* (New York: Crossroad, 1988), 4.

vita, autobiography, and visionary accounts, and *Documenta spiritualium exercitionum* (*Teachings of Spiritual Exercises*), containing
seven liturgically based meditations—are highly erudite and
astute. Gertrude's two works, along with two others (Mechthild
of Magdeburg's *The Flowing Light of the Godhead* and *The Book of
Special Grace* [*Liber specialis gratiae*], associated with Mechthild of
Hackeborn), form the largest extant body of female-authored
writing from that period.[5] Nevertheless, Gertrude studies are still
nascent. Of the valuable scholarly work on Gertrude that has been
conducted, much falls within the four following categories:
history,[6] literariness,[7] gender,[8] and (the largest category of all)

[5] Caroline Walker Bynum, *Jesus as Mother: Studies in the Spirituality of the
High Middle Ages* (Berkeley: University of California Press, 1982), 174.

[6] For examples of historical studies, see Caroline Walker Bynum, "Women
Mystics in the Thirteenth Century: The Case of the Nuns of Helfta," in *Jesus
as Mother: Studies in the Spirituality of the High Middle Ages* (Berkeley: Univer-
sity of California Press, 1982), 186–209; Anna Harrison, "Sense of Community
Among the Nuns at Helfta," Ph.D. dissertation, Columbia University, 2007;
Anna Harrison " 'Oh! What Treasure is in this Book?' Writing, Reading, and
Community at the Monastery of Helfta," *Viator* 39, no. 1 (2008): 75–106; Anna
Harrison, "I Am Wholly Your Own: Liturgical Piety and Community Among
the Nuns of Helfta," *Church History* 78, no. 3 (2009): 549–83; Mary Jeremy
Finnegan, *The Women of Helfta: Scholars and Mystics* (Athens, GA: University
of Georgia Press, 1991).

[7] Claudia Eliass, *Die Frau ist die Quelle der Weisheit: Weibliches Selbstverständ-
nis in der Frauenmystik des 12. und 13. Jahrhunderts*, Frauen in Geschichte und
Gesellschaft, Band 28 (Pfaffenweiler: Centaurus-Verlangsgesellschaft, 1995);
Gertrud Jaron Lewis, "Gertrud of Helfta's *Legatus divinae pietatis* and *ein botte
der götlichen miltekeit*: A Comparative Study of Major Themes," in *Mysticism:
Medieval and Modern*, ed. Valerie Lagorio (Salzburg: Institut für Anglistik und
Amerikanistik, 1986), 58–71.

[8] See for example Mary Jeremy Finnegan, " 'Similitudes' in the Writings of
Saint Gertrude of Helfta," *Mediaeval Studies* 19 (1957): 48–54; Mary Jeremy
Finnegan, "Idiom of Women Mystics," *Mystics Quarterly* 13 (1987): 65–72;
Johanna Schwalbe, "Musik in der Mystik: Zur Sprache der Musik in den
Schriften der hl. Gertrud von Helfta," *Erbe und Auftrag* 71 (1995): 108–24;
Maren Ankermann, "Der 'Legatus divinae pietatis'—Gestaltete Mystik?" in
Freiheit des Herzens: Mystik bei Gertrud von Helfta, ed. Michael Bangert, Mystik
und Mediävistik (Münster: Lit, 2004), 37–56; Maren Ankermann, *Gertrud die
Grosse von Helfta: eine Studie zum Spannungsverhältnis von religiöser Erfahrung
und literarischer Gestaltung in mystischen Werken* (Göppingen: Kümmerle
Verlag, 1997).

spirituality.[9] Yet aside from the brilliant work of Michael Bangert, Laura Grimes, and, most recently, Claire Jones,[10] very few studies on Gertrude belong to the category of theology.

This book has a theological focus. It examines the extensive eucharistic theology and anthropology that Gertrude presents in her visionary accounts and devotional instructions, in particular the innovative relationship she articulates between a person's eucharistic devotion and that person's body. This study attends to her references to the biblical, monastic, and theological traditions, including ideas about the spiritual and corporeal senses, in order to illuminate the positive role she assigns to the body in making spiritual progress.

Chapter one introduces Gertrude and her writings, and chapter two discusses the relevant details of her monastic context, with the next two chapters situating Gertrude within the tradition of

---

[9] Jean Leclercq, "Liturgy and Mental Prayer in the Life of Saint Gertrude," *Sponsa Regis* 32, no. 1 (September 1960): 1–5; Maria Teresa Porcile Santiso, "Saint Gertrude and the Liturgy," *Liturgy* 26, no. 3 (1992): 53–84; Cyprian Vaggagini, "The Example of a Mystic: St. Gertrude and Liturgical Spirituality," in *Theological Dimensions of the Liturgy* (Collegeville: Liturgical Press, 1976), 740–803; Gertrud Jaron Lewis, "*Libertas Cordis*: The Concept of Inner Freedom in St. Gertrud the Great of Helfta," CSQ 25, no. 1 (1990): 65–74; Michael Casey, "Gertrud of Helfta and Bernard of Clairvaux: A Reappraisal," *Tjurunga* 35 (1988): 3–23; Miriam Schmitt, "Freed to Run with Expanded Heart: The Writings of Gertrud of Helfta and RB," CSQ 25, no. 3 (1990): 219–32; Ann W. Astell, " 'Hidden Manna': Bernard of Clairvaux, Gertrude of Helfta, and the Monastic Art of Humility," in *Eating Beauty: the Eucharist and the Spiritual Arts of the Middle Ages* (Ithaca, NY: Cornell University Press, 2006), 62–98; Sabine Spitzlei, *Erfahrungsraum Herz: Zur Mystik des Zisterzienserinnenklosters Helfta im 13. Jahrhundert* (Stuttgart-Bad Canstatt: Frommann-Holzboog, 1991); Spitzlei's work remains the standard study on the sacred heart at Helfta.

[10] Michael Bangert, "A Mystic Pursues Narrative Theology: Biblical Speculation and Contemporary Imagery in Gertrude of Helfta," *Magistra* 2, no. 2 (Winter 1996): 3–20; see also his German work, *Demut in Freiheit: Studien zur geistlichen Lehre im Werk Gertruds von Helfta*, Studien zur systematischen und spirituellen Theologie 21 (Würzburg: Echter, 1997); Laura Marie Grimes, "Theology as Conversation: Gertrude of Helfta and her Sisters as Readers of Augustine," Ph.D. diss., University of Notre Dame, 2004; Claire Jones, "*Hostia jubilationis*: Psalm Citation, Eucharistic Prayer and Mystical Union in Gertrude of Helfta's *Exercitia Spiritualia*," *Speculum* 89, no. 4 (2014): 1005–39.

the doctrine of spiritual senses. She integrates the legacy of the doctrine of spiritual senses into her theology of the Eucharist while making some important innovations of her own. Specifically, chapter three provides an overview of the legacy of the doctrine of the spiritual senses, with a focus on the doctrines that Gertrude used as source and authority in her own writings, those of Origen, Augustine, and Bernard of Clairvaux. Chapter four turns to Gertrude's teaching on the spiritual senses, demonstrating the way she left behind some of the more dualistic aspects of her sources while exploiting the more affirmative concepts for bodily forms of divine union.

Chapter five goes deeper in its textual analysis of Gertrude's doctrine. It takes seriously the devotional genre of Gertrude's writings and the mode in which she teaches her innovative eucharistic theology and anthropology. Gertrude's writings are overtly liturgical. They rely upon epistemological principles and pedagogical techniques beyond those used by the schoolmen in theological treatises, recognized in the traditional sense. Her writings presuppose an epistemology based upon her liturgical experience and that of her intended audience. She painstakingly constructs her eucharistic theology and anthropology with conscious use of multiple references to sensory language, ritual actions, and liturgical tropes and images. Mary Carruthers' scholarship on medieval monastic contemplative texts provides the hermeneutical key here for examining Gertrude's rhetorical strategy, as she argues that medieval meditative texts are best viewed as a "craft of thinking," because, as she points out, they entail more than "mental contemplation" but in fact frequently use "tools . . . made of language and image, primarily the tropes and figures and schemes discovered in the Bible, the liturgy, and the arts." In the idiom of medieval monasticism, Carruthers says, people do not " 'have' ideas, they 'make' them."[11] Of necessity, then, in order to more fully examine Gertrude's theology, chapter

---

[11] Mary Carruthers, *The Craft of Thought: Meditation, Rhetoric, and the Making of Images, 400–1200*, Cambridge Studies in Medieval Literature, 34 (Cambridge: Cambridge University Press, 1998), 3–5.

five carefully considers the function and place of the liturgical tropes and images that she weaves throughout her texts.

The work of chapter five paves the way for chapter six, which discusses the gender implications of Gertrude's use of liturgical tropes and images. Her works, specifically her *Spiritual Exercises*, demand this examination, as she writes them consciously from the feminine perspective, using feminine grammatical endings (e.g., *captiva* for "prisoner"). The chapter again considers the tools of sensory language and liturgical image that Gertrude uses to craft her works, but here the focus is on significant moments when Gertrude inserts feminine nouns or uses feminine grammatical endings. In the final analysis, the chapter shows that the way Gertrude crafts her *Spiritual Exercises* transforms fixed dichotomies between male and female.

Yet the question remains as to whether Gertrude's innovations build upon previous understandings of being a woman. Chapter seven takes up this question, looking beyond Gertrude to her female religious contemporaries and considering the gender conventions modern historians have identified in the writings of these women. For instance, Caroline Walker Bynum has shown that many medieval women writers exploited the ancient association of the female with the flesh as the means by which women could achieve union with the humanity of Christ and therefore sanctification.[12] In addition, Barbara Newman has identified the "womanChrist" model in women's writings, which claims the possibility that woman qua woman could imitate Christ by using feminine inflections and thus achieve a high-ranking religious status in the spiritual realm.[13] Indeed Gertrude is not alone as a medieval woman reimagining deeply rooted institutions in the structure of Christian thought to manipulate male/female di-

[12] Caroline Walker Bynum, *Holy Feast and Holy Fast: The Religious Significance of Food to Medieval Women* (Berkeley: University of California Press, 1987), 260–69.

[13] Barbara Newman, *From Virile Woman to WomanChrist: Studies in Medieval Religion and Literature*, Middle Ages Series (Philadelphia: University of Pennsylvania Press, 1995), 3.

chotomies.[14] The chapter shows how elements of Gertrude's rhetorical strategy both correspond with and depart from that of her female religious contemporaries. For example, like many of her contemporaries, she was able to retain an impeccably orthodox piety while also and at the same time creatively claiming a female religious identity and ranking herself equal to, if not above, men. She also claimed an association with Christ's humanity, yet unlike so many of her contemporaries, she does not gender this association, playing on the connection of femaleness with flesh. The chapter concludes by suggesting socio-cultural reasons for Gertrude's understanding of being a woman.

Ultimately, Gertrude's affirmative embodied spirituality is what speaks to the current wave of excitement about other medieval women mystics like Hildegard of Bingen. What is attracting contemporary readers to them is what Bynum alluded to in her ground-breaking work a few decades ago, that these women's voices—which are alongside and distinct from the prevailing male voices of medieval religion—stress continuity and reconciliation between concrete earth and ethereal divine, and they emphasize the role of physicality in religiosity.[15] For this reason, their voices can point today's people in the direction of a search for positive religious symbols of the human person. This book aims to contribute to that work.

---

[14] Both medieval men and women challenged and broke down gender dichotomies through their self-presentations and writings. See especially Elizabeth L'Estrange and Alison More, "Representing Medieval Genders and Sexualities in Europe: Construction, Transformation, and Subversion, 600–1530," in *Representing Medieval Genders and Sexualities in Europe: Construction, Transformation, and Subversion, 600–1530* (New York and London: Routledge, 2011), 1–13.

[15] Caroline Walker Bynum, ". . . And Women His Humanity: Female Imagery in the Religious Writing of the Later Middle Ages," in *Gender and Religion: On the Complexity of Symbols*, ed. Caroline Walker Bynum, Steven Harrell, and Paula Richman (Boston: Beacon Press, 1986), 257–88; see especially 280. See also Bynum, *Jesus as Mother*; Bynum, *Holy Feast and Holy Fast*; Bynum, *Fragmentation and Redemption: Essays on Gender and the Human Body in Medieval Religion* (New York: Zone Books, 1991).

xxii   *This Is My Body*

Yet the overarching aim of the book, which I have sought to make transparent at its outset, is to show that Gertrude's highly nuanced and sophisticated theology merits a place in the canon of medieval theological works because of its originality. Her eucharistic theology is different from traditional forms, because it is delivered in hybrid form—i.e., as a blend of scholastic and vernacular theology. Gertrude writes in Latin and draws from scholastic sources, but she does so in the genre of visionary literature and devotional instruction. As she depends on both traditions, her theology cannot be characterized as belonging wholly to one or the other. In this regard, Gertrude contributes in a distinctive way to what Gary Macy has called "the legacy of diversity" in thirteenth- and fourteenth-century eucharistic thought. Macy, of course, tries to overturn the stubborn notion that all medieval eucharistic theology may be reduced to the thought of one influential Dominican, Thomas Aquinas.[16] With his focus on theology done in the traditional sense, Macy's studies uncover a great deal of theological diversity but still exclude female writers.

Because of the recovery project of the last few decades, a goldmine of female-authored texts is now available for contemporary theology. Yet the scholarly bias against devotional texts still has to be shed. Through attention to the sophisticated, creative, and complex theology of one medieval woman, other readers and scholars may be prompted not only to recognize but also to turn to the devotional writings of women in history for the innovative theological insights they offer today.

---

[16] Gary Macy, *Treasures from the Storeroom: Medieval Religion and the Eucharist* (Collegeville, MN: Liturgical Press, 1999), 36–58.

CHAPTER ONE

Gertrude of Helfta and Her Writings

The honorary title *la magna* ("the Great") was accorded to Gertrude of Helfta in 1738 by Cardinal Prosper Lambertini in his treatise *De servorum Dei beatificatione et beatorum canonizatione*, making her the only woman in monastic history to receive the title. The cardinal, who would later become Benedict XIV, the "scholar pope," was at that time acting as the *promotor fidei*, popularly known as the "Devil's advocate," or the canon lawyer appointed to argue against the case of a candidate for beatification and canonization.[1] It is curious that as Devil's advocate he would bestow the honorary title on Gertrude, especially in view of the lack of details surrounding her life and work. Gertrude is a woman whose surname and birthplace are unknown, who never held an official position in her religious community, who is not credited with any remarkable prophecies or miracles,[2] who had

---

[1] Ludwig von Pastor, *The History of the Popes*, trans. E. F. Peeler (St. Louis: Herder, 1949), 35:25; Mary Jeremy Finnegan, *The Women of Helfta: Scholars and Mystics* (Athens, GA: University of Georgia Press, 1991), 70.

[2] The *Herald* attributes to Gertrude only two prophecies: the first concerns the results of an imperial election, and the second is Gertrude's foreknowledge of her community's safety, during the region's assault by armed forces. Editions and translation of Gertrude's works cited in this book are listed in the List of Abbreviations (pp. ix–xii) and in the Bibliography (pp. 213–36) (Gertrude, *Herald* 1.2.3 [CF 35:43; SCh 139:128–30]; Gertrude, *Herald* 3.48.1 [CF 63:153; SCh 143:214]). Gertrude is also credited with only two miracles: stopping a rainstorm and finding a writing pen in a haystack (Gertrude, *Herald* 1.13.1–3 [CF 35:79–80; SCh 139:190, 192]).

no real prominence in the history of her country, whose burial site is not recorded,[3] and whose original writings have been lost. In the void of information about Gertrude, all that remains are late medieval copies of only two of her works. It could only have been these writings, then, that impressed the studious cardinal enough to call Gertrude "the Great."

Gertrude follows the model of Jesus himself, who left behind only his words. The Helfta nuns relate that in one of Gertrude's encounters with him, after she had expressed her desire for a relic of his cross, he told her that "the most precious relics you can have are the words that express the deepest love of my heart."[4] Like Jesus, the best surviving memorial of Gertrude is not a piece of her habit or bones, but rather her words.[5]

Shortly after Gertrude's death, several distinguished theologians and lecturers of her day examined and approved her writings. As the *approbatio doctorum* appended to some of the copies of her manuscripts indicates, one university professor was so inspired by her words that "From then onwards he happily spent his whole life in wonderful devotion and longing for God."[6] Although Gertrude was never formally canonized, the memorial of her holy and erudite words caused her feast day, November 16, to be included in the Roman martyrology in 1678 and to be extended to the entire Roman Catholic Church on July 20, 1738.[7]

Because Gertrude was a medieval nun and not a schoolman, her authority as a writer and theologian had to be established. Thus the kind of theological authority she developed and claimed and the strategy she used to creatively reinforce it are noteworthy.

---

[3] Curiously enough, Gertrude wrote a prayer for a mystical death in her *Exercises* petitioning that her tomb be unknown (Gertrude, *Exercises* 4.240–43 [CF 49:66; SCh 127:140]).

[4] Gertrude, *Herald* 4.52.3 (CF 85:258; SCh 255:434).

[5] Finnegan, *The Women of Helfta*, 70.

[6] Gertrude, *Herald* 1, Endorsement and Authorization (CF 35:29; SCh 139:104, 106).

[7] Pierre Doyère, "Introduction," in Gertrude, *Herald* (SCh 139:31). Gertrude's feast day was first proposed for November 17 but had to be moved because of a full liturgical calendar (Finnegan, *The Women of Helfta*, 149).

Early Life: From a Grammarian to a Theologian

Information about Gertrude's life is limited to her *vita* in Book One of the *Herald*, composed by one or two anonymous writers, presumably contemporary to Gertrude at Helfta, sometime between 1290 and the time of Gertrude's death in 1301 or 1302.[8] It is a typical hagiography in that it testifies to the impeccable character and extraordinary virtue of the saint's life. But it lacks details commonly found in a *vita* (e.g., surname, testimonies of miracles, prophecies). Moreover, it also seems to have been written in conversation with Gertrude herself, who reflected upon and related her experiences to the writers. Unfortunately, all other chronicles, documents, and letters containing evidence for Gertrude's life were destroyed in the disasters that struck the Helfta community.[9]

What is known of Gertrude is that she was born on the feast of the Epiphany in 1256,[10] and that she appeared at the door of the monastery at Helfta as an orphan, just shy of five years old.[11] The Helfta nuns received Gertrude in the monastery school and recounted that she quickly distinguished herself from the other girls there with her keen intellect and innate charm. They marveled at the wisdom she showed at such a young age: "She was indeed tender in years and body, but in her perceptiveness old and wise: lovable, quick, articulate, and so consistently easy to teach that all those who heard her were astonished. In this way she passed the years of childhood and youth with a pure heart and an eager delight in the liberal arts, shielded by the Father of mercies from the many childish aberrations that often occur at that age."[12]

---

[8] The authorship of the *Herald* is discussed further below. Gertrude, *Herald* 1 Prol.1–8 (CF 35:31–34; SCh 139:108–16).

[9] Finnegan, *The Women of Helfta*, 4–5.

[10] Pierre Doyère, "Introduction," in Gertrude, *Herald* (SCh 139:13).

[11] Passages in the *Herald* suggest Gertrude was an orphan (Gertrude, *Herald* 1.16.5; 5.17.1 [CF 35:92; SCh 139:216; 331:176]). That Gertrude's surname was not recorded at Helfta, coupled with the fact that her hagiography does not celebrate her as forgoing family wealth, also supports the conclusion that Gertrude was an orphan (Finnegan, *The Women of Helfta*, 69).

[12] Gertrude, *Herald* 1.1.1; 2.1.2 (CF 35:38; 101; SCh 139:118, 120; 230).

In her adolescence, Gertrude joined the community as a religious sister. Her decision to take monastic vows, however, seems to have been motivated by her desire for further education rather than sanctity. Both the *vita* and Gertrude's spiritual autobiography recount that she was excessively devoted to literary studies and indifferent about her religious vocation when she became a nun.[13] Indeed, for an intellectual woman in the thirteenth century with no family ties to nobility, the monastery offered a library and instruction that she could not obtain elsewhere. Gertrude describes her departure from the monastic ideal as leaving her anxious and melancholy: "I bore—an empty boast—the name and habit of religious life."[14]

Eventually, at the age of twenty-six, Gertrude underwent a profound conversion, which was kindled by a vision of Christ on January 27, 1281. She reports that he appeared to her as a handsome young man, around the age of sixteen. And although this revelation came to her in the dormitory, it seemed to her as if she were in the choir, in the corner—the place where she used to make her "lukewarm devotions." Jesus then took her by the hand, and said to her, "I shall free you and I shall deliver you; do not fear." He added: "You have licked the dust with my enemies, and you have sucked honey among thorns; return to me at last, and I shall make you drunk with the rushing river of my divine pleasure!"[15] The *vita* describes this revelation to cause a change in Gertrude:

> From it she then realized that she had been far from God, in a land of unlikeness, for while clinging too closely to the liberal arts, she had until that moment failed to adjust the eye of her mind to the light of spiritual understanding. By attaching herself too eagerly to the pleasure of human wisdom, she had deprived herself of the most delightful taste of true Wisdom. All outward things now suddenly seemed worthless to her, and rightly so, for the Lord then led her into

---

[13] Gertrude, *Herald* 1.1.2 (CF 35:38–39; SCh 139:120).

[14] Gertrude, *Herald* 2.1.1 (CF 35:101; SCh 139:230). See also Gertrude, *Herald* 2.1.2 (CF 35:101; SCh 139:230).

[15] Gertrude, *Herald* 2.1.2 (CF 35:101; SCh 139:228, 230).

a place of joy and gladness, to Mount Sion, that is, to the vision of himself. There she put off her old nature with its deeds and put on the new nature which is created after God's likeness in true righteousness and holiness.[16]

From this point on, Gertrude declares, she constantly felt the presence of Christ within her soul.[17]

Clearly Gertrude's religious conversion was not associated with her body, as if she had turned away from lust toward chastity. Instead, it was her intellectual focus that was concerned. Her mental preoccupations turned away from exterior toward interior ones. As the Helfta nuns describe her conversion, "No longer a student of literature, then, she became a student of theology and tirelessly ruminated on all the books of the Bible which she could obtain."[18]

After her conversion, Gertrude gave herself fully to her theological vocation. Her sisters say that she worked quickly and with pleasure,[19] and that she "tirelessly ruminated on the books of the Bible which she could obtain. The basket of her heart she packed to the very top with the more useful, and honey-sweet, texts of holy Scripture, so that she always had at hand an instructive and holy quotation. Hence she could give a ready and suitable answer to anyone who came before her, and turn aside any kind of error with scriptural witnesses so appropriate that almost no one could refute her."[20] According to the *vita*, Gertrude was not only a theological scholar, but also a teacher: "Elucidating and clarifying what lesser minds found obscure, she made compilations from the sayings of the saints, gathered as a dove gathers grain, and committed to writing many books filled with all sweetness, for the general profit of all those who wished to read them."[21] "For the same reason, if she found anything useful in holy Scripture

---

[16] Gertrude, *Herald* 1.1.2 (CF 35:38–39; SCh 139:122).

[17] Gertrude, *Herald* 2.3.3 (CF 35:106–7; SCh 139:238).

[18] Gertrude, *Herald* 1.1.2 (CF 35:39; SCh 139:230).

[19] Gertrude, *Herald* 1.11.9 (CF 35:74; SCh 139:178).

[20] Gertrude, *Herald* 1.1.2 (CF 35:39; SCh 139:122).

[21] Gertrude, *Herald* 1.1.2 (CF 35:39; SCh 139:122).

which seemed hard for the less intelligent to understand, she would alter the Latin and rewrite it in a more straightforward style, so that it would be more useful to those who read it. She spent her whole life in this way, from early morning until night, sometimes in summarizing lengthy passages, sometimes in commenting on difficulties in her desire to promote God's praise and her neighbor's salvation."[22]

The images Gertrude's sisters employ in detailing her conversion are significant. As Laura Grimes points out, they spin the images into a web of associations with Saint Augustine, especially his similar conversion from spiritually empty "scholarship transformed through grace."[23] For instance, in his *Confessions*, Augustine describes himself as a gifted young student, who also excelled far beyond the talents and abilities of his classmates.[24] And he too expresses the state in which his proud and empty scholarship left him before his conversion, as a "region of unlikeness."[25] In addition, in *On Christian Doctrine*, Augustine warns about mistaking secular knowledge for divine sweetness,[26] which closely resembles the description of Gertrude's "pleasure of human wisdom" which had deprived her "of the most delightful taste of true Wisdom." Moreover, also in *On Christian Doctrine*, Augustine portrays the model Christian preacher as being formed by God's incarnate and scriptural Word,[27] an image that is again taken up by Gertrude's sisters in the picture they paint of her after her conversion:

---

[22] Gertrude, *Herald* 1.7.1 (CF 35:57–58; SCh 139:152, 154).

[23] Laura Marie Grimes, "Theology as Conversation: Gertrude of Helfta and her Sisters as Readers of Augustine," Ph.D. dissertation, University of Notre Dame, 2004, 141. Grimes also notes that the model of converted scholarship is commonplace for male monastics (e.g., Augustine, Jerome, Augustine), but an innovative one for a woman (Grimes, "Theology as Conversation," 133, 145).

[24] Augustine, Conf 1.17.27 [PL 32:673]; Grimes, "Theology as Conversation," 143.

[25] Augustine, Conf 7.10.16 [PL 32:742]; Grimes, "Theology as Conversation," 146–47.

[26] Augustine, De doc 1.4.4 [PL 34:20–21]; Grimes, "Theology as Conversation," 151.

[27] Augustine, De doc 4.4–6 [PL 34:91]; Grimes, "Theology as Conversation," 152.

She also possessed a sweet and piercing eloquence, an articulate tongue, and speech so persuasive, effective and gracious that most of those who heard her words testified, by the miraculous softening of their hearts and the change in their wills, that God's spirit was speaking in her. It was the Word—living, effectual and sharper than any two-edged sword, piercing to the division of the soul and the spirit—dwelling in her, which did all this. Some she goaded by her words to salvation, others she enabled to see both God and their own shortcomings; to some she brought the help of consoling grace, and the hearts of others she caused to burn more brightly with divine love.[28]

In another instance, Gertrude's sisters describe the influential power of her words: "There are many people who could testify that they once felt greater pangs of remorse at a single word of hers than at a lengthy sermon by seasoned preachers."[29]

Of course, Gertrude did not teach in the same manner and mode as Augustine, the esteemed bishop and preacher. Rather, she taught and advised a large number of her religious sisters at Helfta and apparently many outsiders who visited her for spiritual direction.[30] Yet it is clear that the Helfta nuns regarded her as a theologian of equal authority and rank with Augustine. As they record it, in an account from Book Four of the *Herald*, Gertrude once made a visual odyssey to heaven, right up to God's throne, and found herself standing next to Saint Augustine, with Saint Bernard of Clairvaux closely beside him.[31]

In her vision Gertrude saw Augustine's words, deeds, sayings, and writings appear in the form of sunrays, which Jesus drew into his sacred heart. Jesus then poured back into Augustine's heart all the learning that had flowed into his readers' hearts,

---

[28] Gertrude, *Herald* 1.1.3 (CF 35:40; SCh 139:122).
[29] Gertrude, *Herald* 1.12.1 (CF 35:78; SCh 139:186).
[30] Gertrude, *Herald* 1.1.3 (CF 35:40; SCh 139:124). See also Gertrude, *Herald* 2.73.13–14; 3.72.4; 3.76.1; 3.89.1 (CF 63:200; 208–9; 217; 239–40; SCh 143:292; 310, 312; 324; 344, 346).
[31] Gertrude, *Herald* 4.50.1 (CF 85:239; SCh 255:402).

including Gertrude's, on heaven and earth. Later, on another occasion, Augustine appeared again to Gertrude, this time opening his heart and presenting it to God in the form of a fragrant rose. Gertrude greeted him and prayed for all those who had a devotion to him. Augustine then asked God to make the hearts of his devotees smell also like fragrant roses.[32]

This vignette suggests that Gertrude was devoted intellectually and spiritually to both Augustine and Bernard but that her teaching was influenced mostly by the former. Indeed, her sisters begin the account by stating, "Mindful of the glorious bishop Augustine, toward whom she had always felt great affection from an early age, she also gave devout thanks to God for all the blessings performed in him."[33] Like Augustine, Gertrude knows the misery of living in the "land of unlikeness," because of an early career in spiritually empty studies. It is significant, therefore, that as a theologian she is united to Augustine (and Bernard) in her heart rather than her mind, and that the union occurs through the sacred heart of Jesus. Yet most important is that Gertrude is depicted as not just writing about Augustine or Bernard: the account also underlines the fact that she herself has become an author of God's words; she stands beside the two men as a theological authority in her own right.

Writings

Gertrude expressed her vocation to teach theology in her writing. Her sisters say that she was "committed to writing many books" and that in addition to the biblical commentaries and translations mentioned above, she also wrote letters, "compilations from the sayings of the saints," "many prayers, . . . and many other examples of spiritual exercises."[34] Unfortunately, because of the wholesale destruction of the convent during the

[32] Gertrude, *Herald* 4.50.2–3 (CF 85:240–41; SCh 255:404).
[33] Gertrude, *Herald* 4.50.1 (CF 85:239; SCh 255:402).
[34] Gertrude, *Herald* 1.1.2 (CF 35:39; SCh 139:122).

Peasants' Revolt of 1525, all of these works have been lost. Only outside copies made of her two major works have survived.

The only extant work written entirely in Gertrude's own hand is her *Documenta spiritualium exercitionum* (*Teachings of Spiritual Exercises*). While no autograph remains, the earliest manuscript copy that survives today was written in 1536 by the Carthusian Lanspergius (Johannes Gerecht of Landsberg, Bavaria).[35] This manuscript is therefore the basis for the current critical editions of Gertrude's *Exercises* in Latin and its French translation, published together in 1967 in the Sources Chrétiennes series.[36] Their first English translation appeared in 1956, just over a decade too early to make use of this publication.[37] Later, in 1989, Gertrud Jaron Lewis and Jack Lewis completed the task of translating the new critical edition into English.[38]

The book seems to be what Gertrude's sisters were referring to when they mentioned her writing "many other examples of spiritual exercises,"[39] as it follows from the tradition of spiritual exercise in Christian history. Indeed, the term *exercitium spirituale* was commonly known in early Latin Christianity,[40] and the sayings of the Desert Fathers and Augustine's *Confessions* are obvious examples. Moreover, in Gertrude's day and even a bit earlier, in the twelfth and thirteenth centuries, writers like William of Saint-Thierry, Saint Dominic, Guigo the Carthusian, David of Augsburg,

---

[35] Gertrud Jaron Lewis, "Introduction," in *Exercises*, CF 49:3; Bernard McGinn, *The Flowering of Mysticism: Men and Women in the New Mysticism (1200–1350)* (New York: Crossroad, 1998), 446, n. 11. For a list of manuscripts published from the sixteenth through the twentieth century in Latin and their translations into German, Italian, Spanish, French, and English, see Jacques Hourlier and Albert Schmitt, "Appendice 1," in SCh 127:52–53.

[36] Gertrude, *Exercises* (SCh 127). An earlier critical edition is included in *Revelationes Gertrudianae ac Mecthildianae*, vol. 1, ed. Louis Paquelin (Poitiers-Paris, 1875).

[37] Gertrude the Great of Helfta. *The Exercises of Saint Gertrude*, trans. Columba Hart (Westminster, MD: Newman, 1956).

[38] Gertrude, *Exercises*.

[39] Gertrude, *Herald* 1.1.2 (CF 35:39; SCh 139:122). It seems that Gertrude wrote this book during the late 1280s and early 1290s, when she began to write her spiritual autobiography.

[40] Lewis, "Introduction," in Gertrude, *Exercises* (CF 49:1).

Bonaventure, and especially Aelred of Rievaulx and Ludolph the Carthusian were developing the tradition. They composed exercises that incorporated the practice of *lectio divina*, including the stages of *lectio, meditatio, oratio,* and *contemplatio.* Perhaps Ignatius of Loyola's sixteenth-century version of *Spiritual Exercises,* which also witnessed the three stages of growth through life in prayer—the *via purgativa, via illuminativa,* and *via unitiva*—is best known today. However, it depends very much on the works before him.[41]

Gertrude's *Exercises* are structured according to the stages of life. The bookends of her work, the first and seventh exercises respectively, focus on the themes of rebirth and life in death. Between these exercises she progresses from the stages of spiritual conversion to a dedication of self, and then to the themes of following Christ, mystical union, and *jubilus.* These interim stages are the sources of spiritual renewal in this life. As if defining human life backwards, she teaches that life gains meaning through its certain end—that is, consummation in death.[42]

Gertrude divides her work into seven chapters, probably because of the number seven's signification of fullness and perfection. Yet each chapter has a distinct theme and liturgical basis. The first exercise is based on the sacrament of baptism and is intended as a renewal of the foundation of Christian life. The second, third, and fourth exercises recall rites of passage important to the monastic life—i.e., clothing with the habit, consecrating virgins, and professing of vows, respectively. Throughout these three exercises, Gertrude indicates that readers outside her community could adapt the monastic customs into rites of passage specific to their own life circumstances.[43] Gertrude's fifth exercise freely draws from the seven canonical hours and is intended to

[41] Ignatius's *Exercises* depend on two twelfth-century works by Aelred of Rievaulx, followed by Ludolph the Carthusian's *Vita Christi.* On this genealogy, see Marsha L. Dutton, "The Cistercian Source: Aelred, Bonaventure, and Ignatius," in *Goad and Nail: Studies in Medieval Cistercian History X,* ed. E. Rozanne Elder, CS 84 (Kalamazoo, MI: Cistercian Publications, 1985), 151–78.

[42] Lewis, "Introduction," in Gertrude, *Exercises* (CF 49:9).

[43] For example, see Gertrude's parenthetical remark in Gertrude, *Exercises* 3.21 (CF 49:41; SCh 127:94).

deepen one's union with Christ. The sixth exercise is intended to be performed during reception of Holy Communion,[44] while the seventh and final exercise aims to prepare the reader to meet Christ at the moment of death.

Gertrude composed each of the seven exercises with great care. As a master of Latin, she aptly expressed herself in rhythmic prose and even verse, especially in exercise seven. Moreover, because of her monastic upbringing and daily participation in the Mass and Divine Office, she peppers each exercise with biblical images and liturgical tropes. Gertrude's exercises, however, should not be misunderstood simply as pious devotions prescribed for achieving union with God. Of course they are spiritual exercises in the traditional sense of the term, but in composing them she also engages and make innovations to important theological teachings. For example, in her fifth exercise, which at first blush appears to be a prayerful and ecstatic discourse on the *unio mystica*, Gertrude presents an original doctrine of the spiritual senses, teaching that the corporeal and spiritual senses perceive God together, in tandem, in eucharistic communion. Indeed, as Andrea Dickens notes, Gertrude's doctrine seems to rescind Augustine's warning that the corporeal senses are neither the means God chooses to initiate divine union nor the means through which humans should respond to God's invitation.[45]

Gertrude's other extant work is her *Legatus memorialis abundantiae divinae pietatis* (*The Memorial Herald of the Abundance of Divine Love*). The autograph of the *Herald*, like that of the *Exercises*,

[44] This purpose has been recently pointed out in Claire Jones, "*Hostia jubilationis*: Psalm Citation, Eucharistic Prayer and Mystical Union in Gertrude of Helfta's *Exercitia Spiritualia*," *Speculum* 89, no. 4 (2014): 1032.

[45] Andrea Janelle Dickens, "*Unus Spiritus cum Deo*: Six Medieval Cistercian Christologies," Ph.D. dissertation, University of Virginia, 2005, 277. Pierre Doyère has also noted that Gertrude teaches that the activity of the corporeal and spiritual senses is harmonious. This harmony distinguishes Gertrude's doctrine of spiritual senses from Origen's and calls for theological study of her innovative writings (Pierre Doyère, "Sainte Gertrude et les sens spirituels," *Revue d'ascétique et de mystique* 144 [1960]: 429–46, especially 445–46). See also Pierre Doyère, "Appendice VI: Les sens spiritual," in Gertrude, *Herald* [SCh 143:359–66].)

has been lost, although five manuscripts survive from the fifteenth century along with one that was recently discovered from the fourteenth century, University Library of Leipzig MS. 827.[46] The Latin critical edition uses the first five manuscripts and was published in four volumes between 1968 and 1986 in Sources Chrétiennes, alongside Gertrude's *Exercises*.[47] A full English translation of the *Herald* was first printed in 1862, based on an older critical edition.[48] An English translation based on the Sources Chrétiennes critical edition was published by Paulist Press in 1993, although it contains only various parts of the *Herald*.[49] The fullest English translation is in progress with Cistercian Publications; the first four of the *Herald*'s five parts have been published with the fifth currently in press.[50]

The composition of the book and the story of how its five parts were brought together is complex. Gertrude seems to have been inspired on Holy Thursday 1289 by an overwhelming desire to write down her visionary experiences, almost eight years after she first received that life-changing vision of Christ in January 1281.[51] As the Helfta sisters recount it, Gertrude was waiting with the community to take communion to a nun in the infirmary: "Compelled by the Holy Spirit, she snatched up the tablet hanging at her side. Out of the overflowing abundance of thanksgiving, to his praise, she described with her own hand in these words

---

[46] Almuth Märker and Balázs Nemes were the first scholars to draw attention to this newly discovered manuscript. For a description, see http://bilder .manuscripta-mediaevalia.de/hs//projekt-Leipzig-pdfs/Ms%20827.pdf. Three other Latin editions of the *Herald* appeared in the sixteenth century, and several other translations followed during the sixteenth and seventeenth centuries, in German, Dutch, Spanish, Italian, and French (Jacques Hourlier and Albert Schmitt, "Appendice 1," in Gertrude, *Herald* [SCh 127:52–53]).

[47] SCh 139, 143, 255, and 331.

[48] Gertrude, *The Life and Revelations of St. Gertrude: Virgin and Abbess, of the Order of St. Benedict*, trans. M. Frances Clare Cusack, 2nd ed. (London: Burns and Oates, 1876). This translation is based on a Latin edition of the *Herald* from 1662; it was published in 1865, just ten years shy of Louis Paquelin's critical edition in 1875 (Finnegan, *The Women of Helfta*, 76).

[49] Gertrude the Great of Helfta, *Gertrude of Helfta: The Herald of Divine Love*, trans. and ed. Margaret Winkworth (New York: Paulist Press, 1993).

[50] Gertrude, *Herald*, trans. Alexandra Barratt, CF 35, 63, 85.

[51] Gertrude, *Herald* 1 Prol.1 (CF 35:31; SCh 139:108).

that follow her sensations when she held intimate converse with her Beloved."[52] What she began to write then was her spiritual autobiography, entitled *Memoriale abundantiae divinae suavitatis*.

The other part of what would be included in the final version of the book began to be written some twenty years after Gertrude received her first vision of Christ in 1281.[53] By this time, because of her frequent illnesses, which would eventually lead to her death at the age of forty-five, writing had become too painful for her, and this book, entitled *Legatus divinae pietatis*, was written by one or more Helfta nuns in conversation with her. In accord with the pattern of monastic anonymity, the authorship of this book is never stated, and it refers to its writers with both singular and plural pronouns.[54] Therefore my study also refers to the authors of this work with plural nouns and pronouns.

Sometime around Gertrude's death, either shortly before or afterward, the two books were compiled to form the final version of the book, titled in full *Legatus memorialis abundantiae divinae pietatis* (*The Memorial Herald of the Abundance of Divine Love*). As the writers' prologue to the compilation asserts, God willed this title and the union of the two books. In fact, the compilers record God's words to them: "Just as the birth of a lovely child sometimes leads each of its parents to look on the other more affectionately, so I have preordained that this book should result from a union of both parts."[55] Grimes remarks on the significance of this childbirth metaphor: "Like the child of a marriage, the final text of the *Herald* is connected to, yet distinct from, each of its parent books; it has a fullness that could never have been achieved without their union. This highlights the main point of the composite work: the intricate interplay between individual and community, and the fruitfulness of sharing through spiritual conversation, here extended to writing."[56]

---

[52] Gertrude, *Herald* 2 Prol.1 (CF 35:99; SCh 139:226).
[53] Gertrude, *Herald* 1 Prol.1 (CF 35:31; SCh 139:108).
[54] See Gertrude, *Herald* 5.1.16; 5.34.1; 5.35.1 (SCh 331:36, 226, 268–73).
[55] Gertrude, *Herald* 1 Prol.5 (CF 35:33; SCh 139:112).
[56] Laura M. Grimes, "Writing as Birth: The Composition of Gertrud of Helfta's *Herald of God's Loving Kindness*," CSQ 42, no. 3 (2007): 332. Anna

This final work comprises five books: Book One takes the form of a *vita*, recounting Gertrude's life and detailing her exceptional character, Book Two is her spiritual autobiography, Book Three describes and reflects theologically on her visions, Book Four relates visions she had on the days of particular liturgical feasts, and Book Five tells of revelations she received about departed souls from her community and its circle of friends, as well as recounting some of the consolations Gertrude received before her own death.[57] In this final compilation, therefore, Books One and Three through Five are originally from the *Legatus memorialis abundantiae divinae pietatis*, and Book Two is from Gertrude's *Memoriale abundantiae divinae suavitatis*.

Grimes has made an important contribution to Gertrude studies, which have previously regarded Book Two, Gertrude's spiritual autobiography, as the central and most valuable part of the full compilation, and Books Three through Five as less important because they contain mere "dictations" of Gertrude, written down by other nuns. In the previous view, Book One is regarded as an introduction to the final compilation and not even a part of the parent book, the *Legatus memorialis abundantiae divinae pietatis*. Grimes has shown, however, that this opinion betrays the evidence found in the Prologue and perpetuates a false priority given to sole authorship over collaborative composition. Indeed, the Prologue makes it clear that the nuns working on the *Herald* with Gertrude were active authors and not merely writing down her dictations.[58] For instance, one night, when one of the writers

---

Harrison's work has followed Grimes's in focusing in detail on the collaborative authorship at Helfta and its implications about the interaction between individual and community (Anna Harrison, "Sense of Community Among the Nuns at Helfta," Ph.D. dissertation, Columbia University, 2007; Anna Harrison " 'Oh! What Treasure is in this Book?' Writing, Reading, and Community at the Monastery of Helfta," *Viator* 39, no. 1 [2008]: 75–106; Anna Harrison, "I Am Wholly Your Own: Liturgical Piety and Community Among the Nuns of Helfta," *Church History* 78, no. 3 [2009]: 549–83).

[57] The description of the five books written by the compilers is in Gertrude, *Herald* 1 Prol.7 (CF 35:34; SCh 139:114).

[58] Grimes "Writing as Birth," 334–35. As Grimes notes, Doyère established this view in Doyère, "Introduction" in SCh 139:22–24; he refers to the Helfta

was complaining to God about her workload, God soothed her, saying,

> "I have given you as a light for the nations, that you may be my salvation from the uttermost ends of the earth." When she understood that he was speaking of this book, which at the time had scarcely been started, she said in astonishment, "And how, God, can anyone be enlightened by means of this little book when it is not my intention to write any more and I shall certainly not allow even what little I have already written to be made public?" The Lord replied, "When I chose Jeremiah to be a prophet he thought he did not know how to speak and that he lacked the necessary powers of discernment; but by means of his eloquence I brought nations and kingdoms back to the right path. In the same way, whatever I have arranged to illuminate through you by the light of knowledge and truth will not be frustrated, for no one can thwart my eternally predestined plan. I shall call those whom I have predestined and I shall justify those whom I have called, in any way that pleases me."[59]

As Grimes points out, the passive verbs used for writing, along with the shift to the third person in Book Three of the final compilation, demonstrate that the nuns are full literary partners in the book, in conversation with Gertrude.[60]

Yet this account also flags the important issue of female authorship. Indeed, the doubts expressed therein by one of the compilers were probably fueled by the ideas of her day about female writing—e.g., that it had to be justified by visionary experience—and that she was not the visionary, but Gertrude. Moreover, the writer of this passage is more than Gertrude's secretary. God reminds her that authority comes from its divine origin and that the fruits of her work are bound in the same way as that of the

---

writers who assisted in compiling and writing the *Herald* as "secretaries" (Grimes, "Theology as Conversation," 23; Grimes "Writing as Birth," 337–42). Ensuing scholarship seemed to embrace Doyère's view uncritically; see e.g., Winkworth, "Introduction," 12, in *Gertrude of Helfta.*

[59] Gertrude, *Herald* 1 Prol.3 (CF 35:32; SCh 139:110).

[60] Grimes, "Theology as Conversation," 52–53, 60.

prophets to the project of instructing and saving souls. The Helfta nuns were not naïve about the fact that they had to consider the issue of how Gertrude's and their own female authorship would be received.

The Authority of Female Authorship

While Gertrude and her sisters had no problem seeing her as a theological authority in her own right, even one who joined the heavenly ranks of Saint Augustine and Saint Bernard, for others outside of the convent walls to regard Gertrude as a premier theologian in the thirteenth century was another matter altogether. The fact that she was a woman meant that her authority had to be authenticated in a distrustful world.

For this reason, the Helfta nuns remind the readers of the *Herald* that God regarded Gertrude as a key player in the work for his salvation project in their time. They insist on the prolific nature of her writing: "In fact no one in our day has produced in greater profusion than she the floods of that instruction which leads to salvation."[61] Just like the compilers, the Helfta nuns carefully underline the scriptural basis of Gertrude's words: "She also composed many prayers . . . and many other examples of spiritual exercises, in a style so fitting that it was impossible for any authority [*nulli magistrorum*] to find fault with it, or do anything except delight in it its aptness, which was founded on such honey texts from holy Scripture that no one, theologian or believer, could scorn it."[62] Moreover, in the Prologue, they assert the Scriptural authority of the *Herald*, beginning by citing Hugh of St. Victor:

> As Hugh says, "I hold suspect all truth which is not confirmed by scriptural authority," and again, "No revelation, however truthful it appears, should be endorsed without the witness of Moses and Elijah, that is, without the authority of Scripture," I have therefore recorded in the margin what my simple wit and inexperienced understanding could recall

[61] Gertrude, *Herald* 1.1.3 (CF 35:40; SCh 139:122).
[62] Gertrude, *Herald* 1.1.2 (CF 35:39; SCh 139:122).

on the spur of the moment, in the hope that if anyone of
keener wit and more experienced understanding should
come across it, he would be able to cite far more credible and
appropriate witnesses.[63]

Here the writers of the Prologue state their intention to provide
marginal notations for the many scriptural passages and theological authorities that Gertrude referenced in her theological
conversations with them. That they invite future readers to add
to or correct their original citations indicates their sense of inadequacy in determining precisely which authorities Gertrude's
encyclopedic mind was referencing in any given moment when
she was conversing about theology with them. As a matter of fact,
the reference to Hugh of St. Victor in this account should be to
another Victorine, Richard, from his *Benjamin Minor*.[64] In considering the two complete manuscripts of the *Herald* that survive from
the fifteenth century, one finds that the nuns and the later scribes
who made emendations penned anywhere between 150 and
200 marginal citations in this book alone.[65] Clearly Gertrude's
sisters worked to bolster their reports of her words with scriptural
and theological citations.

Adding to Gertrude's religious authority, of course, is her report that she receives visions and revelations directly from God.
As she declares in her spiritual autobiography, she continued to
enjoy regular visions of Christ after his first manifestation to her
in 1281. Perhaps the two most extraordinary experiences she details are her reception of interior stigmata and the transverberation
of her heart.[66]

---

[63] Gertrude, *Herald* 1 Prol.8 (CF 35:34; SCh 139:116).

[64] Gertrude, *Herald* (SCh 139:116, n. 8).

[65] Doyère observes that of the two complete surviving manuscripts of the
Legatus, both dating from the fifteenth century, the Munich codex (B) contains
approximately two hundred marginal notations, while the Vienna codex (W)
contains one hundred and fifty, virtually all of which are present in Doyère,
"Introduction," Gertrude, *Herald* (SCh 139:83–91).

[66] Barbara Newman provides an excellent discussion of these phenomena
in their context at Helfta and in the general devotion to the Sacred Heart at
the time. See Barbara Newman, *"Iam cor meum non sit suum*: Exchanging

The first instance occurred not long after Gertrude's conversion, when she was thinking of a devotional prayer to the Sacred Heart that she had recently discovered and begun praying with regularly: "Most merciful Lord, write your wounds in my heart with your precious blood, that I may read in them your suffering and your love alike." She goes on to say that she was sitting in the convent's refectory, talking to a spiritual confidant, when she had a premonition that the prayer had been granted and the wounds conferred on her: "Inwardly in my heart, as if in physical places, I realized the Spirit had impressed the worshipful and adorable imprint of your most holy wounds."[67]

In addition to receiving this interior, invisible stigmata, about seven years later Gertrude experienced another similar gift. She had asked a friend to pray daily these words for her: "By your heart that was wounded through and through, most loving Lord, pierce her heart with the shafts of your love, so much so that it may be unable to possess anything that is of this earth, but may be possessed by the unique power of your divinity." During Mass on the third Sunday of Advent before Christmas that year, Gertrude recounts that she herself prayed, "Lord, I admit that, as far as my merits go, I am not worthy to receive the least of your gifts. But by the merits and earnest longing of all those around I beseech your loving-kindness to pierce my heart with the arrow of your love."[68] And with those words she became aware that her petition might actually be granted. After she received communion, she was looking upon a picture of the crucified Christ, and from the wound in his side she saw a ray of light in the form of an

Hearts from Heloise to Helfta," in *From Knowledge to Beatitude: St. Victor, Twelfth-Century Scholars, and Beyond: Essays in honor of Grover A. Zinn, Jr.*, ed. E. Ann Matter and Lesley Smith (Notre Dame, IN: University of Notre Dame Press, 2013), 290–92. For more on the devotion to the Sacred Heart at Helfta, see Sabine Spitzlei, *Erfahrungsraum Herz: Zur Mystik des Zisterzienserinnenklosters Helfta im 13. Jahrhundert* (Stuttgart-Bad Canstatt: Frommann-Holzboog, 1991); Gabriele Winter, "Die Herz-Jesu-Mystik bei Mechtild von Magdeburg, Mechtild von Hackeborn, und Gertrud von Helfta," *Jahrbuch für Salesianische Studien* 17 (1981): 72–82; Finnegan, *The Women of Helfta*, 131–42.

[67] Gertrude, *Herald* 2.4.1–3 (CF 35:109–10; SCh 139:242, 244).

[68] Gertrude, *Herald* 2.5.1 (CF 35:112; SCh 139:248).

arrow emerge toward her and linger. This experience only further enkindled her desire for the transverberation of her heart, but she still had to wait for her petition to be granted. Eventually, on the following Wednesday after Mass, when the annunciation and incarnation were commemorated with recitation of the Angelus, Christ granted Gertrude the mystical wound.[69]

In these accounts, Gertrude is clear that her union with Christ is so intimate that her heart resembles his own. As Christ's heart was pierced by the lance that wounded his side, hers too is pierced by a wound of love. She participates closely in the wounds on his hands and feet as well, as they are also imprinted upon her heart. In addition, the context of the transverberation of her heart is important. She receives the wound while commemorating Mary's reception of Jesus in her womb. Thus she seems to understand her heart as resembling not only Christ's, but also his mother's.

In Book Five of the *Herald*, Gertrude's sisters hark back to these experiences when they report that after the entire compilation was finished, Jesus appeared to Gertrude in a vision in which he took the manuscript and placed it on his heart, expressing his desire that the work be made fruitful by his five wounds.[70] What is noteworthy here is that Gertrude's sisters deemed it necessary, even given her visionary status, to reinforce her spiritual authority and that of the book. As a result of the extraordinary graces she received, they insist, Gertrude and her book have authority in their resemblance to the humanity of Christ; the connection of both her and her book to him is so close that they share his five wounds.

As Caroline Walker Bynum has shown, the concern to join to Christ through physicality is commonplace in the writings of medieval women religious. They drew from the longstanding association of women with matter—sometimes coopting it, sometimes subverting it—to argue for their spiritual authority.[71] Hildegard

[69] Gertrude, *Herald* 2.5.1–2 (CF 35:112–13; SCh 139:248, 250).

[70] Gertrude, *Herald* 5.3.1 (SCh 331:264, 266).

[71] Caroline Walker Bynum, *Holy Feast and Holy Fast: The Religious Significance of Food to Medieval Women* (Berkeley: University of California Press, 1987), 260–69.

of Bingen, for example, referred to herself as a "poor little female"
in a move to exploit conventional ideas connecting women with
weakness and thus claim for herself the biblical paradox that "the
humble will be exalted." As Hildegard wrote, her female inferiority allowed her to be identified with Christ's humble human
nature. Therefore, as his human nature was eventually raised to
miraculous heights, so was her female inferiority.[72] Other medieval
women writers like Julian of Norwich, Catherine of Siena, and
Catherine of Genoa located their authority as instruments of God's
salvation in physical pain and sacrifice. They understood their
bodily pain to unite them to—or, more accurately, to allow them
to participate in—Christ's own redemptive, physical pain. Commenting on these women, Bynum remarks: "The pain/blood/
self [these] women offer to God yearns to subsume and incorporate the pain of others and to become the pain/blood/life of Christ
himself."[73]

Gertrude is, therefore, not alone among medieval female writers in seeking to transcend the need to authenticate her authority
by reinforcing her visionary status with a claim to be closely
united to Christ's humanity.[74] However, she stands out among

[72] Barbara Newman, *Sister of Wisdom: St. Hildegard's Theology of the Feminine,
With a New Preface, Bibliography, and Discography* (Berkeley: University of
California Press, 1987), 1–41. Newman notes here that Hildegard also utilized
important figures in sapiential theology to affirm her authority.

[73] Caroline Walker Bynum, *Wonderful Blood: Theology and Practice in Late
Medieval Northern Germany and Beyond* (Philadelphia: University of Pennsylvania Press, 2007), 204. Other scholars have illustrated how medieval women
routinely offered their suffering to God (often physical suffering and sometimes voluntary physical suffering) in their purgatorial piety, in order to
imitate the crucified Christ, and thus to incorporate and co-redeem the sufferings of others. See for example Robert Sweetman, "Christine of St. Trond's
Preaching Apostolate," *Vox Benedicta* 9 (1992): 67–99; Jo Ann McNamara, "The
Need to Give: Suffering and Female Sanctity in the Middle Ages," in *Images
of Sainthood in Medieval Europe*, ed. Renate Blumenfeld-Kosinski and Timea
Szell (Ithaca: Cornell University Press, 1991), 199–221, esp. 213–21; Barbara
Newman, "On the Threshold of the Dead: Purgatory, Hell, and Religious
Women," in *From Virile Woman to WomanChrist: Studies in Medieval Religion
and Literature* (Philadelphia: University of Pennsylvania Press, 1995), 120–22;
Bynum, *Holy Feast and Holy Fast*, 120–21, 127–29.

[74] See for example Gertrude, *Exercises* 6.107 (CF 49:97; SCh 127:208).

her contemporaries in the way she handles the strategy. Her joining herself to Christ's humanity is accomplished almost exclusively in and through eucharistic communion rather than by gendered weakness and suffering. As Gertrude explains it, the Eucharist offers a kind of reincarnation of the Logos to each and every communicant. In receiving the Host, one encounters both Christ's *humanitas* and his *divinitas*. The Eucharist is, therefore, the paramount opportunity for persons in this life to achieve union with God. As she articulates it, when a person makes physical contact with Christ's humanity in the eucharistic Host, he or she, regardless of gender, concomitantly makes spiritual contact with Christ's divinity. This belief is based on the traditional doctrine of the real presence or, in Gertrude's words, the fact that the "fullness of the divine dwells bodily" (*habitat corporaliter omnis plenitudo divinitatis*), in the sacred Host.[75] Thus she writes a prayer in her *Exercises* for "receiving communion of the *life-giving* body and the blood of the spotless Lamb, Jesus Christ" that petitions Jesus,

> Let your pleasant embodiment [*incorporatio*] be for me *today*
> . . . eternal salvation,
> . . . and the enclosing of my life sempiternally in you.[76]

Gertrude teaches that when Christ incorporates her, or any believer, into his humanity by way of his "pleasant embodiment" in the Eucharist, that person is enclosed in his divinity. Clearly this incorporation into Christ's divinity grants Gertrude a status with which no one can argue, as it is something available to anyone, male or female. Therefore, it is the traditional doctrines of and devotions to the Eucharist that ultimately form the basis of Gertrude's female literary authority.

Indeed, in Book Five of the *Herald*, it is not only Christ's five wounds that the Helfta nuns associate with Gertrude's book, but also his eucharistic body and blood. In the abovementioned account, after Christ had placed the manuscript on his heart and

---

75 Gertrude, *Herald* 2.7.1 (CF 35:119–20; SCh 139:260).
76 Gertrude, *Exercises* 1.178–79, 189–90, 193–95 (CF 49:29–30; SCh 127:72–74).

impressed his wounds upon it, the Helfta nuns report that he gave it the same blessing that effectively transubstantiates bread and wine for the salvation of all.[77] Moreover, in a later account, one of the compilers describes taking the completed manuscript to Mass with her one day, and tucking it into the sleeve of her habit so that no one would notice; as she approached the altar to receive communion, she presented the book to God in a spiritual oblation and heard him respond, "I will penetrate and enrich every word of this book with divine sweetness."[78] By recounting these benedictions, the Helfta nuns seem to be saying that the book is not just *like* the Eucharist, but is itself sacramental. Gertrude herself uses eucharistic imagery at the end of her spiritual autobiography, crying out to God, "I long to praise you so that some people who read this account may take delight in the sweetness of your loving-kindness . . . . In the same way, may they be led by these pictures, so to speak, that I have painted, to taste within themselves that hidden manna."[79]

It thus becomes clear that both Gertrude's book and her body are aligned with the humanity of Christ, and in particular with his wounds and in the Eucharist. The authority of Gertrude's book, then, is legitimated in her body's close union with God. Because she is a female writer, even her visionary status has to be reinforced. But unlike so many of her female contemporaries, Gertrude does not present a self-image of inferiority because of her gender in order to vindicate herself; nor does she denigrate her body in physical suffering. Her stigmata are interior, and her physical union with God is carried out by way of eucharistic communion rather than by a literal *imitatio crucis*. Perhaps this departure from the common trend is what led the translator of the 1662 edition of Gertrude's *Herald* to conclude that her style is "not feminine, but is not contemptible."[80]

---

[77] Gertrude, *Herald* 5.33.1 (SCh 331:264).

[78] Gertrude, *Herald* 5.34.1 (SCh 331:266, 268). Translation my own.

[79] Gertrude, *Herald* 2.24.1 (CF 35:172; SCh 139:290).

[80] Gertrud d'Helfta, *Insinuationes divinae pietatis seu revelationes S. Gertrudis virginis et abbatissae ordinis S. Benedicti*, vol. 1, trans. Nicholas Canteleu (Paris: Léonard, 1662), 4; Finnegan, *The Women of Helfta*, 81.

Gertrude clearly had theological resources readily available to her, and she did not doubt her ability to utilize them, as a source for her own distinctive theories. But she was a grammarian turned into a theologian and mystic, a contemplative who achieved divine union in and through Jesus' humanity, particularly in visions of his sacred heart and in receiving the eucharistic host. She thus understands God to be remarkably accessible, not only to her, but to anyone seeking him. And ultimately this is what her *Exercises* and *Herald* seek to relate. Thus Gertrude, blending principles from the doctrines of the spiritual senses and the Eucharist, was able to construct a complex, nuanced, and positive theological anthropology.

CHAPTER TWO

The Monastery of St. Mary at Helfta

Because Gertrude of Helfta appeared at the doorstep of St. Mary at Helfta as a five-year-old girl, the monastery was the only home she ever remembered. Upon her arrival, she was entrusted to the care of another Gertrude—probably her namesake—Gertrude of Hackeborn, who was the abbess at the time and responsible for establishing the robust curriculum for which the monastery became well known. The Helfta nuns described Abbess Gertrude in this way: "Whenever she could, she read the divine Scripture studiously and with wonderful delight, requiring her subordinates to love the sacred lessons and recite them from memory. She bought her church all the good books that she could, or else had the sisters copy them. She also zealously promoted education so the girls would acquire knowledge of the liberal arts. If zeal for learning were to perish, she used to say, once they no longer understood the divine Scripture, religious devotion would perish too."[1] It was during the tenure and under the care of this abbess that young Gertrude developed into a prominent theologian.

---

[1] Mechthild, *Liber* 6.1 (LSG 375–76; BSG 204). Commentators still depend on the 19th-century edition discussed below: Mechtild of Hackeborn, *Liber Specialis Gratiae*, ed. Monks of Solesmes (Louis Paquelin), *Revelationes Gertrudianae ac Mechtildianae*, vol. 2 (Poitiers-Paris: Oudin, 1877) [LSG]. For a French edition, see Mechtild of Hackeborn, *Le Livre de la Grâce Spéciale: Révélations de Sainte Mechtilde, Vierge de l'Ordre de saint-Benoit*, trans. nuns of Wisques from the Latin edition of Solesmes (Tours: A. Mame, 1921). For a partial English translation, which was used in this book, see Mechthild of Hackeborn and the Nuns of Helfta, *The Book of Special Grace*, trans. Barbara Newman. The Classics of Western Spirituality (New York: Paulist Press, 2017) [BSG]. My citations sometimes only include the LSG, when the BSG does not contain the translation for the corresponding section.

Gertrude the Great was not the only woman to whose formation the abbess contributed. During her abbacy the monastery
was in its heyday of literary and visionary activity. In addition to
creating Gertrude's *Exercises* and *Herald*, the Helfta nuns wrote
the *Book of Special Grace* (*Liber specialis gratiae*), associated with
Mechthild of Hackeborn, and they helped to complete *The Flowing Light of the Godhead* (*Fliessende Licht der Gottheit*), written by
Mechthild of Magdeburg. These four works taken together com-
prise the largest surviving collection of women's visionary writing
from the thirteenth century.[2] Gertrude's *Exercises* is the only one
of these four works that is the product of sole authorship. The
Herald and the *Book of Special Grace* are communal collaborative
works in their entirety; they recount the mystical experiences of
Gertrude and of Mechthild of Hackeborn, respectively, in addition
to the theological analysis that ensued when small circles of
women discussed the revelations within the monastery. Because
of the education the nuns received at Helfta, the *Herald* and the
Book of Special Grace draw upon the thought of Origen, Augustine,
Gregory the Great, Bernard of Clairvaux, Thomas Aquinas, Albert
the Great, and the Victorines.[3] These two books, therefore, are

[2] Caroline Walker Bynum, *Jesus as Mother: Studies in the Spirituality of the
High Middle Ages* (Berkeley: University of California Press, 1982), 174.

[3] Teresa Halligan, "The Community at Helfta: Its Spirituality and Celebrated
Members," in *The Booke of Gostlye Grace of Mechtild of Hackeborn* (Toronto:
Pontifical Institute of Medieval Studies, 1979), 34–35; Miriam Schmitt,
"Gertrud of Helfta: Her Monastic Milieu (1256–1301) and her Spirituality,"
in *Cistercian Monastic Women–Hidden Springs*, vol. 3, CS 113B (Kalamazoo,
MI: Cistercian Publications, 1995), 476. Several scholars have commented on
the literary culture at Helfta and the high level of education of its women:
Mary Jeremy Finnegan, *The Women of Helfta: Scholars and Mystics* (Athens,
GA: University of Georgia Press, 1991), 8–9; Bernard McGinn, *The Flowering
of Mysticism: Men and Women in the New Mysticism (1200–1350)* (New York:
Crossroad, 1998), 267; Lina Eckenstein, *Women under Monasticism: Chapters
on Saint Lore and Convent Life between A.D. 500 and A.D. 1500*, reprint ed. (New
York: Russell and Russell, 1963), 328–53, esp. 329; Louis Paquelin, "Praefatio,"
in *Sanctae Gertrudis Magnae, virginis ordinis sanctae Benedicti, Legatus divinae
pietatis, accedunt ejusdem Exercitia spiritualia*, vol. 1 of *Revelationes Gertrudianae
ac Mechtildianae*, xii–xiii; Sabine Spitzlei, *Erfahrungsraum Herz: Zur Mystik des
Zisterzienserinnenklosters Helfta im 13. Jahrhundert* (Stuttgart-Bad Canstatt:
Frommann-Holzboog, 1991), 53–57.

fruits of a thriving community of intellectual women, who were well read and who supported and cross-pollinated one another's thought.

Furthermore, it is noteworthy that the visions of both Gertrude and Mechthild are often triggered by the community's liturgical celebrations and are thus inclusive of the devotions and achievements of their religious sisters. For example, one account from the *Herald* relates Gertrude's vision of Christ appearing in the center of the nuns during Mass one year on Ember Saturday in Advent:

> all the women of the community who were standing round the Lord were drawing in the divine grace, each according to her capacity, as it were through the reeds bestowed in them. Some appeared to draw directly from the depths of the Divine Heart. But to others what they received came through the hands of the Lord and so the greater the distance they drew from the Heart, the more difficult it was for them to obtain their desires. And the nearer to the Lord's Heart they tried to come, the more easily, sweetly and abundantly they drank.[4]

The Helfta nuns, who wrote the account, provide this interpretation of Gertrude's vision:

> Whence, by those women who drank immediately and directly from the Lord's Heart, are symbolized those who completely conform and subdue themselves to the divine will, desiring above all that the most praiseworthy will of God concerning themselves may be completely performed, in both spiritual and physical things. And these move the divine Heart toward themselves with such great efficacy that at a time foreordained by the Lord they receive a flood of divine delight as fully and delightfully as they have unreservedly entrusted themselves to his will. But by those who were trying to draw something through the Lord's other limbs, are signified those who according to their own desire

[4] Gertrude, *Herald* 3.30.1 (CF 63:103; SCh 143:132, 134).

attempt to win certain gifts of graces or fruits of virtues, according to the disposition of their own good pleasure. The more they rely on their own will, and the less they entrust themselves to divine Providence, the harder they have to work for their own desires.[5]

This vignette provides a window into the nuns' daily worship at Helfta and how they interpreted it. They understood the material stuff of worship—i.e., its physical gestures, books, chanted responses—as the chief opportunity for intimacy with Christ. The Helfta nuns thus considered communal worship to be efficacious not just for their own individual spiritual lives, but also for all of the women in their monastery and the broader church considered as a whole. As visionaries, Gertrude and Mechthild did not always play a major role in their visions; as is the case in the account above, sometimes the part they played was not discernible at all. Their revelations were recorded and interpreted in a deliberate effort to establish the collective reputation of the community and to hand down its spiritual teaching to the next generation of nuns and readers outside of the monastery.[6] The Helfta literature is therefore influenced wholly by the spiritual orientation of the closely knit community of Helfta nuns, in whose self-consciously literary and theologically sophisticated monastery they were rooted.[7]

The Monastery of St. Mary: History

One evening in 1229 in northern Saxony, Count Burchard of Mansfeld had a dream warning him that he would not be saved unless he put some of his enormous wealth toward a monastery for women in honor of Mary, the Mother of God and Mother of

---

[5] Gertrude, *Herald* 3.30.1 (CF 63:103; SCh 143:132, 134).

[6] Bynum, *Jesus as Mother*, 180.

[7] In general, on the communal collaborative composition of the Helfta literature, see Anna Harrison, " 'Oh! What Treasure is in this Book?' Writing, Reading, and Community at the Monastery of Helfta," *Viator* 39, no. 1 (2008): 75–106.

mercy.[8] Heeding the admonition, just before his death that same year, he and his wife, Countess Elisabeth Schwarzburg, founded the monastery of St. Mary in their castle precincts at Mansfeld. Its first inhabitants were seven nuns, led by Cunegund (who eventually became their abbess) from the nearby Cistercian monastery of St. Jacob and St. Burchard, about forty-five kilometers away in the city of Halberstadt.[9] Five years later, the nuns and the widowed Countess relocated to Rodarsdarf, only a few kilometers away.[10] This move was probably for reasons of safety, since the castle precincts would have implicated the nuns in the local conflicts surrounding them. Imperial politics in Saxony at that time were unstable and turbulent, to say the least. During the thirteenth century, Saxony saw

[8] *Urkundenbuch der Klöster der Grafschaft Mansfeld*, ed. Max Krühne, Geschichtsquellen der Provinz Sachsen und angrenzender Gebiete, 49 vols. (Halle: Otto Hendel, 1888), 20:223. This work comprises the fifteenth-century "Narratio" or chronicle of the convent, written by its then-abbess, Sophia of Stolberg (1409–1459?), and its surviving charters. The "Narratio" is reproduced in the book containing the nineteenth-century edition of the *Book of Special Grace*: "Narratio abbatisse Sophiae de Stolberg conscripta anno 1451 de fundatione monasterii novae-Helfta incepti anno 1229," in *Sanctae Mechthildis, virginis ordinis sanctae Benedicti, Liber specialis gratiae accedit sororis Mechthildis ejusdem ordinis Lux divinitatis*, vol. 2 of *Revelationes Gertrudianae ac Mechtildianae*, ed. Louis Paquelin (Paris: H. Oudin, 1877), 714–17. For the details surrounding the foundation and history of the monastery and its institutional affiliation, I have relied heavily upon Anna Harrison, "Sense of Community Among the Nuns at Helfta," Ph.D. dissertation, Columbia University, 2007, 12–51; Finnegan, *Women of Helfta*, 1–10; Hermann Grössler, "Die Blütezheit des Kloster Helfta bei Eisleben," *Jahres-Bericht über das Königliche Gymnasium zu Eisleben von Ostern 1886 bis Ostern 1887* (Eisleben, 1887), 1–38; Michael Bangert, "Die sozio-kulturelle Situation des Klosters St. Maria in Helfta," in *"Vor dir steht die leere Schale meiner Sehnsucht": Die Mystik der Frauen von Helfta*, ed. Michael Bangert and Hildegund Keul (Leipzig: Benno, 1998), 29–47; and Bynum, *Jesus as Mother*, 174–76.

[9] The circumstances surrounding the nuns' departure from Halberstadt are not mentioned. On their monastery there, see Franz Schrader, "Die Zisterzienserkloster in den mittelalterlichen Diozesen Magdeburg und Halberstadt," *Cîteaux: commentarii cistercienses* 21 (1970): 271.

[10] Although she never took vows, Countess Elisabeth lived with the community until her death in 1240 (Finnegan, *The Women of Helfta*, 2).

the disintegration of the Hohenstaufen empire, the fight for communal independence in episcopal cities, and anarchy during the so-called Great Interregnum between the death of Frederick II in 1254 and the election of Rudolph of Hapsburg in 1273.[11] In any case, the move placed the nuns conveniently near another noble family of patrons, that of Gertrude of Hackeborn, who would eventually become the abbess, and her younger biological sister, Mechthild of Hackeborn, who later joined her sister's highly intellectual and spiritual community.[12] Donations of land from their family allowed the growing community to found a daughter house in Hedersleben in 1253 and to move their motherhouse again in 1258, when they were faced with a water shortage, to its third site, at Helfta, two or three kilometers southeast of Eisleben. There the monastery remained for nearly the next hundred years.[13]

Yet even at Helfta the monastery walls did not shield the nuns from the surrounding political turbulence. During their one hundred years there, the monastery multiple times endured involvement in local conflicts and ecclesiastical trials, usually because of the family ties and noble lineage of many of the nuns. For instance, for unclear reasons, the monastery was invaded in 1284 by Gerhard of Mansfeld, the great grandson of the founders, and also the brother and cousin of two contemporary members of the community.[14] In 1342 the monastery was pillaged and set on fire

---

[11] Clearly concerned about this political instability, Gertrude prayed for and prophesied the result of the election for King Rudolph's successor (Gertrude, *Herald* 1.2.3 [CF 35:43; SCh 139:128, 130]). For a thorough account of the local and imperial politics surrounding the monastery, see Harrison, "Sense of Community Among the Nuns at Helfta," 34–37.

[12] For more on the patronage of the Mansfeld and Hackeborn families, see Harrison, "Sense of Community Among the Nuns at Helfta," 15–21. In addition to the "Narratio," Harrison's meticulous study considers the additional charters, letters, tax records, financial transactions, and documents associated with the convent.

[13] Krühne, *Urkundenbuch*, 225; Finnegan, *The Women of Helfta*, 2–3, 12.

[14] Harrison, "Sense of Community Among the Nuns at Helfta," 18. It is probably this attack to which Gertrude refers in her prayers to God for "certain persons who had damaged the monastery by despoiling it and were in addition oppressing it excessively" (Gertrude, *Herald* 3.67.1–2 [CF 63:188–89; SCh 143:272, 274]). Under the threat of another imminent attack, Gertrude

by Albert of Brunswick, the brother of then-Abbess Luitgard. The attack, which of course included the scriptorium, destroyed the nuns' precious charters and writings. Apparently Albert had become enraged upon learning that after he had not been elected bishop of Halberstadt, Pope Clement VI had suggested someone else, and Albert decided to take out his anger on the monastery. Fortunately, the abbess's noble relations benefited her four years later, in 1346, when she convinced her father, Burchard IV of Mansfeld, to transfer the community to Eisleben, its fourth and final site.[15]

Much later, in this location, Abbess Catherine of Watzdorff reformed the abbey's rule, with the result that Martin Luther described her as a "second Jezebel." He used the term in a pamphlet he circulated in 1524, which told the story of a young nun who escaped from a convent in Wittenberg to join the Lutherans. The monastery was then caught up in the Protestant Reformation and attacked the following year during the Peasant Revolt in 1525. This attack included the second wholesale destruction of the community's books and manuscripts. The monastery's leadership was so weakened during these Post-Reformation years that another intrusion in 1546, this time by a heretical prelate, concluded with the community's becoming extinct.[16]

Over 300 years later, in 1868, the monastery was restored as a Benedictine monastery. But the death of its first prioress soon afterward, and the May Laws of 1874, which took the property from the community, led to another closing. In 1890 the property was repurchased to build a church dedicated to Gertrude.[17] Finally, the monastery was re-founded and rebuilt as a Cistercian women's monastery in 1999, as it still exists today.

Given the chaotic history of the monastery of St. Mary, it is notable that Gertrude the Great was part of the community during

---

predicted correctly that the danger would be averted by a juridical decision (Gertrude, *Herald* 1.2.4 [CF 35:43; SCh 139:130]).

[15] Krühne, *Urkundenbuch*, 225; Finnegan, *The Women of Helfta*, 3–5.

[16] Finnegan, *The Women of Helfta*, 5; Grössler, *Die Blüzheit des Klosters Helfta bei Eisleben*, 35.

[17] Finnegan, *The Women of Helfta*, 5–6.

its longest period of stability, the one hundred years' period in which the monastery was located at its third foundation at Helfta. Although the Helfta nuns continued to suffer from constant threat of attack, because of the imperial political situation of thirteenth-century Saxony, they did not have to re-locate their home again. Such stability may be attributed to the community's first abbess at Helfta, Gertrude of Hackeborn. During her long office (1251–1291), the monastery reached its zenith of intellectual and visionary activity. This achievement is a result of her steady and calm work, in the midst of surrounding political pandemonium, to ensure the uninterrupted pursuit of learning and sanctity at her monastery. The ethos certainly had a positive impact on the life and writing of Gertrude the Great, as the monastery at Helfta was the only home she ever really knew.

Institutional Affiliation

Abbess Gertrude would also have probably been concerned about the frequent lootings of the monastery and its library, especially given the wealth with which her family had endowed the monastery. She may have even sought to retain an autonomous status for it, independent of any institutional affiliation, in order to protect her family's patronage from the hands of monks, who would otherwise have exercised financial supervision.[18]

Historians have discussed at length the thorny question to which religious order, if any, the monastery of St. Mary and its renowned nuns officially belonged. That both Benedictines and Cistercians have claimed the monastery since its extinction indicates them as the two principal possibilities. For example, because the founding nuns were Cistercian and the charter chronicles refer to them as such (e.g., "nuns of the gray order"), many scholars have claimed a Cistercian association for the monastery of St. Mary.[19]

[18] Harrison, "Sense of Community Among the Nuns at Helfta," 24.

[19] Reference to the founding women as *moniales grisei ordinis* is in the "Narratio." See Krühne, *Urkundenbuch*, 224. For scholarship on the monastery's Cistercian affiliation, see for example Ailbe J. Luddy, *St. Gertrude the Great: Illustrious Cistercian Mystic* (Dublin: M. H. Gill and Son, 1930), 33;

Others, however, such as Louis Paquelin, have assumed a Benedictine association, based on the Cistercian General Chapter's prohibition against the incorporation of nunneries into the Order the year before the founding of St. Mary at Helfta.[20] This prohibition, which was passed in 1228 and reaffirmed in 1235, also banned any new affiliations of existing houses of women. The monastery of St. Mary would have been a case of such a new affiliation, given that its founding nuns were from the Cistercian monastery of Saints Jacob and Burchard.[21]

Yet in addition to formal affiliation, it seems that female houses in the thirteenth century could be recognized as Cistercian by other criteria. According to the Decree of 1228, nuns could adopt and follow Cistercian customs without receiving any kind of oversight or visitation from the Order. In fact, unincorporated convents had been adopting Cistercian customs since the middle of the twelfth century.[22] Moreover, as Elizabeth Freeman notes, recent scholarship on Cistercian women's history reveals an inconsistency between the 1228 prohibition against incorporations of nun-

---

Markus Dombi, "Waren die hll. Gertrud und Mechtild Benedikterinnen oder Cistercienserinnen?" *Cistercienser-Chronik* 25 (1913): 257–68; and R. P. Émil Michael, "Die hl. Mechtild und die hl. Gertrud die Grosse Benedictinerinnen?" *Zeitschrift für katholisches Theologie* 23 (1899): 548–52.

[20] Paquelin, "Praefatio," xxvii–xxxi. See also Pia Schindele, "Elemente der Benediktinerregel in den Offenbarungen der heiligen Gertrud von Helfta," in *Und sie folgten der Regel St. Benedikts: die Cistercienser und das benediktinische Mönchtum: Eine Würdigung des abendländischen Mönchsvaters als Nachlese zum Benediktusjubiläum 1980*, ed. Ambrosius Schneider with Adam Wienand (Cologne: Wienand, 1981), 156–68.

[21] See Sally Thompson, "The Problem of Cistercian Nuns in the Twelfth and Early Thirteenth Centuries," in *Medieval Women*, ed. Derek Baker (Oxford: Blackwell, 1978), 227–53; Brigitte Degler-Spengler, "The Incorporation of Cistercian Nuns into the Order in the Twelfth and Thirteenth Century," in *Hidden Springs: Cistercian Monastic Women*, 2 vols., ed. John Nichols and Lillian Thomas Shank, Medieval Religious Women Series, 1, CS 113 (Kalamazoo, MI: Cistercian Publications, 1995), 85–135.

[22] See Degler-Spengler, "The Incorporation of Cistercian Nuns," 85–135; Constance H. Berman, "Were there Twelfth-Century Cistercian Nuns?" *Church History: Studies in Christianity and Culture* 68, no. 4 (December 1999): 824–64; and Constance H. Berman, *The Cistercian Evolution: The Invention of a Religious Order in Twelfth-Century Europe* (Philadelphia: University of Pennsylvania Press, 2000).

neries and the codifications of Cistercian legislation at the same time that pay growing attention to nuns and mention the incorporation of many nunneries.[23] As was true of the St. Mary foundation, Freeman explains,

> Many of the new thirteenth-century foundations were initiated by royal and noble women. But even though the statutes mention the incorporation of many houses, other female houses being accepted as Cistercian did so thanks to other mechanisms of support. Evidence for this is most readily found in local administrative sources such as charters, in papal and episcopal documents, in records from local Cistercian monks' houses and, of course, in surviving documentation from nunneries themselves. This means that we can rarely point to one single piece of evidence which can demonstrate that a medieval nunnery was a Cistercian nunnery. We are better served if we accept the lack of homogeneity in Cistercian nunnery affairs, and examine various pieces of evidence and criteria in order to establish that a nunnery was a member of the Cistercian Order.[24]

In light of the evidence in surviving Helfta literature, it appears that the monastery of St. Mary from the time it was founded through Gertrude's time was an unincorporated house. The charter chronicles themselves from that period refer to the monastery as Cistercian.[25] In addition, the fact that in 1262 Abbess Gertrude of Hackeborn sent twelve of the nuns to a Cistercian monastery founded by her brothers at Hedersleben in Harz suggests a continuing association with the Cistercian way of life.[26] Still the identification does not seem to be an official one. This conclusion seems evident in the mention in Gertrude's *Herald* of the importance of her keeping the "rigor of the Order's rule-governed life," because she was "professed in a cenobite order," without mentioning a

---

[23] Elizabeth Freeman, "Nuns," in *The Cambridge Companion to the Cistercian Order*, ed. Mette Birkedal Bruun (Cambridge, UK: Cambridge University Press, 2013), 102–3.

[24] Freeman, "Nuns," 103.

[25] Krühne, *Urkundenbuch*, 140.

[26] Krühne, *Urkundenbuch*, 133; Harrison, "Sense of Community Among the Nuns at Helfta," 24.

particular religious order.[27] The literature is also silent in regard to the monastery's financial and administrative ties, giving no indication that the monastery was under the jurisdiction of the general chapter.[28] Again, this may have been Abbess Gertrude's choice, seeking to safeguard her family's benefactions.

In addition, in discussing the nuns' pastoral care, the *Book of Special Grace* states that Masses were offered for the community by "religious brothers [*religiosi fratres*] and devoted priests," without mentioning their affiliation. Anna Harrison has proposed that the use of the word *fratres* here might suggest Franciscan friars.[29] In addition, the *Approbatio doctorum* appended to some of the early manuscript copies of the *Herald* states that male theologians from both the Franciscan and Dominican Orders approved of Gertrude's writings and respected her for her spiritual counsel.[30] Moreover, as Mary Finnegan notes, the proximity of Dominican houses to Helfta makes it likely that Dominican friars were responsible for the regular preaching at the monastery of St. Mary. If this was the case, the content of the sermons the nuns heard would have been Thomistic, since in 1278 the Dominican general chapter imposed Thomas Aquinas's teachings on all Dominicans.[31] This hypothesis seems likely, given the honor the Helfta literature grants to both Thomas and Albert the Great, who had not yet been canonized.[32]

Furthermore, the fact that the Dominicans were under papal order and the 1256 ruling of the Chapter of Florence to act as spiritual directors not just to Dominican nuns but also to other

---

[27] Gertrude, *Herald* 3.44.2 (CF 63:143; SCh 143:200).

[28] The monastery would ultimately have been under the authority of the local bishop. During Gertrude's life, the bishop of Halberstadt, as the "Narratio" mentions, was Vulrad of Kranichfeld (1255–1296) (Krühne, *Urkundenbuch*, 140, 144–45, 148, 225; Harrison, "Sense of Community Among the Nuns at Helfta," 26–27).

[29] Mechthild, *Liber* 5:25 (LSG 329); Harrison, "Sense of Community Among the Nuns at Helfta," 27.

[30] Gertrude, *Herald* 1, Endorsement and Authorization (CF 35:29; SCh 139:104, 106). For more on the Dominican pastoral care of the nuns, see Kurt Ruh, *Geschichte der abendländischen Mystik* (Munich: Beck, 1990), 326.

[31] Finnegan, *Women at Helfta*, 6–7.

[32] Mechthild of Hackeborn's *Book of Special Grace* suggests familiarity with both scholars and includes a tribute to both (Mechthild, *Liber* 5.9 [LSG 333; BSG 191–92]; Finnegan, *Women at Helfta*, 7).

religious women's orders makes it quite probable that the Dominicans were hearing the nuns' confessions at Helfta and providing them with spiritual counsel. The Provincial of the Friars
Preachers from 1286 to 1290, Hermann of Minden, recommended
that the well-educated friars in the order be assigned as the spiritual directors of learned nuns, a description certainly befitting the
women at Helfta.

At this point it becomes clear that while historians have de-
bated whether the monastery of St. Mary was technically Cistercian or Benedictine, an easy categorization of one or the other
affiliation is impossible.[33] Moreover, it seems that the scholarly
focus on this debate draws attention away from the significant
manner in which Abbess Gertrude used the unincorporated status
of the monastery to her advantage, drawing from a variety of
monastic traditions, selectively choosing only those customs most
helpful for her own spiritual project.[34] It is clear from the Helfta
literature that her nuns drew freely from Cistercian customs and
followed the Benedictine Rule.[35] In addition, Abbess Gertrude
seems to have welcomed the opportunity for supportive Francis-
cans and well-read Dominicans to administer the sacraments,
preach, and provide spiritual counsel to her nuns. Given that the
monastery was without official supervision from any religious
order, the success that it enjoyed during its height of scholarly
and visionary activity must be connected with the financial capa-
bility and administrative competence of Abbess Gertrude.[36]

In this regard, it is important to remember the critical role
Abbess Gertrude played in Gertrude the Great's intellectual and
spiritual formation. Having been received by the abbess at such

[33] Bynum, *Jesus as Mother*, 174, n. 12; John B. Freed, "Urban Development
and the 'Cura monialium' in Thirteenth-Century Germany," *Viator* 3 (1972):
311–27; Micheline de Pontenay de Fontette, *Les religieuses à l'âge classique du
droit canon* (Paris: J. Vrin, 1967), 27–63.

[34] Bangert, "Die sozio-kulturelle Situation," 32–33.

[35] For references to Saint Benedict and the RB, see for example Gertrude,
Herald 4.3.1; 4.11.1–3 (CF 85:21, 65–67; SCh 255:48, 126–31).

[36] Anne Lester makes this point about Cistercian women's monasteries in
general from this time period (Anne E. Lester, *Creating Cistercian Nuns: The
Women's Religious Movement and Its Reform in Thirteenth-Century Champagne*
[Ithaca: Cornell University Press, 2011], 173).

a young age, Gertrude would not have remembered her biological mother; instead, she was to a great extent formed by the abbess, for whom scholars presume she was named. It seems that in watching the abbess selectively choose from a variety of monastic traditions for her monastery—and in following this variety of customs herself—Gertrude the Great learned how to freely and confidently mine a variety of liturgical and theological sources for her own spiritual aims.

The Convent at Helfta:
Liturgical Piety and Literary Education

At the age of nineteen, Gertrude of Hackeborn was unanimously elected abbess at Helfta. Though her election was probably influenced by her family's benefactions, her effective ministry soon verified the choice. The liturgical privileges and educational opportunities she provided for her nuns ushered the monastery of St. Mary into its golden age. In fact, by the time of her death in 1291, she had drawn more than a hundred women to Helfta, including her younger sister, Mechthild of Hackeborn, Mechthild of Magdeburg, and of course Gertrude the Great.[37]

Unfortunately, Gertrude of Hackeborn left no writings of her own, but both Gertrude the Great's *Herald* and Mechthild of Hackeborn's *Book of Special Grace* provide details about the abbess's life and death. For instance, Book Five of the *Herald* reports many of Gertrude the Great's visions of the abbess and describes the death of the abbess, at whose bedside Gertrude the Great was present.[38]

Because of the similarity of their names, Gertrude the Great has sometimes been mistakenly identified as Abbess Gertrude of Hackeborn. In the commemoration of Gertrude the Great's feast day, for instance, the Roman breviary perpetuates the error by making Gertrude the Great an abbess. This confusion is also evident in numerous artistic images of Gertrude the Great holding

---

[37] Finnegan, *The Women of Helfta*, 11.

[38] Gertrude, *Herald* 5.1 (SCh 331:16–62). Mechthild of Hackeborn also had a vision of the abbess after her death. See Mechthild, *Liber* 6.9 (LSG 389; BSG 213–15).

the crozier of a medieval abbess.[39] The first English translation of the *Herald* even replaces Book One with a fabricated hagiography confusing the two Gertrudes. It stresses the nobility and wealth of the von Hackeborn family, as well as the admirableness of Gertrude the Great's renunciation of that nobility.[40] These conflations are errors, as the textual evidence in the *Herald* and *Book of Special Grace* clearly distinguishes between the two women.

As one of her primary goals, Abbess Gertrude of Hackeborn worked to nourish the spiritual lives of the nuns at the monastery of St. Mary with the Eucharist and liturgical prayer. She saw to it that the Divine Office and Mass were the Helfta nuns' principal activities and the center of their daily routine. Anna Harrison points to the intensity of the nuns' religious observance: "The sisters sometimes attended Mass twice in one day, and they may have spent the majority of their waking moments chanting the eight canonical hours. Supplementary liturgical observances, such as the office of the dead, and quasi-liturgical gatherings, including chapter . . . further filled their schedule. The liturgy was, to the nuns, marked off as an occasion for concentrated praise of God; it was shot through with opportunities to move closer to Christ, especially when he was received in communion."[41] What is most striking about this liturgical culture, especially in view of the broader context of the church at the time, is the abbess's insistence that her nuns not only attend Mass often but also receive the eucharistic Host frequently, even though that was unusual in her day.[42]

---

[39] Finnegan, *Women at Helfta*, 12.

[40] Gertrude of Helfta, *The Life and Revelations of Saint Gertrude*, 2–3. Her election as abbess is discussed in *The Life and Revelations of Saint Gertrude*, 13.

[41] Anna Harrison, "I Am Wholly Your Own: Liturgical Piety and Community Among the Nuns of Helfta," *Church History* 78, no. 3 (2009): 555.

[42] The *Book of Special Grace* relates a vision of Mechthild of Hackeborn in which Abbess Gertrude was rewarded after her death with sweet kisses from Christ for her faithful insistence upon frequent communion at the monastery (Mechthild, *Liber* 5.24 [LSG:319]). In addition, both the *Book of Special Grace* and the *Herald* provide further textual evidence about the frequent communion practice at Helfta, as they both mention and bemoan an interdict that was imposed on the community in 1296, which silenced the organ and chant and deprived the women of the Mass and reception of communion (Mechthild,

Indeed, reception of the Host had been declining since the sixth century, and by the abbess's time in the thirteenth century, it had fallen out of fashion almost entirely. Several theological ideas contributed to the trend. For one thing, the common image of God at the time was a distant and fear-provoking royal figure, as is evident in the twelfth-century sequence *Dies Irae*, used in the liturgy of the Mass for the dead, which referred to God as the "King of terrifying majesty."[43] Adding to this fearful distance between God and self was the heightened suspicion of the flesh and awareness of personal sinfulness. This notion was doubtlessly influenced by the teaching of the Cathars and other dualists, but also by clergymen's incessant preaching on penance, fasting, and conjugal abstinence before eucharistic communion.[44] Stern warnings against receiving the Host invalidly referred to the Pauline threat in 1 Corinthians 11:29—that those who ate and drank Christ's body and blood unworthily ate and drank condemnation upon themselves.

In addition, eucharistic theology by that time had created a wider distance between the altar of the priest and the laypeople, both in actual worship space and in common perceptions about their respective levels of holiness.[45] All these factors accumulated

---

Liber 1.27 [LSG 94; BSG 101–2] and Gertrude, *Herald* 3.16.1–4 [CF 63:62–65; SCh 143:66, 68, 70, 72]). For scholarship on the frequency of the nuns' communion at Helfta as more often than once a week, see Camille M. Hontoir, "La dévotion au Saint Sacrement chez les premiers cisterciens (XIIe–XIIIe siècles)," in *Studia Eucharista. DCC anni a condito festo Sanctissimi Corporis Christi 1246–1946*, ed. Stephanus Axters (Antwerp: De Nederlandsche Boekhandel, 1946), 144–47; Olivier Quenardel, *La communion eucharistique dans* Le Héraut de L'Amour Divin *de sainte Gertrude d'Helfta: situation, acteurs et mise en scène de la divina pietas* (Turnhout: Brepols, 1997); Gilbert Dolan, *St. Gertrude the Great* (London: Sands, 1913), 26.

[43] Adriaan H. Bredero, *Christendom and Christianity in the Middle Ages* (Grand Rapids, MI: Wm. B. Eerdmans Publishing, 1994), 344.

[44] These reasons for eucharistic fear are discussed in David Noel Power, *The Eucharistic Mystery: Revitalizing the Tradition* (New York: Crossroad, 1993); Miri Rubin, *Corpus Christi: The Eucharist in Late Medieval Culture* (Cambridge: Cambridge University Press, 1991), 84–85, 149.

[45] Gary Macy, *The Theologies of the Eucharist in the Early Scholastic Period: A Study of the Salvific Function of the Sacrament According to the Theologians, c. 1080–c. 1220* (Oxford; New York: Clarendon Press, 1984), esp. 119–20.

into a general notion that average men and women were so impure, distant from, and unworthy of God that they should stop receiving the Eucharist altogether. So instead of eating the Host, many anxious laypeople began the practice of either gazing at it, making an "ocular communion,"[46] or allowing the priest to receive for them, in what Josef Jungmann calls a "vicarious communion."[47] Of course, these devotional movements led the Fourth Lateran Council in 1215 to establish as canon law the well-known "Easter duty," requiring the faithful to confess their sins and to receive the Host at least one time a year, during Easter.[48]

Given this trend, it is remarkable that there is no hint in the Helfta literature that the nuns used any kind of peripheral form of liturgical devotion as a substitute for eating the communion wafer.[49] The writings produced at Helfta during Gertrude of

[46] See for example Rubin, *Corpus Christi*, 155–63; and Nathan Mitchell, *Cult and Controversy: The Worship of the Eucharist Outside Mass* (New York: Pueblo, 1982), 106, 164–66, 169–70; Edouard Dumoutet, *Le Christ selon la chair et la vie liturgique au Moyen-Age* (Paris: Beauchesne, 1932), 120–21, 147–80.

[47] See Josef Jungmann, *The Mass of the Roman Rite: Its Origins and Development (Missarum Sollemnia)*, trans. F. A. Brunner, 2 vols. (New York: Benzinger, 1951, 1955), 2:364–65. On the doctrine of vicarious communion and the practice of women in particular, see Bynum, *Holy Feast and Holy Fast*, 56–57, 227–37.

[48] On this canon see Thomas M. Izbicki, *The Eucharist in Medieval Canon Law* (Cambridge: Cambridge University Press, 2015), 137.

[49] Cheryl Clemons has illustrated this point in "The Relationship between Devotion to the Eucharist and Devotion to the Humanity of Jesus in the Writings of St. Gertrude of Helfta," Ph.D. dissertation, Catholic University of America, 1996, 479–89, 575–76, 614–16, and 709–11. Of course, Helfta was not entirely alone in its frequent reception of communion. David Knowles notes that the ancient custom of weekly Sunday communion was preserved in some Benedictine communities in England (David Knowles, *The Monastic Order in England: A History of its Development from the Times of St. Dunstan to the Fourth Lateran Council, 940–1216*, 2nd ed. [Cambridge: Cambridge University Press, 1963], 468–69). And Macy speaks of the monthly requirements for Benedictines at Cluny and Cîteaux (Macy, *Theologies of the Eucharist*, 206–7). In addition, Dumoutet points out that several of the great female visionaries of the thirteenth and fourteenth centuries were able to receive communion weekly or even more frequently. In addition to Gertrude the Great and Mechthild of Hackeborn, he mentions Lutgard of Aywières, Angela

Hackeborn's abbacy reveal confident images of both God and self[50] and—especially in the case of Gertrude the Great's writings—depict the recipient of the host with her own priestly accoutrements.

For instance, when it came to the elevation rite at Mass, rather than gazing upon the Host to replace receiving it, Gertrude tended to envision herself in her visions as a priest: when he raised the host over the chalice to make his oblation, she made her own. In doing so, she quite literally adopted the thirteenth-century rubrics of the Mass, which directed the priest to offer thanks for souls in heaven, in purgatory, and on earth, when he held the host over the chalice.[51] For instance, during one elevation rite Gertrude prayed, "Holy Father, I offer this host to you for this soul on the part of all in heaven, on earth, and in the deep." She then saw the soul for whom she had prayed as if it, like the communion Host, was "elevated higher and higher by the prayers of the Church."[52] On another occasion during Mass, the *Herald* reports that when the priest raised the Host, Gertrude lowered her eyes from the raised Host out of humility, only to hear Christ reassure her of her divinely ordained priestly mission: "I have set you in a higher place to make you take part in this Mass. If you gladly applied your will to this labor, however difficult, you were willing to serve so that this offering [*oblatio*] may share its full effect in all Christians, living and dead, according to its dignity; then in your way you have helped me best in my work."[53]

---

of Foligno, Margaret of Cortona, Catherine of Siena, Emilie Bricchieni, and Bridget of Sweden (Dumoutet, *Le Christ selon la chair*, 120–21).

[50] Bynum, "Woman Mystics in the Thirteenth Century: The Case of the Nuns of Helfta," in Bynum, *Jesus as Mother*, 170–262.

[51] See Rubin, *Corpus Christi*, 51; and Brian Patrick McGuire, "Purgatory, the Communion of Saints, and Medieval Change," *Viator* 20 (1989): 83. Generally, on the priest's actions accompanying the consecration and the *Memento* of the dead at the Liturgy of the Eucharist, see Jungmann, *Mass of the Roman Rite*, 202–47.

[52] Gertrude, *Herald* 5.5.6 (SCh 331:114, 116). Translation my own.

[53] Gertrude, *Herald* 3.6.1 (CF 63:37; SCh 143:28). For an example of Mechthild of Hackeborn's similar kind of oblations at the elevation rite, see Mechthild, *Liber* 5.3 (LSG 320–21; BSG 188).

In other visions, Gertrude claimed the practice of vicarious communion, not as a substitute for her own reception of the host, but rather as an opportunity to receive it for others for whom she prayed. As the Helfta nuns recount it, at one Mass God bade her, "Bring before me those whom you prepared . . . for they are about to feast with me."[54] Gertrude then became inspired to pray "For the amendment of all the sins ever committed by the universal church." The *Herald* reports that "the granting of her prayer was immediately given her soul in the form of a piece of bread, which she immediately offered the Lord with thanksgiving. The Lord, accepting it gratefully, and with upraised eyes giving devout thanks[55] to God the Father, *blessed* it[56] and then gave it back to her to distribute to the whole church."[57] In another account, from the *Book of Special Grace*, Christ tells Mechthild, after she received communion and saw his heart given to her in the form of a spectacular chalice, "Through my divine heart you shall always praise me. Go and offer the living cup of my heart to all the saints, so they can be happily intoxicated with it."[58] Indeed, the Helfta nuns were so confident in their proximity to God in the Eucharist that they believed they had the capacity by virtue of this union to make the boundary between the living and dead permeable. They were confident about their abilities because they saw God not as an angry judge, but rather as a benevolent and merciful giver of grace.

Within the community it seems that Gertrude the Great was most renowned for her trust in God's mercy. In her *vita*, the Helfta nuns declare this as her most extraordinary gift,[59] and they say

---

[54] *Herald* 4.21.1 (CF 85:109; SCh 244:200). In her doctoral dissertation, Cheryl Clemons provides descriptions of Gertrude's visionary experiences in other parts of the Mass (e.g., the introit, Kyrie, readings, offertory, elevation, communion procession, and prayers after communion) (Clemons, "The Relationship between Devotion to the Eucharist," 465–94).

[55] See John 6:11.

[56] See Matt 14:19.

[57] Gertrude, *Herald* 4.21.2 (CF 85:110; SCh 244:200–2). Translator's emphasis.

[58] Mechthild, *Liber* 1.1 (LSG 10; BSG 40); Bynum, *Jesus as Mother*, 210.

[59] Gertrude, *Herald* 1.10 (CF 35:66–69; SCh 139:164, 166, 168, 170).

that she exercised her gift most often in an apostolate of frequent communion: "she possessed such grace concerning the reception of communion, that reading in Scripture or hearing from anyone about the danger run by those who receive communion unworthily could not prevent her from always receiving communion gladly, with a firm hope in the Lord's loving-kindness." Gertrude's religious sisters go on to say that she even received the Host on occasions when she had neglected the proper preparation, because "she placed her trust in the unchanging nature of divine generosity as better than any preparation."[60] They report that Gertrude understood worthiness of and preparation for communion with God in the Eucharist as both impossible and unnecessary. For her, what was more important (and actually possible) was confident trust in God's condescension to unworthy souls.[61] She desired that everyone approach the altar with the kind of confidence before God that she had. In fact, she recommended frequent communion to others with such eagerness, the Helfta nuns say, that "Sometimes she almost forced them!"[62]

Of course, Gertrude was aware of the cautionary words of 1 Corinthians 11:29 that were being used in her day to warn against invalid communion. Against these threats, she claimed that Christ himself had once told her as she was approaching the eucharistic table, no less, that the faithful should seek to share in his body and blood out of love for his glory, "even to the extent, if it is possible, of receiving in that sacrament their own condemnation." She says that Christ explained to her, "Then the divine loving-kindness may shine out the more, in that God did not disdain to give himself in communion to someone so unworthy."[63]

[60] Gertrude, *Herald* 1.10.3 (CF 35:67; SCh 139:166).

[61] Gertrude, *Herald* 2.20.2 (CF 35:151; SCh 139:310).

[62] Gertrude, *Herald* 1.14.2 (CF 35:82; SCh 139:196).

[63] Gertrude, *Herald* 2.19.2 (CF 35:149; SCh 139:304, 306). When Gertrude sought further clarification, particularly wondering about what would happen if she encouraged someone to receive communion who really was sinful enough to abstain, Christ put her concern to rest, assuring her that he would never allow someone in that position to seek her counsel (*Herald* 2.20.1 [CF 35:150; SCh 139:308]).

Perhaps the Helfta nuns' confidence before God in the liturgy owes to their familiarity with it. Abbess Gertrude had ensured that the rhythm of every one of their days followed the hours of the Office, and that the cycles of their years turned through the liturgical calendar of feasts and seasons.[64] Communal celebrations of the Liturgy of the Eucharist and the Divine Office became the most common triggers for the mystical visions and ecstasies of both Gertrude the Great and Mechthild of Hackeborn.[65] The liturgy so permeated the nuns' worldviews that its images give the language and its calendar provides the framework for all of the Helfta literature.[66]

The nuns' intellectual productivity at Helfta was clearly fueled by the liturgy. For example, when Mechthild of Hackeborn sought more fully to understand the collect *Infirmitatem nostram respice, quaesumus*, Christ instructed her to tease out the meaning of each word and craft something like a gloss on the liturgical prayer.[67] Gertrude too engaged in such work; her *Exercises* at times takes the form of a *cento*, composed of an artful blending of scriptural references and liturgical tropes.[68] Since the Helfta nuns knew Latin well, they could easily adapt their prayer to the liturgical celebrations that pervaded their days.[69]

[64] Harrison, "I Am Wholly Your Own," 558.

[65] Their individual experiences seem to have contributed to rather than to have disrupted their communal liturgical devotion. Anna Harrison is the leading authority on the relationship between self and other in the Helfta nuns' liturgical piety. About this, see Harrison, "I Am Wholly Your Own," 565–82.

[66] Felix Vernet declares that few works of mysticism "are more overtly liturgical" than the Helfta literature (Felix Vernet, "Gertrude la Grande," in *Dictionnaire de théologie catholique*, 6 [Paris: Letouzey, 1909–1950], 220–23, 270). In addition, Sabine Spitzlei identifies Mechthild and Gertrude as "liturgical mystics" (Spitzlei, *Erfahrungsraum Herz*, 77). In general, the most comprehensive introduction to liturgical piety at Helfta is Cyprian Vaggagini, "The Example of a Mystic: St. Gertrude and Liturgical Spirituality," in *Theological Dimensions of the Liturgy* (Collegeville: Liturgical Press, 1976), 742, 794–96.

[67] Mechthild, *Liber* 1.20 (LSG 75; BSG 86–87); Harrison, "Sense of Community Among the Nuns at Helfta," 158.

[68] Vaggagini, "The Example of a Mystic," 742.

[69] One passage from *The Book of Special Grace* illustrates that their visions of God came in Latin. When Mechthild saw a dove on a nest and asked Christ

The Helfta nuns' knowledge of Latin was due to the fact that in addition to their rich liturgical milieu, Abbess Gertrude associated religious life with education. That she explicitly expressed this objective is evinced in her words cited on the first page of this chapter: "She also zealously promoted education so the girls would acquire knowledge of the liberal arts. If zeal for learning would perish, she used to say, once they no longer understand the divine Scripture, religious devotion would perish too."[70] She saw to it that the monastic school at Helfta included instruction in the courses of the *trivium*—grammar, rhetoric, and logic—as well as in the advanced courses of the *quadrivium*—arithmetic, geometry, astronomy, and music.[71] This practice is significant given that at the time the University of Paris was being renowned as a center of higher learning.[72] Women were banned from admittance to the university, but Abbess Gertrude of Hackeborn offered the Helfta nuns an alternative of equal intellectual caliber. Indeed, the library and educational opportunities at Helfta seemed to influence the initial decision of the intellectual Gertrude the Great to join the order, rather than a desire for religious life.

At Helfta, Abbess Gertrude ensured that what was left of the nuns' busy daily schedule after they attended Mass, chanted the eight canonical hours, went to chapter, and cared for the sick in the infirmary was given to teaching girls in the monastic school, transcribing manuscripts, and writing.[73] The Helfta literature often makes reference to the writing tablets the nuns carried around

---

about the egg (*ovum*) in the nest, he replied: "Egg is a two-syllable word. The *O*-syllable symbolizes my majesty and divinity, the *vum* the depths of your baseness. Unite these and rest like a bird on its egg" (Mechthild, *Liber* 3.42 [LSG 245; BSG 161]). Bynum has translated and quoted this passage to make the same point in *Jesus as Mother*, 214.

[70] Mechthild, *Liber* 6.1 (LSG 375–76; BSG 204).

[71] Finnegan, *The Women of Helfta*, 9.

[72] Prudence Allen, *The Concept of Woman*: Volume II: *The Early Humanist Reformation, 1250–1500* (Grand Rapids, MI: Eerdmans, 2002), 331.

[73] Lucie Félix-Faure Goyau, *Christianisme et culture féminine: sainte Radegonde, la culture de la femme au Moyen Age, les femmes de la Renaissance, regards de femmes sur l'au-dela, sainte Gertrude, sainte Mechtilde, le livre des recluses, Juliane de Norwich* (Paris: Perrin et cie, 1914), 168–76.

with them, which allowed them to write without a desk and even outdoors. For instance, in one charming passage from the *Herald*, Gertrude seems to have been at work writing outside while seated on top of a high pile of hay. When she dropped her pen, she said cheekily to God, "There is no use in my searching for it; help me to find it." And then, without even looking, she stuck her hand into the straw and pulled out the pen.[74] Noteworthy about this passage is that some translators have rendered the item that Gertrude lost, a *stylus vel acus*, to be a "needle," rather than a "pen."[75] Perhaps the translators had the proverbial "needle in a haystack" image in mind. Or maybe they were influenced by the misleading notion that medieval nuns all engaged in spinning rather than writing. Whatever the case, this mistranslation highlights the damaging presuppositions that have concealed the writings of women from the tradition, dismissing them as having little theological value.

It is clear from the Helfta literature itself that the nuns themselves did not seem to grant much value to sewing. As Mechthild of Hackeborn puts it in the *Book of Special Grace*, the best way to use one's hands is to raise them in prayer or to write.[76] Her judgment that writing is as important as praying points to Abbess Gertrude's conviction about her nuns' formation that if they neglected learning, their biblical interpretation and spirituality would suffer. She did not fear learning and writing as a hindrance to spiritual progress nor prize it above the religious life, as Gertrude the Great had before her conversion. Instead, prayer and reading and writing positively supported one another. The literature the nuns wrote was the fruit of both prayer and well-informed thought. Their writings emerged from a community that was both deeply intellectual and religious, containing significant theology.

---

[74] Gertrude, *Herald* 1.13.4 (CF 35:80–81; SCh 139:192, 194).

[75] Finnegan has pointed out this translation mistake (*The Women of Helfta*, 67).

[76] Mechthild, *Liber* 3.48 (LSG 251; BSG 162). For a brief discussion on the work of copyists and the female contribution to it in the Middle Ages, see Finnegan, *Women of Helfta*, 10.

Helfta Literature

The *Book of Special Grace* provide accounts and theological analysis of the visions of Mechthild of Hackeborn (1240–ca. 1298), who was the younger biological sister of Abbess Gertrude of Hackeborn. Apparently, when Mechthild went to visit her sister Gertrude at the monastery in 1248, when she was seven years old, she was so taken with the intellectual and visionary activity there that she insisted upon joining the community.[77] Mechthild was educated at the monastic school and became consecrated as a nun in due course, under the abbacy of her sister. At Helfta, Mechthild developed a great intellect and an ability to effectively teach, counsel, and intercede for her religious sisters as well as for outside friars and lay persons. Besides her visionary experiences, Mechthild was most known for her beautiful singing voice, which led her to be given the sobriquet "nightingale of Christ" and to be elected to the position of Lady Chantress (*Domna Cantrix*), the choir director within the community.[78]

Serving in this prominent role within the community, Mechthild would have led the choir nuns in chanting the psalms of the Divine Office, and she would have assisted the novices in memorizing long liturgical texts. As David Knowles explains, "Until the fourteenth century the choir was in darkness save for candles on the lectern, except on great feasts; it was therefore essential that the monk should know by heart not only the whole psalter with the customary canticles and hymns, but the versicles also, the anthems, and the whole of the 'common' office of saints."[79] The cantor in medieval monasticism functioned as a kind of librarian, in charge of the liturgical books. In particular, the cantor would be on hand with the *Antiphonarium* and the *Office Lectionary*, ready to correct mispronunciations as soloists gathered around the

---

[77] Mechthild, *Liber* Prol. (LSG 5–7; BSG 35–36); Finnegan, *Women of Helfta*, 26.

[78] Finnegan, *Women of Helfta*, 36–38.

[79] David Knowles, *The Religious Orders in England* (Cambridge: Cambridge University Press, 1948), 285.

books to practice their pieces.[80] The medieval cantor, therefore, possessed a high level of Latin literacy and liturgical mastery, and Mechthild of Hackeborn was no exception.

Mechthild's *Book of Special Grace* comprises over a thousand manuscript pages of Latin, composed by one or more anonymous nuns at Helfta. They began recording Mechthild's visionary experiences and theological reflections around 1291—at first without her knowledge—and worked for over a decade to complete the sprawling opus.[81] Some scholars have identified Gertrude the Great as the book's primary compiler, yet there is no textual evidence upon which to base this conjecture.[82] As Laura Grimes has convincingly argued, *The Book of Special Grace* was written in the 1290s, the same time that Gertrude experienced the health challenges that led her to turn over the work she had started in her own spiritual autobiography to her religious sisters. For this reason, it is difficult to imagine Gertrude recording Mechthild's visionary experiences at the same time as other sisters in the community were working to describe her own.[83] Assigning Gertrude as the main compiler of *The Book of Special Grace* also has the

---

[80] Martinus Cawley, "The Ancient Usages as 'Cantorial Science,' " CSQ 34, no. 1 (1999): 8–9. For more on Mechthild's role as cantor, see Ella Johnson, "The Nightingale of Christ's Redemption Song: Mechthild of Hackeborn's Musical Apostolate," in *Music, Justice and Theology*, ed. Michael O'Connor, et al. (Lanham, MD: Lexington Books, 2017), 181–96.

[81] These statements concerning the book's authorship are based on internal textual evidence. Mechthild, *Liber* 5.31 (LSG 370). Throughout *The Book of Special Grace* (as with the *Herald*), both singular and plural pronouns are used to refer to its author or authors. See for example Mechthild, *Liber* 2.43 (LSG 193); 5.22 (LSG 354); 5.25 (LSG 358).

[82] For example, Mechthild, *Liber* (LSG 355, n. 1) refers to one author as Gertrude the Great, though naming her is an interpolation, not based on textual evidence. The assertion is repeated in Doyère, "Introduction," 21, and Finnegan, *Women of Helfta*, 35–36. Sometimes the assertion has been based on an assumed close spiritual friendship between Mechthild and Gertrude the Great. But as Grimes points out, this conjecture too lacks textual evidence (Grimes, "Theology as Conversation," 14–15).

[83] Grimes, "Theology as Conversation," 13–16. As Grimes indicates, the *Herald* and *Book of Special Grace* also differ significantly in style, suggesting different authors.

unfortunate effect of downplaying the fruitful collaborative communal writing that occurred at Helfta. The conjecture implies that Gertrude was the only visionary or capable writer at Helfta. More accurately, as the writings themselves attest, Gertrude should be seen as one of many women at the monastery whom Mechthild trusted, to whom she disclosed her visions, and with whom she could ruminate theologically.

As the title suggests, *The Book of Special Grace* is most concerned with manifesting the special grace Mechthild received from God and imparting it to others. The book has seven parts: Book One follows a brief prologue and memoir of Mechthild's childhood, considers the Annunciation, and then provides the visionary's devotional instructions; Books Two, Three, and Four relate Mechthild's visions; Book Five treats the afterlife, referring to deceased members and friends of the Helfta community; and Books Six and Seven recount the joyful death of Mechthild in 1298 and that of her biological and religious sister, Abbess Gertrude, in 1291. *The Book of Special Grace*, like the *Herald*, has no extant autograph, but survives in the form of a copied manuscript dating from the fourteenth century.[84] It was condensed and translated into Middle English in the fifteenth century as the *Booke of Gostlye Grace*; in this version, the book became the most widely circulated and influential piece of Helfta literature.[85]

[84] For the manuscript, translation, and transmission history of the text, see Jacques Hourlier and Albert Schmitt, "Appendice 1," in SCh 127:52–53. It is noteworthy that Book Four contains Mechthild's letters to an anonymous laywoman friend, the only extant words known to be written by Mechthild herself. These letters are not in the BSG but have been translated into English in Mechthild of Hackeborn, "Letters from Mechthild of Hackeborn to a Friend, a Laywoman in the World Taken from the 'Book of Special Grace' Book IV, Chapter 59," in *Vox Mystica: Essays on Medieval Mysticism in Honor of Professor Valerie M. Lagorio*, ed. Anne Clark Bartlett, et al. (Cambridge: D. S. Brewer, 1995), 173–76. On the epistolary genre in late medieval women's religiosity generally, see the following collection of essays: Karen Cherewatuk and Ulrike Wiethaus, eds., *Dear Sister: Medieval Women and the Epistolary Genre* (Philadelphia: University of Pennsylvania Press, 1993).

[85] The critical edition of this translation is still Theresa A. Halligan, ed., *The Booke of Gostlye Grace of Mechtild of Hackeborn* (Toronto: Pontifical Institute of Mediaeval Studies, 1979). For textual notes and commentary on the transla-

The Book of Special Grace, like Gertrude's works, evinces positive images of both God and self, and it also describes Mechthild in a priestly role. But given her role as cantor, her priestly apostolate is depicted more often with images from liturgical chant than from the Eucharist.[86] One intriguing visionary account, for instance, relates how Christ's heart once manifested itself to Mechthild while she was singing in the choir, in the form of a ten-stringed harp. It seemed to her that as she was chanting the notes of the Psalter, she was plucking the corresponding strings of Christ's harp. After she had plucked the first nine strings, "she desired that all creatures in heaven and earth should be made sharers in the grace of God."[87] When she plucked the tenth string, she was able to take his hand, and thus redeem souls on earth and in purgatory: "And, taking the Lord's hand, she made such a great cross that it seemed to fill heaven and earth. From this the host of heaven received greater joy, the guilty pardon, the sorrowful comfort, and the righteous, strength and perseverance, while souls in purgatory were granted absolution and relief of their pains."[88]

Thus Mechthild's *Book of Special Grace* provides a further glimpse into the monastery that was Gertrude the Great's home and shows that the formation that Abbess Gertrude provided her nuns contributed to their strong and confident sense of intellectual, literary, and spiritual authority. This authority, for Mechthild as for Gertrude, was based in eucharistic communion and the deep intimacy they claimed with God through it. In addition, both

---

tion, see Halligan, *The Booke of Gostlye Grace*, 25–32, 79–107. Halligan notes the circulation records of this manuscript, as well as the many devotional materials that contained excerpts of her prayers. Halligan, *The Booke of Gostlye Grace*, 47–52.

[86] Indeed, in one eucharistic vision, when Mechthild received communion, Christ seemed to offer her his heart in the form of a chalice, which he instructed her to offer to the saints in heaven (Mechthild, *Liber* 1.1 [LSG 7–10; BSG 39–40]).

[87] 2 Pet 1:4.

[88] Mechthild, *Liber* 2.35 (LSG 182–83; BSG 142); Ann Marie Caron, "Mechthild of Hackeborn, Prophet of Divine Praise: To Sing God's Praise, To Live God's Song," CSQ 36 (2001): 157. See Johnson, "The Nightingale of Christ's Redemption Song," 183–85.

women exhibit positive images of God and self that resist the
dominant paradigm of their day. One might conjecture that these
images are also a fruit of the socialization the nuns experienced
at the monastery of St. Mary and the liturgical and educational
privileges they received under Abbess Gertrude's care.[89]

The final piece of Helfta literature, also written during Gertrude
the Great's life, is Mechthild of Magdeburg's *Flowing Light of the
Godhead* (*Fliessende Licht der Gottheit*).[90] This Mechthild (ca. 1208–
ca. 1282/1294) was born into a noble family and reported having
been visited by the Holy Spirit since the age of twelve. She continued to receive these divine greetings throughout her adolescence, probably leading her to adopt the life of a Beguine when
she was twenty-three.[91] Beguines (and their male counterparts,
the Beghards) were part of the larger spiritual renewal movement
of the thirteenth century, which sought to radically imitate the
life of Christ through voluntary poverty, religious devotion, and
pastoral care. Beguines publicly practiced charity and piety, and
even some bodily austerities, without taking vows in a religious
order. Generally, during the time of their novitiate, they lived with
other Beguines, and then they moved to their own individual
dwellings afterward, usually in urban centers, so they could be
of service to the poor.[92] As *Flowing Light* indicates, Mechthild lived
this solitary lifestyle for about forty years as a Beguine in the city

[89] Bynum, *Jesus as Mother*, 184–85; 252–55.

[90] The critical edition of this version, cited in this study [Licht], is Hans
Neumann and Gisela Vollmann-Profe, eds., *Mechthild Von Magdeburg, "Das
Fliessende Licht Der Gottheit"* (Munich: Artemis Verlag, 1990, 1993). The
modern English translation of Neumann's edition, also used in this study
[FL], is Mechthild of Magdeburg, *The Flowing Light of the Godhead*, trans. and
introduced by Frank Tobin (New York: Paulist Press, 1998).

[91] Mechthild, *Flowing Light* 4.2 (FL 139; Licht 110). Mechthild's noble lineage
is conjectured from details in her book, esp. Mechthild, *Flowing Light* 1.44 (FL
58–62; Licht 27–32); 4.2 (FL 139; Licht 110); 7.27 (FL 296–98; Licht 276–77).

[92] On the Beguines in general, see Michel Lauwers and Walter Simons,
*Béguins et Béguines à Tournai au bas Moyen Age: les communautés béguinales à
Tournai du XIIIe au XVe siècle* (Tournai and Louvain-la-Neuve: Archives du
chapitre cathédral; Université Catholique de Louvain, 1988); Saskia Murk-
Jansen, *Brides in the Desert: Spirituality of the Beguines* (Maryknoll, NY: Orbis
Books, 1998); Walter Simons, *Cities of Ladies: Beguine Communities in the Medieval*

of Magdeburg, Saxony, not too far away from the monastery of St. Mary at Helfta.

In 1270 Mechthild fled to the monastery to seek refuge from the isolation, alienation, and persecutions that she had endured because of her harsh clerical criticisms and involvement with the Beguines.[93] As one instance of her bold criticism of clergy, Mechthild writes in *Flowing Light*, "our Lord speaks thus: 'my shepherds of Jerusalem have become murderers and wolves. Before my very eyes they murder the white lambs, and the old sheep are all sick in the head because they cannot eat from the healthy pasture that grows in the high mountains, which is divine love and holy teaching.'"[94] Writing such caustic words about priests and bishops in Mechthild's time was dangerous. The lay women's movement was becoming increasingly suspect for its lack of ecclesial affiliation, approbation, and supervision. These were among the charges that led the church officially to forbid and dissolve the Beguines at the Council of Vienne in 1312. Mechthild probably experienced opposition preceding the crackdown, since a synod

---

Low Countries, 1200–1565, Middle Ages Series (Philadelphia: University of Pennsylvania Press, 2001).

[93] Although Mechthild's instructions to other Beguines (Mechthild, *Flowing Light* 3.14–15 [FL 121–24; Licht 93–97]; 3.24 [FL 134–35; Licht 106–7]; 5.5 [FL 184–85; Licht 159–60]) demonstrate her contact with the broader Beguine community in Magdeburg, her book indicates little sense of communal identity and an overriding sense of solitariness. On her sense of isolation, see Elizabeth Andersen, *The Voices of Mechthild of Magdeburg* (Oxford and New York: Peter Lang, 2000), 82; Bynum, *Jesus as Mother*, 235. On the presence of the Beguines in Magdeburg, see Murk-Jansen, *Brides in the Desert*, 66. For Mechthild's references to the persecutions she endured, see Mechthild, *Flowing Light* 1.31 (FL 55; Licht 23); 2.4 (FL 72–75; Licht 41–44); 2.26 (FL 96–98; Licht 68–70); 3.3 (FL 108–10; Licht 80–82); 3.16 (FL 124; Licht 97); 5.21 (FL 195–96; Licht 171); 6.28 (FL 253–54; Licht 235–36); 6.36 (FL 261–62; Licht 244–45); 7.17 (FL 288–89; Licht 268–70).

[94] Mechthild, *Flowing Light* 6.21 (FL 250; Licht, 232). On Mechthild's clerical criticisms, see Marianne Heimbach, *"Der ungelehrte Mund" als Autorität: mystische Erfahrung als Quelle kirklich-prophetischer Rede im Werk Mechthilds von Magdeburg* (Stuttgart-Bad Cannstatt: Frommann-Holzboog, 1989), 152–57; Sara S. Poor, *Mechthild of Magdeburg and her Book: Gender and the Making of Textual Authority*, Middle Ages Series (Philadelphia: University of Pennsylvania Press, 2004), 41–48.

held in Magdeburg in 1261 threatened Beguines with excommunication if they disobeyed their parish priests.[95]

Yet while still living in Magdeburg as a Beguine, Mechthild attained some spiritual and literary support from at least one priest, her Dominican confessor, Heinrich of Halle. At some point in her forties, she disclosed her visionary experiences to him, and he reportedly encouraged her to write them down in a book, as if her words came "out of God's heart and mouth."[96] Mechthild's *Flowing Light* comprises 7 books and 267 subdivisions, and it includes a variety of literary forms (i.e., courtly love poetry, dialogue, drama, folk and wedding song, and allegory). Her confessor, Heinrich of Halle, edited the original version of her book and circulated it widely. It seems that, lacking the influence of monastic vows, Mechthild had to seek out a male cleric to bolster her female religious authority more directly than did the women writers at Helfta.

Although the autograph of *Flowing Light* is lost, a translation of the book into Middle High German, completed shortly after Mechthild's death, is extant; this book therefore serves as the basis for the modern critical edition and its numerous translations.[97] It is also significant that after having penned the first six books of *Flowing Light* as a Beguine in Magdeburg, Mechthild finished her

[95] Ernest W. McDonnell, *The Beguines and Beghards in Medieval Culture, with Special Emphasis on the Belgian Scene* (New York: Octagon Books, 1969), 508.

[96] Mechthild, *Flowing Light* 4.2 (FL 144; Licht 114). As Ursula Peters notes, readers should not take Mechthild's assertions that she wrote under the prompting of and in obedience to her Dominican confessor at face value. She thinks it more probable that these are fictive assertions adhering to a common female literary convention common in spiritual texts written by women (Ursula Peters, *Religiöse Erfahrung als literarisches Faktum: zur Vorgeschichte und Genese frauenmystischer Texte des 13. und 14. Jahrhunderts* [Tübingen: Niemeyer, 1988], 53–67, 116–29. For more on Mechthild's authority and audience, see Poor, *Mechthild of Magdeburg and her Book*; Frank J. Tobin, "Audience, Authorship and Authority in Mechthild von Magdeburg's 'Flowing Light of the Godhead,' " *Mystics Quarterly* 23, no. 1 (March 1997): 8–17; Andersen, *The Voices of Mechthild of Magdeburg*; Elizabeth A. Andersen, "Mechthild von Magdeburg: Her Creativity and Her Audience," in *Women, the Book and the Godly*, ed. Lesley Smith and Jane H. M. Taylor (Cambridge: D. S. Brewer, 1995); Heimbach, *"Der ungelehrte Mund" als Autorität*.

[97] Tobin, "Introduction," in *Flowing Light*, 6–9.

work at Helfta. In fact, when she was struck by blindness and entered her last illness, she dictated the seventh book to the Helfta nuns.[98]

Within the established women's community of theological discourse at Helfta, Mechthild was supported in her literary efforts and sought after for her spiritual wisdom. While she never officially joined the community, she is probably responsible for deepening the monastery's relationship with the Dominicans and for catalyzing the devotion to the Sacred Heart of Jesus taken up by the younger nuns, especially Gertrude of Helfta.[99] Despite all of this, though, Mechthild says that she always felt inferior to the Helfta nuns. Ignorant of Latin and lacking an education from the monastic school at Helfta, she writes that she could not suitably advise her religious sisters on any matter.[100] Her self-doubt, suggests Caroline Walker Bynum, may have been due to the sociohistorical fact that Mechthild had seen the corruption in the church and had internalized the persecutions she had endured for asserting religious authority to teach and criticize the clergy.[101]

Flowing Light is peppered with images of suffering, alienation, and deprivation. Such language helps Mechthild to describe her experience of divine union, which knew deep union with Christ primarily through suffering. This experience is illustrated in a beautiful couplet from Book Four of the *work*, which seems to

---

[98] Mechthild, *Flowing Light* 7.64 (FL 334; Licht 309–10).

[99] Scholars generally agree that members of the Order of Preachers informed Mechthild's religiosity, that she maintained contact with her confessor and editor of her work after she entered Helfta, and that her biological brother, Baldwin, entered the Dominican Order, becoming a sub-prior at the friar's house in Halle. See, for example, Frank J. Tobin, *Mechthild von Magdeburg: A Medieval Mystic in Modern Eyes*, 1st ed. (Columbia, SC: Camden House, 1995), 128–31; Tobin, "Introduction," 4–6. On Mechthild's influence on the Sacred Heart at Helfta, see Rosalyn Voaden, "All Girls Together: Community, Gender, and Vision at Helfta," in *Medieval Women and Their Communities*, ed. Diane Watt (Toronto: University of Toronto Press, 1997), 76–77. Finally, both Mechthild of Hackeborn and Gertrude of Helfta speak highly of Sister M. in their books, which is probably a reference to Mechthild of Magdeburg. See for example Gertrude, *Herald* 5.7.1–4 (SCh 331:122–26) and Mechthild, *Liber* 4.8 (LSG 226; BSG 168); *Liber* 5.3 (LSG 320–21).

[100] Mechthild, *Flowing Light* 2.3 (FL 72; Licht 40).

[101] *Jesus as Mother*, 184–85, 252–55.

encapsulate the entirety of her spiritual project: "The deeper I sink, / The sweeter I drink."[102] Bynum characterizes Mechthild's spirituality as one of suffering: "Moments outside the ecstasy of union are secure only if they are experienced as alienation and deprivation; to her the structure of the universe *is* the rhythm of oneness and loss."[103]

While the writings of Gertrude the Great and Mechthild of Hackeborn focus on the immediate quality of divine union the women enjoy during liturgical celebration, Mechthild of Magdeburg emphasizes union with God through loss—even being deprived of routine ministerial care and the sacraments. Accordingly, in Book Three of *Flowing Light*, she laments, "Oh, Lord, now I am extremely destitute in my sickly body and am so miserable in my

---

[102] Mechthild, *Flowing Light* 4.12 (FL 156; Licht 127).

[103] Bynum, *Jesus as Mother*, 247 (author's emphasis). On the general place of suffering and asceticism in Mechthild's spirituality, see Amy M. Hollywood, *The Soul as Virgin Wife: Mechthild of Magdeburg, Marguerite Porete, and Meister Eckhart* (Notre Dame: University of Notre Dame Press, 1995), 57–89, 173–206; Ulrike Wiethaus, "Suffering, Love and Transformation in Mechthild of Magdeburg," *Listening* 22 (1987): 139–57. For Mechthild's spirituality in general, and her visions, see Alois Maria Haas, "Mechthilds von Magdeburg dichterische heimlichkeit," in *Gotes und der werlde hulde: Literatur im Mittelalter und Neuzeit: Festschrift für Heinz Rupp zum 70. Geburtstag*, ed. Rüdiger Schnell (Bern/Stuttgart: Francke, 1989), 206–23; Hildegund Keul, "Du bist ein inniger Kuss meines Mundes. Die Sprache der Mystik—eine Sprache der Erotik. Am Beispiel Mechthilds von Magdeburg," in *"Vor dir steht die leere Schale meiner Sehnsucht": Die Mystik der Frauen von Helfta*, ed. Hildegund Keul and Michael Bangert (Leipzig: Benno, 1998), 95–111; Frank Tobin, "Hierarchy and Ponerarchy: Mechthild von Magdeburg's Visual Representations of Spiritual Orders," in *Nu lôn' ich iu der gâbe: Festschrift for Francis G. Gentry*, ed. Ernst Ralf Hintz (Göppingen: Kümmerle Verlag, 2003), 241–53; Tobin, *Mechthild von Magdeburg: a Medieval Mystic in Modern Eyes*; Tobin, "Medieval Thought on Visions and its Resonance in Mechthild von Magdeburg's Flowing Light of the Godhead," in *Vox Mystica: Essays on Medieval Mysticism in Honor of Mary E. Giles*, ed. Robert Boenig (Burlington, NY, and London: Ashgate, 2000). For an exhaustive bibliography of scholarship on the life and work of Mechthild von Magdeburg (as well as that of Gertrude of Helfta and Mechthild of Hackeborn), see Gertrud Jaron Lewis, Frank Willaert, and Marie-José Govers, *Bibliographie zur deutschen Frauenmystik des Mittelalters* (Berlin: Erich Schmidt, 1989), 159–223.

soul which is so lacking in spiritual order that no one recites the hours of the office in my presence and no one celebrates holy mass for me!"[104]

As Bynum has shown, the Helfta literature offers an interesting case for comparison on the effect of socio-cultural influences on religious images. While Mechthild of Hackeborn and Gertrude the Great, who had entered the cloister as child oblates, knew nothing other than the liturgical and intellectual woman-centered community that Abbess Gertrude worked to provide, Mechthild of Magdeburg experienced the scathing effects of living within a misogynistic culture for most of her life. Bynum attributes the differences between Mechthild of Magdeburg's negative images of self and the positive, even priestly ones, of Mechthild of Hackeborn and Gertrude the Great to their social contexts. While some degree of misogyny may have been internalized by the nuns at Helfta, given their close contact with the theological tradition, the constant and courageous persecution Mechthild of Magdeburg endured throughout her life would certainly have made her more prone than Mechthild of Hackeborn and Gertrude the Great to be affected by stereotypes defining women as morally and intellectually inferior to men.[105]

It is significant that Gertrude was a stronger advocate of frequent communion and a more regular imaginer of herself as a priest than Mechthild of Hackeborn, who lived within the same social setting. Why is this so? Of course, personality distinctions and different roles within the monastery may provide some of the reasons. While Mechthild drew from her leadership authority within the community as cantor, Gertrude drew hers primarily from her recognized spiritual gift of trust in God's merciful kindness. But the answer seems to have to do with something more, that is, Gertrude's profound and formative conversion experience. Indeed, Gertrude was a grammarian turned theologian. As she reports, before her conversion she paid as much attention to her inner life as she did to the soles of her feet; her experience of mo-

---

[104] Mechthild, *Flowing Light* 3.5 (FL 111; Licht 83).
[105] Bynum, *Jesus as Mother*, 184–85, 252–55.

nastic life was empty. Going through the motions in her monastic routine, she says, left her melancholic and anxious, and her intellect and soul were isolated from one another, as if in a duality. For this reason, it seems that after her conversion she had a heightened sense of awareness about the integration of her soul and intellect and the relationship between her exterior actions and interior motivations. Not only did monastic customs and liturgical celebrations elicit her visions, but she also worked carefully to promote them by integrating them into her spiritual instructions and theological writings.

In comparing Mechthild of Magdeburg with Gertrude the Great and Mechthild of Hackeborn, it is critical to avoid juxtaposing the latter two by overstating their similarities, as was suggested in scholars' mistaken identification of Gertrude as the compiler of *The Book of Special Grace*. While their socialization at Helfta doubtlessly influenced them, they also are individuals who, as in any community, were valued for their own individual ideas and spiritual projects. Both Mechthild of Hackeborn and Gertrude stress the incarnation of Christ more than the passion, for which Mechthild of Magdeburg has a predilection. But Gertrude's anthropology is influenced by her conversion experience and the way it affected the hermetical lens through which she read the theological tradition. Therefore the theology she puts forth is significantly original, different even from that of Mechthild of Hackeborn.

Finally, that Gertrude the Great is also known as Gertrude the Great "of Helfta" points to the significance of the place she lived, conducted her ministry, and wrote her books. In other words, a satisfactory analysis of the innovations Gertrude made in eucharistic theology and anthropology depends upon a thorough understanding of her life experiences, of the women with whom she lived and wrote, and of the way her books were formed.

CHAPTER THREE

The Doctrine of Spiritual Senses
According to Gertrude's Sources

Inspired by the language of Scripture, writers throughout
Christian history have drawn extensively from the vocabulary of
the five bodily senses to discuss how humans know God.[1] They
say that divine union includes the experience of seeing,[2] hearing,[3]
smelling,[4] tasting,[5] and touching God.[6] Biblical commentators

---

[1] For recent work on the importance of the doctrine of the spiritual senses
in religious writing and theology in the later Middle Ages, see Boyd Taylor
Coolman, *Knowing God by Experience: The Spiritual Senses in the Theology of
William of Auxerre* (Washington, DC: Catholic University of America Press,
2004); Rachel Fulton, " 'Taste and See that the Lord is Sweet' (Ps. 33:9): The
Flavor of God in the Monastic West," *Journal of Religion* 86, no. 2 (2006):
169–204; Rosemary Drage Hale, " 'Taste and See, for God is Sweet': Sensory
Perception and Memory in Medieval Christian Mystical Experience," in *Vox
Mystica: Essays on Medieval Mysticism in Honor of Professor Valerie M. Lagorio*,
ed. Anne Clark, et al. (Cambridge: D. S. Brewer, 1995), 3–14; Gordon Rudy,
Mystical Language of Sensation in the Later Middle Ages, Studies in Medieval
History and Culture, vol. 14 (New York: Routledge, 2002). For a study in early
Christianity, see Susan Ashbrook Harvey, *Scenting Salvation: Ancient Chris-
tianity and the Olfactory Imagination*, Transformation of the Classical Heritage,
42 (Berkeley: University of California Press, 2006).

[2] Ps 18:9; Eph 1:18.

[3] Matt 13:9; 2 Cor 12:2.

[4] 2 Cor 12:15.

[5] Ps 33:9; John 6:32.

[6] John 1:1. Several other biblical narratives are perennial favorites in relation to the spiritual senses (e.g., Moses' event on Mt. Sinai [Exod 24:9-18;
34:29-35], Ezekiel's visions of the chariot [Ezek 1:1-28], Isaiah's celestial altar

have also, of course, frequently read the vividly sensual book, the Song of Songs, as an allegory for the divine-human encounter.[7]

Yet this sensory language has also posed problems for many authors in the history of Christian thought. They have had to consider its theological appropriateness and implications with questions like "How can terms that manifest bodily existence and the perception of material things apply to an immaterial, incorporeal God? What is the role of the body, if any, in the pursuit of knowing and loving a transcendent God, who is entirely beyond the material and physical realm?"

Beginning with Origen of Alexandria (ca. 185–252), Christian theologians have tried to work out systematic solutions to these questions. As one of the first leading contributors to the tradition, Origen established an influential doctrine on the spiritual senses that was underpinned by a thoroughly dualistic anthropology and cosmology. Above all, he was concerned to refute any notion of God as bodily and to counter any interpretation of the Bible's sensory language as physical. He thus sharply distinguished between the senses of the body and the senses of the soul, having the effect of radically opposing the ways persons know material things and spiritual things.[8]

[Isa 6:1-7], the disciples' witness of the Transfiguration of Christ on Mt. Tabor [Mark 9:2-8; Matt 17:1-8; Luke 9:28-36], and the apostle Paul's experience of being caught up into Paradise [2 Cor 12:2-4]).

[7] The doctrine of the spiritual senses should not be confused with the "spiritual sense" of Scripture developed in medieval exegesis. In the latter, the "spiritual sense" is defined as distinct from the "literal sense," in which the words signify things, because it refers to the fact that the things signified by the words signify other things. For this definition, see Thomas Aquinas's *Summa Theologiae*, p. 1, 1, a. 10. See also Henri de Lubac, *Medieval Exegesis: The Four Senses of Scripture*, vol. 2 (Grand Rapids, MI: Wm. B. Eerdmans, 2000); Friedrich Ohly, "On the Spiritual Sense of the Word in the Middle Ages," in *Sensus spiritualis: Studies in Medieval Significs and the Philology of Culture*, ed. Kenneth J. Northcott (Chicago: University of Chicago Press, 2005), 1–30; Beryl Smalley, "Use of the 'Spiritual' Senses of Scripture in Persuasion and Argument by Scholars in the Middle Ages," *Recherches de théologie ancienne et médiévale* 44 (1985): 44–63.

[8] Rudy, *Mystical Language of Sensation*, 1, 3, 17–35; Karl Rahner, "The 'Spiritual Senses' According to Origen," in *Experience of the Spirit: Source of the Theology*, Theological Investigations, vol. 16 (New York: Crossroad, 1979), 81–103.

Even when Christian writers after Origen departed from his Middle Platonic presuppositions, they still tended to be influenced by his dualism when they engaged the doctrine of the spiritual senses. Several later Western theologians, for example, agreed with him that sensual language is ultimately inappropriate for God.[9] If they used any sensory language at all to describe how persons know or perceive God, they used sight. In this regard, they assumed the Aristotelian sensory schema in which sight and hearing are ranked as the superior and most spiritual senses, and taste and touch as the lowest and most bodily ones.[10] The ranking was also convenient for writers seeking to uphold the established tradition, as it easily agreed with Origen's basically dualist anthropology and his influential association between sight and the intellect that "sees."[11]

---

[9] The most complete study of the development of the doctrine of the spiritual senses in the West remains Karl Rahner, "The Doctrine of the Spiritual Senses in the Middle Ages: The Contribution of Bonaventure," in *Theological Investigations*, vol. 16 (New York: Crossroad, 1979), 109–28. See also Hans Urs Von Balthasar, *The Glory of the Lord: A Theological Aesthetics*, ed. John Riches, trans. Andrew Louth and Francis McDonagh, Studies in Theological Style, vol. 2 (San Francisco: Ignatius Press, 1982), 309–26; Coolman, *Knowing God by Experience*; M. Olphe-Galliard, "Les sens spirituels dans l'histoire de la spiritualité," in *Nos sens et Dieu: Études carmélitaines* (Bruges: Desclée de Brouwer, 1954), 179–93; Gregorio Penco, "La dottrina dei sensi spirituali in Gregorio Magno," *Benedictina* 17 (1970): 161–201; John Giles Milhaven, *Hadewijch and her Sisters: Other Ways of Loving and Knowing* (Albany, NY: State University of New York Press, 1993).

[10] See Aristotle, "On Sense and Sensible Objects," in *On the Soul: Parva naturalia* (Cambridge: Harvard University Press, 1957), 219. On this schema in the Western monastic tradition, see Fulton, " 'Taste and See that the Lord is Sweet' " 190; Elizabeth Sears, "Sensory Perception and Its Metaphors in the Time of Richard of Fournival," in *Medicine and the Five Senses*, ed. W. F. Bynum and Roy Porter (Cambridge: Cambridge University Press, 1993), 17–39; Nelson Pike, *Mystic Union: An Essay in the Phenomenology of Mysticism*, Cornell Studies in the Philosophy of Religion (Ithaca, NY: Cornell University Press, 1992), 45.

[11] Rahner points out that several medieval writers (with the exception of Bonaventure) were concerned to maintain Origen's identification of the spiritual senses of sight and hearing with the incorporeal intellect (Rahner, "The Doctrine of the Spiritual Senses in the Middle Ages," 109–28). See Janet Martin Soskice, "Sight and Vision in Medieval Christian Thought," in *Vision*

Even writers like Augustine of Hippo and Bernard of Clairvaux, who put forth fresh ideas about the structure of the person, were still influenced at times by Origen's dualistic thought, especially when they used sensory language. Thus their ideas about the spiritual senses are difficult to classify as either wholly affirmative of the role of the body in knowing God or disparaging of it. Complex as they are, the writings of Augustine and Bernard are important to consider—not only for their profound influence on medieval Western thought in general, but also for their influence on the writings of Gertrude of Helfta.[12] Gertrude seizes upon the more body-affirmative language and holistic ideas within Augustine's and Bernard's teachings on the spiritual senses, in order to use them as source and authorization for her own innovative anthropology and epistemology, which are based on her idea that the body and soul of the person unite with the body and soul of Christ in the liturgy of the Eucharist. Gertrude ultimately jettisons the dualism of Origen's concept of the spiritual senses and any of its traces left over in Augustine's and Bernard's sensory language.

Origen's Legacy:
The Corporeal and Spiritual Senses
as Radically Opposed

Origen's doctrine of the spiritual senses is first and foremost about how to interpret the carnal language found in the Scriptures. For him, when the Bible speaks about knowing God through

---

in Context: Historical and Contemporary Perspectives on Sight, ed. Teresa Brenna and Martin Jay (New York and London: Routledge, 1996), 29–43; Suzannah Biernoff, *Sight and Embodiment in the Middle Ages* (Basingstoke, UK: Palgrave Macmillan, 2002); David F. Appleby, "The Priority of Sight according to Peter the Venerable," *Mediaeval Studies* 60 (1998): 123–57; Rudolph E. Siegel, *Galen on Sense Perception. His Doctrines, Observations and Experiments on Vision, Hearing, Smell, Taste, Touch and Pain, and their Historical Sources* (Basel: Karger, 1970).

[12] As was discussed in the previous chapter, the Helfta nuns were familiar with the writings of Augustine and Bernard, and also Origen. Moreover, because of the influence of the three thinkers' writings, one can also rightly assume that their ideas would have been available to Gertrude in the reception history (*Wirkungsgeschichte*) of the established tradition.

the five senses, it refers to a "spiritual" kind of sensory faculty, wholly different from the physical one. The names of the five spiritual senses (i.e., sight, hearing, smell, taste, and touch), he says, are the only thing they have in common with their corporeal counterparts:

> So also will you find the names of the members of the body transferred to those of the soul; or rather the faculties and powers of the soul are to be called its members. . . . It is perfectly clear that in these passages the names of the members can in no way be applied to the physical body, but must be referred to the parts and the powers of the invisible soul. The members have the same names, yes; but the names plainly and without any ambiguity carry meaning proper to the inner, not the outer man.[13]

Therefore, as an exegete and guide of souls, Origen is quick to spiritualize any bodily language of seeing, hearing, smelling, tasting, or touching God in the Bible. About the physical intimacy written about in the Song of Songs, for example, he says, "We find there a certain sensation of an embrace *by the spirit*."[14] He thus teaches that the spiritual senses belong to the organs and actions of the "inner" person, the soul, and are analogous but completely separate from the bodily senses of the "outer" person.

Origen derives his sharp distinction between the inner and outer persons from Paul's New Testament letters:[15]

> since the Apostle frequently writes in a way that indicates that in each one there are two human beings, one of whom he calls the external, the other the internal, calling one of them according to the flesh and the other according to the Spirit (following, I think, what is written in Genesis where one was created in God's image and the other formed from

---

[13] Origen, Cant Prol.2.9; Origen, *The Song of Songs: Commentary and Homilies*, trans. R. P. Lawson, Ancient Christian Writers, vol. 26 (New York: Paulist Press, 1957), 27–28.

[14] Origen, Cant 1.2; Origen, *The Song of Songs: Commentary and Homilies*, 65 (my emphasis).

[15] For example, 2 Cor 4:16; Rom 7:22; Eph 3:16.

the dust of the earth) . . . it must be observed that each of these is set up so as to be in some things different and in others similar. For some things begin with the internal human being and move on to the external, and others which have their beginning in the external human being move on to the internal.[16]

Basing his view on Paul, therefore, Origen concludes that the soul has a "kind of sense faculty which is immortal, spiritual and divine."[17] He is emphatically clear that this spiritual faculty is radically opposed to the corporeal one.[18] It is a higher-sense faculty, which is not bodily, because it refers to "a sensuality which has nothing sensual in it."[19]

This opposition of the spiritual and corporeal senses in Origen's thought is predicated upon the Platonic tradition and its basic cosmological and anthropological assumptions that oppose spirit to material body and knowledge of spiritual things to knowledge of material things.[20] According to this view, God, who is pure spirit, exists apart from all matter—without any intermixture—and is thus not discernable by the corporeal senses. Put simply, spirit can know spirit; matter cannot. As Origen declares, "God is not

[16] Origen, Comm in Rom 2.12; Hans Urs von Balthasar, ed., *Origen, Spirit and Fire: A Thematic Anthology of His Writings* (Washington, DC: Catholic University of America Press, 1984), 208–9.

[17] Origen, Princ 1.1.4; Origen, *On First Principles*, trans. G. W. Butterworth (Gloucester, MA: Peter Smith, 1973), 9. See also Origen, Cels 1:48; Origen, *Contra Celsum*, trans. Henry Chadwick (Cambridge: University Press, 1953), 44; Rahner, "The 'Spiritual Senses' According to Origen," 85.

[18] Mariette Canévet points to some of the theories on the relation between the corporeal and spiritual senses (e.g., as "radical opposition," as "separate parallelism," and in some cases as "transformative evolution" from physical to spiritual sense perception). I use her categories here to draw a distinction between the thought on the one hand of Origen, who maintains the first kind of relationship, and on the other of Augustine and Bernard, who maintain the third kind of relationship (Mariette Canévet, "Sens spirituel," in *Dictionnaire de spiritualité ascétique et mystique doctrine et histoire*, ed. Marcel Viller, et al. [Paris: Beauchesne, 1937], 15:598–619).

[19] Origen, Cels 1.48; Origen, *Contra Celsum*, 44.

[20] Rahner, "The 'Spiritual Senses' According to Origen," 93; Harvey, *Scenting Salvation*, 101–5.

in a place but is indescribable, ineffable and invisible." So "we obviously approach him by something invisible in us. And what is invisible in us if not the human being hidden in the heart which scripture calls the 'inner human being?' This is what can come near to God."[21] For Origen, knowledge of God is beyond humans and "is better than the body."[22] He even declares, "they do wrong even to God himself in supposing that he can be understood through a bodily nature, since according to them, that which can be understood or perceived through a body is itself a body; and they are unwilling to have it understood that there is a certain affinity between the mind and God, of whom the mind is an intellectual image, and that by reason of this fact the mind, especially if it is purified and separated from bodily matter, is able to have some perception of divine nature."[23]

For Origen, then, the process of gaining divine knowledge requires that the spirit of the person be separated from the body, so that it is able to ascend to the immaterial God, who is pure Spirit. In order to make any kind of spiritual progress, the person must eschew the body and all material things. Origen asserts of the soul, "the Word of God . . . exhorts her to arise and come to Him, that is to say: to forsake things bodily and visible and to hasten to those that are not of the body and are spiritual. For *the things which are seen are temporal, but the things which are not seen are eternal.*"[24] In addition, he interprets *the inward man is renewed day by day*[25] to mean that when the person's soul (*psuchē*) uses its spiritual senses to learn from the Logos, the "inward man" of the person is transformed.[26] He points to the "names" (*epinoia*) of the Logos, especially Wisdom (*Sophia*), as the proper spiritual objects

---

[21] Origen, Cels 3.41; Origen, *Contra Celsum*, 426. This passage contains another allusion to Rom 7:22. See also Cels 1.48; 7.37–38.

[22] Origen, Cels 1.48; Origen, *Contra Celsum*, 45.

[23] See Origen, Princ 1.1.7–9; Origen, *On First Principles*, 12–13. See also Rudy, *Mystical Language of Sensation*, 19–24.

[24] Origen, Cant 3.13; Origen, *The Song of Songs: Commentary and Homilies*, 234 (translator's emphasis).

[25] 2 Cor 4:16.

[26] See Origen, Cant Prol.2; Origen, *The Song of Songs: Commentary and Homilies*, 22–26. See also Rudy, *Mystical Language of Sensation*, 30–31.

to which the soul should direct its attention, rather than the bodily actions and works of Jesus Christ: "the Son is the Word, and therefore we must understand that nothing in him is perceptible to the senses."[27]

Origen's devaluing of the human body of Jesus Christ originates in his dualistic understanding of the Fall. Origen understands the experience of Paradise as wholly spiritual. The universe was populated only by pre-existent spiritual intellects—angelic, human, and demonic. Because of his interpretation of Romans 8.6, *The mind set on the flesh is death, but the mind set on the Spirit is life and peace,* he reasons that in Paradise the human intellect (*nous*) was focused entirely on union with the fiery Holy Spirit. When the intellect (*nous*) of the person fell, because of its "fatal sin of self-satisfaction," its immaterial spirit (*pneuma*) was placed in a body (*soma*), and the intellect became cold. Thus Origen's understanding of structure of the person in the fallen state is complex; it comprises the spirit (*pneuma*), soul (*psuchē*), intellect (*nous*), and body (*soma*). He identifies the soul (*psuchē*, derived from *psychros* or "cold") with the "cooled" state of the fallen intellect (*nous*).[28]

Moreover, Origen teaches that the soul (*psuchē*) is a two-part composite: it has both a higher part, associated with the spirit (*pneuma*), and a lower part, associated with the body (*soma*).[29] What this means for persons in regard to knowing God in this fallen state is that the soul (*psuchē*) is able to be either redirected above to the immaterial God and heated by God's primal fire, or

[27] Origen, Princ 1.1.9; Origen, *On First Principles*, 19. Origen understands the body of Christ and the material body of the person as divinely created, precisely because these bodies provide a way for the fallen intellect to return to God. Yet for Origen, the chief function of the incarnation is to reveal the Logos, in order to direct fallen humanity to a nonobvious spiritual referent. See Origen, Princ 4.1.6; 4.2.3; Rudy, *Mystical Language of Sensation*, 33–35; Marguerite Harl, *Origène et la fonction révélatrice du verbe incarné* (Paris: Éditions du Seuil, 1958), 340–45.

[28] See Henri Crouzel, *Origen*, trans. A. S. Worrall (San Francisco: Harper and Row, 1989), 123–47, esp. 124–26.

[29] See Origen, Princ 2.8; Rudy, *Mystical Language of Sensation*, 30. Crouzel notes that it is difficult to define Origen's definition of *psuchē*, because he associates it so closely with *pneuma* (Crouzel, *Origen*, 123–37, esp. 124–26).

dragged down below by the material body (*soma*) and numbed by the cold absence of love.[30] The eternal Logos, who was already present in the created world and Jewish Scriptures, only took on a body so that fallen intellect (*nous*) of the person might be led back to its original state—that is, immaterial spirit (*pneuma*).[31] Origen asserts that the body of the person is the result of the Fall and a concession for the fallen intellect and soul to return to God: when "the soul is in the house of this body, she cannot receive the naked and plain wisdom of God, but beholds the invisible and the incorporeal by means of certain analogies and tokens and images of visible things."[32]

In accordance with his anthropology and epistemology, Origen conceives the relationship between the corporeal and spiritual senses to be one of radical opposition.[33] Even when the spiritual senses are properly trained, they do not renew the corporeal senses. Instead, they slough them off, because he regards the corporeal as completely nonspiritual. They can never become spiritual in any kind of transformation, because they belong to the lower part of the soul and are directed to bodily and material things, which are opposed to God.

This relationship of radical opposition between the spiritual and corporeal senses is illustrated in Origen's words about the faculty of sight. In his *Fragments on Luke*, for example, he writes: "This is how I understand what God said: 'Who makes him . . . seeing blind? Is it not I, the Lord?'[34] There is an eye of the body with which we view these earthly things, an eye according to the sense of the flesh, of which Scripture says: 'coming in puffed up

---

[30] Origen, Princ 1.6.4, 2.9.7. See also Bernard McGinn, *The Foundations of Mysticism* (New York: Crossroad, 1992), 114; Peter Brown, *The Body and Society: Men, Women, and Sexual Renunciation in Early Christianity*, Twentieth-Anniversary ed. (New York: Columbia University Press, 2008), 163–66.

[31] See Origen, Princ 1.2; 2.6.1; 2.6.3. See also Karen Jo Tørjesen, *Hermeneutical Procedure and Theological Structure in Origen's Exegesis*, Patristische Texte und Studien, Bd. 28 (Berlin: De Gruyter, 1986).

[32] Origen, Cant 3.13; Origen, *The Song of Songs: Commentary and Homilies*, 234.

[33] Rudy, *Mystical Language of Sensation*, 31–32.

[34] Exod 4:11.

without reason by his sensuous mind.'[35] Over against this we have
another, better eye that perceives the things of God. Because it had
become blind, Jesus came to make it see."[36] Here Origen makes an
analogy between corporeal and spiritual sight, but he also depicts
a dichotomous relationship between them.[37] The dichotomy relates
the corporeal and spiritual senses of sight respectively to the pair
of opposite principles—i.e., matter and spirit.

In this way Origen insists that when he speaks of seeing God,
it is only a metaphor; the corporeal sense cannot know God. He
warns about the opposition of corporeal vision to spiritual vision,
"Unless the sight of evil things is first shut off, the view of good
things will not be opened up."[38] Origen bluntly teaches that "seeing" God is only possible in the spiritual realm: "Anyone interested should realize that we need a body for various purposes
because we are in a material place. But in order to know God we
need no body at all. The knowledge of God is not derived from
the eye of the body, but from the mind which sees that which is
in the image of the Creator and by divine providence has received
the power to know God."[39]

---

[35] Col 2:18.

[36] Origen, In Luc Fragm 16; Von Balthasar, ed., *Origen, Spirit and Fire*, 236.
See also Origen, Cels 7.39. It is important to note, as is indicated in this passage, that the proper use and training of the spiritual senses is made possible
by the Logos, who bestows light and grace to the soul and makes room for
himself in the faculties of the "inner man." On this, see Origen, Cels 1.6–7.

[37] As G. E. R. Lloyd explains, analogy and dichotomy are commonly used
in ancient Greek thought to distinguish between two kinds of knowledge:
the former connotes "assimilating or likening one (unknown) object to another that was or seemed to be better known," whereas the latter entails
"relating or reducing phenomena to a pair or pairs of opposite principles"
(G. E. R. Lloyd, *Polarity and Analogy: Two Types of Argumentation in Early Greek
Thought* [Bristol: Bristol Classics, 1987], 236). This sense of *dichotomy* indicates
a form of logical opposition, which is distinct from *dichotomy* understood in
Aristotelian terms as a relationship between two extremities of a given locus
(e.g., contrariety or correlativity). On this see Lloyd, *Polarity and Analogy*,
161–65.

[38] Origen, Hom 1–28 in Num 17.3; Von Balthasar, ed., *Origen, Spirit and Fire*,
236. See also Origen, Cels 1.7, 8.23; Origen, Cant 2.9.

[39] Origen, Cels 7.34; Origen, *Contra Celsum*, 421.

Indeed, Origen grants the body no real or meaningful role in the way humans know and return to God. Because he regards the human as quintessentially spiritual, he maintains that the material body (*soma*) will be left behind at the final *apokatastasis*.[40] There will be another body, a wholly "spiritual body" (*soma pneumatikos*), which will have nothing to do with the material one in which the soul was housed as a result of the Fall. He believes that even Jesus' body will no longer be necessary in the Eschaton: "One will see the Father and the things of the Father for oneself, just as the Son does, no longer merely recognizing in the image the reality of the one whose image it is. And I think this will be the end, when the Son hands over the Kingdom to God his Father, and when God becomes all in all."[41] There and then, at the final *apokatastasis*, when corporeal sight is left behind, the person will finally enjoy a clear vision of God.[42]

Origen is consistent in his view of the incarnation as a concession to embodiment, which he defines as a result of the Fall. Jesus' works and even the Scriptures are helpful for spiritual progress

[40] Origen, Princ 2.3.3; 3.6.8. See also D. G. Bostock, "Quality and Corporeity in Origen," in *Origeniana Secunda*, ed. Henri Crouzel and Antonio Quacquarelli (Rome: Edizioni dell Ateneo, 1980), 333–35.

[41] Origen, Jo 1.16; A. E. Brooke, ed., *The Commentary of Origen on St. John's Gospel*, vol. 1 (Cambridge: Cambridge University Press, 1896), 92. See also Lawrence R. Hennessey, "A Philosophical Issue in Origen's Eschatology: The Three Senses of Incorporeality," in *Origeniana Quinta: Papers of the 5th International Origen Congress, Boston College, 14–18 August 1989*, ed. Robert Daly (Leuven: Peeters Press, 1992), 373–80.

[42] Rahner, "The 'Spiritual Senses' According to Origen," 97. Origen maintains that a few people have attained the *summa perfectionis* in this life and no longer need their corporeal senses to know God; he holds up Isaac, Moses, and the apostles John and Paul as biblical examples. These men reached the point where they did not even need the Scriptures to know God anymore, because their spiritual senses had become so preternaturally sharp that they began to perceive the immaterial Logos directly. Origen, Princ 1.1.9; 1.2.4; Origen, Cels 1.1.48; Others, who have not yet reached the *summa perfectionis*, may develop a particular spiritual sense but never come to full use of all five. The virgins in the Song of Songs (Song 1:3), for example, possess the sense of smell from following the bride (Origen, Cant 1.4). See Origen, Princ 2.3.3; Crouzel, *Origen*, 125; Rudy, *Mystical Language of Sensation*, 31.

only inasmuch as they might assist the person in the embodied and fallen state in becoming separated from matter on the pathway back to the essential state as immaterial spirit. Origen regards the sacraments in the same way. Jesus Christ becomes perceptible in eucharistic communion, for example, to suit the senses of the soul: "He is the Bread of Life, so that the *soul's* palate might have something to taste . . . . For the same reason, He is said to be able to be felt and handled, and is called the Word made flesh, so that the hand of the interior soul may touch concerning the Word of Life."[43] For Origen, the Logos is perceptible to fallen humanity in the sacraments, because humans can no longer perceive the plain Wisdom of the immaterial God without the help of visible things. Their materiality and the way that the five corporeal senses perceive them—especially the lowest and most bodily senses of taste and touch—Origen maintains, should be understood as existing solely as a concession to human materiality: "But all these things are the One Same Word of God, who adapts Himself to the sundry tempers of prayer according to these several guises, and so leaves none of the soul's faculties empty of grace."[44]

Origen's doctrine of the senses is thoroughly dualistic. Based on his view of the fundamental radical opposition between matter and spirit, he regards the relationship between the corporeal and spiritual senses as a dichotomy. He argues that the corporeal senses, as well as Jesus' body, the Scriptures, and the sacraments have no real or lasting meaning in the spiritual life. They are all meant to be discarded after having been used as a necessary step to help the fallen intellect and soul perceive the immaterial God.

Augustine's Doctrine:
The Superiority and Intermediary Potential of Sight

Writing a little over a century after Origen, Augustine was influenced by some of Origen's Middle Platonism while still making

[43] Origen, Cant 2.9; Origen, *The Song of Songs: Commentary and Homilies*, 162.
[44] Origen, Cant 2.9; Origen, *The Song of Songs: Commentary and Homilies*, 162.

some important and lasting advances.[45] For instance, Augustine too derives his language of the spiritual senses from the Pauline distinction between the inner and outer person, as he makes clear in *On the Trinity*: "No one doubts that, as the inner man is endowed with understanding, so the outer man is endowed with the sense of the body. . . . And by the very nature of our condition, whereby we are made mortal and carnal, we apply ourselves more easily and, so to speak, more familiarly with visible than with intelligible things, since the former are external and the latter internal, and we perceive the former through the sense of the body, but the latter through the mind."[46] Here Augustine echoes Origen in teaching that the corporeal senses provide visible or external access to the invisible or internal knowledge of God, which is required for the fallen, "mortal and carnal" person. In this aspect of his doctrine, Augustine agrees with Origen's Middle Platonic belief that God is only perceived by the inner man, who, like God, is also immaterial spirit. Augustine is clear about this parallel in his treatise *On Seeing God*: "*The Lord is spirit*, and *whoever adheres to the Lord is one spirit* [with him].[47] Hence the person who is able to see God invisibly can adhere to God incorporeally."[48]

Because of this transcendent capacity, Augustine, like Origen, regards the spiritual senses as "far superior" to the corporeal

[45] Augustine refers to Origen's doctrine of the spiritual senses in several places in his writing. See Rudy, *Mystical Language of Sensation*, 36; Rahner, "The Doctrine of the Spiritual Senses in the Middle Ages," 102–3, n. 164.

[46] Augustine, De Trin 12.1 (PL 42:984); Augustine, *The Trinity*, trans. Stephen McKenna, Fathers of the Church (Washington, DC: Catholic University of America Press, 1963), 315. Augustine's other main references to the spiritual senses are in Conf 10.6; 10.27–28 (PL 32:782–83, 795–96). For his teaching on the spiritual senses, in addition to Pauline sources, Augustine frequently draws on the Psalms and other Old Testament texts, which describe the longing of humans and personify parts of the body. See Carol Harrison, "Spiritual Senses," in *Augustine through the Ages*, ed. Allan Fitzgerald (Grand Rapids, MI: Wm. B. Eerdmans, 1999), 767–68.

[47] 2 Cor 3:17; 1 Cor 6:17.

[48] Augustine, Ep 147.15.37 (PL 33:613); Bernard McGinn, *The Growth of Mysticism: Gregory the Great through the Twelfth Century* (New York: Crossroad, 1994), 232.

ones.[49] In addition, Augustine is clear about the ranking among
the five spiritual senses themselves. He frequently associates sight
and hearing with the higher, more inward aspects of the inner
person, and smell, taste, and touch with its lower, more bodily
aspects. He reasons that the higher senses bear a greater likeness
to God than the lower senses. For instance, in *On Free Choice of
the Will* he declares, "the objects that we touch, taste, and smell
are less like truth than the things we see and hear."[50] "Let us,
therefore, rely principally on the testimony of the eyes," he says
in *On the Trinity*, "for this sense of the body far excels the rest."[51]
Thus, in this regard, Augustine shares Origen's Platonic inclina-
tion to sharply distinguish matter from spirit, as he associates
truth not with the body, but with the higher spirit that "sees."[52]

---

[49] Augustine, Civ Dei 11.27.2 (PL 41:341). See also Augustine, De Trin 11.1.2
(PL 42:985).

[50] Augustine, Lib arb 2.14.38 (PL 32:1261); David Chidester, *Word and Light:
Seeing, Hearing, and Religious Discourse*, 1st ed. (Champaign-Urbana: University of Illinois Press, 1992), 59. For Augustine, the objects of tasting and touching (e.g., food) are too changeable and unstable to draw analogies from for
immutable truth. Moreover, two persons cannot simultaneously share one
tactile or gustatory experience. In addition, he points out that the senses of
taste and smell alter the objects they perceive after they consume them
(Augustine, Lib arb 2.12.33–34 [PL 32:1259]). For a discussion of this point,
see Chidester, *Word and Light*, 59–62.

[51] Augustine, De Trin 11.1.2 (PL 42:985); Augustine, *The Trinity*, 316.

[52] Augustine's beliefs on this point reflect the Platonic foundation of his
studies and the influence exercised on him by Ambrose of Milan's Neo-
Platonic preaching, which tends to view the material world with a great deal
of suspicion and sometimes rejection (McGinn, *The Growth of Mysticism*, 228).
On the Neo-Platonic background of Augustine, see E. L. Fortin, "Saint
Augustin et la doctrine néo-platonicienne de l'âme," in *Augustinus magister*
(Paris: Études Augustiniennes, 1954), 371–80. Augustine struggled to exclude
from his thinking Manichean views of matter as evil, entrapping the good of
the spirit. On this point, see Paula Fredriksen, "Beyond the Body/Soul
Dichotomy: Augustine on Paul against the Manichees and the Pelagians,"
Recherches augustiniennes 23 (1988): 87–114. But the result is sometimes am-
biguous. Although he argued that material and matter are good in the metaphysical sense, and while he linked the doctrines of the creation, incarnation,
and bodily resurrection to affirm the composite nature of the human, he did
not entirely eschew the Platonic suspicion of body and matter. On this subject,
see Henri Irénée Marrou, *The Resurrection and Saint Augustine's Theology of*

Yet Augustine's epistemology and anthropology depart from Origen's in some significant ways. For instance, Augustine cuts through the tangle of meanings Origen associates with "spirit" (*pneuma*), "soul" (*psuchē*), "intellect" (*nous*), and "body" (*soma*). He opts instead for a clear distinction between "spirit" (*spiritus*) and "mind" (*mens*), a distinction that he derives from his interpretation of 1 Corinthians 14:14-15. He regards the structure of the person as tripartite: body (*corpus*), spirit (*spiritus*), and mind (*mens*) or intellect (*intellectus*).[53]

Moreover, Augustine devised an original theory of knowledge based on this structure. Each of these three parts of the person, he says, obtains knowledge or perceives things by way of its own distinct kind of vision—corporeal (*corporale*), spiritual (*spirituale*), and intellectual (*intellectuale*):[54] "Let us call the first kind of vision corporeal, because it is perceived through the body and presented

---

Human Values, trans. Mary Consolate, Saint Augustine Lecture Series (1966) (Villanova, PA: Villanova University, 1966).

[53] In Civ Dei 10.9.2 (PL 41:286-87), Augustine refers to the Porphyrian distinction between the *intellectualis pars animae*, by which *rerum intelligibilium percipitur veritas, nullas habentium similitudines corporum*, and the *spiritualis* [*pars animae*] *qua corporalium rerum capiuntur imagines*. Markus notes that this Porphyrian analysis of the structure of the person, which itself is derived from Plotinus's, is what prompted Augustine to formulate his own theory of knowledge (R. A. Markus, "The Eclipse of a Neo-Platonic Theme: Augustine and Gregory the Great on Visions and Prophecies," in *Neoplatonism and Early Christian Thought: Essays in Honor of A. H. Armstrong*, ed. H. J. Blumenthal [London: Variorum Publications, 1981], 205). For more on the Porphyrian background to Augustine, see J. Pépìn, "Une nouvelle source de Saint Augustin: le zētēma de Porphyre sur l'union de l'âme et du corps," *Revue des études anciennes* 66 (1964): 53–107. Augustine also grants a significant role to the will and memory in the soul's learning and knowing. In doing so, he distinguishes three specific functions: mind (*mens*) is the soul as knowing, memory (*memoria*) is the soul retaining its contents, and will (*voluntas*) is the soul as acting in any way. See Augustine, De Trin 10.11.18 (PL 42:983).

[54] The schema of the three visions is made explicit in Augustine, Gen lit 12.6.15–12.12.26 (PL 34:458–64); 12.24.51 (PL 34:474). See also Matthias E. Korger, "Grundprobleme der augustinischen Erkenntnislehre: Erläutert am Beispiel von *De Genesi ad litteram* XII," *Recherches Augustiniennes* 2 (1962): 33–57; Steven F. Kruger, *Dreaming in the Middle Ages*, Cambridge Studies in Medieval Literature, 14 (Cambridge: Cambridge University Press, 1992), 182, n. 9.

to the senses of the body. The second will be spiritual, for whatever is not a body, and yet is something, is rightly called spirit; and certainly the image of an absent body, though it resembles a body, is not itself a body any more than is the act of vision by which it is perceived. The third kind will be intellectual, from the word 'intellect.' "[55]

In addition, Augustine teaches that there is a "hierarchy [*ordinem*] in the schema of these [three visions]."[56] At the top is intellectual vision, because it sees "intelligible things in the natural order, in a sort of incorporeal light of its own kind," and the "eye of the flesh" or corporeal vision is at the bottom, because it sees "corporeal light, of which light it is made to be receptive and to which it is adapted."[57] In this regard, Augustine articulates a relationship of polar extremes between corporeal sight and intellectual sight, based on the different realities they perceive: matter and spirit. This polarity accords with his understanding of the outer and inner man, which he associates respectively with sensation and reason.

But this understanding is different from the relationship Origen defines between corporeal and spiritual sight, which is one of radical opposition. Augustine's polarity, on the contrary, seeks mediation. He is explicit about the capacity of spiritual vision to mediate between the poles of corporeal and intellectual visions: "I think that spiritual *visio* can suitably be taken as a kind of intermediary between the intellectual and the corporeal without absurdity. For in my view that which, though not itself corporeal, is similar to corporeal things can appropriately be called an intermediary between that which really is corporeal and that which neither is corporeal nor similar to corporeal things."[58] Steven Kruger explains, "Corporeal vision, the lowest of the three, depends upon spiritual vision, the power by which the likenesses

[55] Augustine, Gen lit 12.7.16 (PL 34:59); Kruger, *Dreaming in the Middle Ages*, 37.

[56] Augustine, Gen lit 12.24.51 (PL 34:474); Kruger, *Dreaming in the Middle Ages*, 37.

[57] Augustine, De Trin 12.15.24 (PL 42:1011); Augustine, *The Trinity*, 366.

[58] Augustine, Gen lit 12.24.51 (PL 34:475); Kruger, *Dreaming in the Middle Ages*, 37.

of bodies are imagined. An external object impinging upon a sense organ is not really 'seen' unless the imaginative faculty, or 'spirit,' forms an image of it. The image, itself, not a body but the likeness of a body, has a status between corporeality and incorporeality, and thus allows the corporeal object to be made present to the incorporeal soul."[59]

In this aspect of his rhetoric of sensation, Augustine's teaching is remarkably different from Origen's. Augustine maintains that there is a continuous relationship between matter and spirit, because of the capacity of the person to reach across from corporeal to intellectual vision, through spiritual vision. As Kruger notes, this view has critical implications for Augustine's anthropology: "By stressing the middleness of spiritual vision . . . as strongly as he does, Augustine moves in essence to remind us of the middle nature of the human being. Made up of both body and soul, humans experience a reality neither wholly corporeal nor fully intellectual."[60]

Unlike Origen, Augustine believes body is necessary and essential to humanity.[61] According to Augustine, humanity's original state in Paradise included the body. He speculates that the bodies of Adam and Eve followed the commands of their souls and minds, just as they themselves followed the commands of God. But when they turned away from God, this properly ordered hierarchy—of God above Adam and Eve and intellect (or mind) and soul above the body—was wrenched out of alignment. The Fall thus triggered a symmetrical punishment for all humanity: the perfectly well-ordered structure of the person became wholly inverted.[62] In Augustine's words, "Man, who by keeping the commandments should have been spiritual even in his flesh, became

---

[59] Kruger, *Dreaming in the Middle Ages*, 37.

[60] Kruger, *Dreaming in the Middle Ages*, 43.

[61] See Fredriksen, "Beyond the Body/Soul Dichotomy," 87–114; Gerard J. P. O'Daly, *Augustine's Philosophy of Mind* (Berkeley: University of California Press, 1987), 70–79; Margaret R. Miles, *Augustine on the Body* (Missoula, MT: Scholars Press, 1979).

[62] Augustine, Civ Dei 13.13–15 (PL 41:383–87). See also Brown, *Body and Society*, 405.

fleshly even in his mind."⁶³ Influenced by his pre-conversion experience, Augustine teaches that in this fallen condition the body
often overwhelms and subjugates the soul and the intellect in an
all-consuming lust for sensual pleasure and corporeal knowledge,
which he respectively calls concupiscence (*concupiscentia carnis*)
and curiosity (*curiositas*):⁶⁴

> Besides the lust of the flesh [*concupiscentiam carnis*] which
> inheres in the delight given by all pleasures of the senses
> (those who are enslaved to it perish by putting themselves
> far from you), there exists in the soul, through the medium
> of the same bodily senses, a cupidity which does not take
> delight in carnal pleasure but in perceptions acquired
> through the flesh. It is a vain inquisitiveness dignified with
> the title of knowledge and science . . . . Pleasure pursues
> beautiful objects—what is agreeable to look at, to hear, to
> smell, to taste, to touch. But curiosity [*curiositas*] pursues the
> contraries of these delights with the motive of seeing what
> the experiences are like, not with a wish to undergo discom-
> fort, but out of a lust for experimenting and knowing.⁶⁵

According to Augustine, the human body, which once was perfect,
is now corrupt and subject to lust and death.

Augustine emphasizes, however, that the body is not the cause
of the Fall. Sin enters Paradise, in the first place, he teaches,
through the will of the person. As Suzannah Biernoff explains,
the will, for Augustine, is a component of the soul, and it is what
first disobeyed God:

⁶³ Augustine, Civ Dei 14.15 (PL 41:423); Augustine, *The City of God*, trans.
Marcus Dods (New York: Modern Library, 1950), 462. See also Augustine,
Civ Dei 13.16; 14.3 (PL 41:387–89, 402–4).

⁶⁴ The entirety of Augustine's *Confessions* may be read as an extended narrative showing that his own fallen flesh's temptation toward sensual pleasure
was the primary obstacle in his pursuit for divine truth. See especially
Augustine, Conf 4.7.12; 10.40.65; 11.9.11 (PL 32:698, 806–7, 813–14).

⁶⁵ Augustine, Conf 10.35.54–55 (PL 32:802); Augustine, *Confessions*, trans.
Henry Chadwick (Oxford: Oxford University Press, 1991), 210–11. See also
Augustine, Civ Dei 14.16; 14.26 (PL 41:424–25, 434–35).

The fall . . . is essentially a movement of the will away from God: a "defection" from God. What results is a "deficiency" or privation of humanity in relation to Supreme Being. . . . Augustine translates the first twinges of disobedience in the will into the stirring of concupiscence [*concupiscentia carnis*] in the flesh. Original sin thus serves as the prototype for all sins of the flesh. . . . At stake in all this is the relationship between body and soul; specifically, the disintegration of their original, harmonious bond.[66]

She goes on to explain the consequence of this disintegration: "The result is that two very different bodies emerge from Augustine's account: one, a purely physical organism, is the corporeal home and help-meet of the soul; the other, marred by original sin, is the seat of rebellious carnality."[67] Augustine refers to the former body generally as the "body," the latter as "flesh" (*caro*). Therefore, according to Augustine, sinful flesh and spirit (in the Pauline sense) are opposed, but, ultimately, body and spirit are not.[68]

For one to live according to the inner person, or to make spiritual progress in this fallen condition, Augustine does not require that the body be sloughed off or sensation be renounced, as Origen does. Instead, he teaches that the "rule of the flesh" should be resisted, so that the body and its senses can be subjugated to the spirit and intellect in their proper order, as they were in their original and harmonious state in Paradise.[69] So, in his three kinds of visions, the power of the middle position of spiritual vision is critical. It has the capacity to turn in one of two directions: either toward the objects of corporeal vision, "judging them to be the only ones," or toward the transcendent things of intellectual vision, "clinging with greater surety to the world beyond bodily forms and beyond the likenesses of bodies."[70] By resisting the

---

[66] Biernoff, *Sight and Embodiment*, 29. Biernoff here quotes from Augustine, Civ Dei 12.7 (PL 41:355).

[67] Biernoff, *Sight and Embodiment*, 26.

[68] See Augustine, Civ Dei 14.2 (PL 41:403–5).

[69] Augustine, Civ Dei 14.2 (PL 41:403–5).

[70] Augustine, Gen lit 12.36.69 (PL 34:484); Kruger, *Dreaming in the Middle Ages*, 42. See also Augustine, Gen lit 12.14.28–30; 12.25.52 (PL 34:465–66, 475–76).

former's concupiscent tendency[71] and instead choosing the latter, spiritual vision prevents the person from remaining mired in the flesh. In this way, the person properly orders the three kinds of vision, placing intellectual vision above spiritual vision, which is in turn above corporeal vision.

Augustine understands this ideal order of the three kinds of vision as characteristic of life in Paradise and also in the Eschaton, when concupiscence will cease: "There will be joy in the things of the intellect, and they will be far more luminously present to the soul than the corporeal forms that now surround us. . . . Everything will be clear without any error and without any ignorance, all things occupying their proper place, the corporeal, the spiritual, and the intellectual, in untainted nature and perfect beatitude."[72] Furthermore, in this perfect condition, he asserts that all things will be held still, in utter unity.[73] So the three kinds of vision will not only be properly ordered; they will be identical: corporeal, spiritual, and intellectual vision will be one and the same. He says,

> we shall in the future world see the material forms of the new heavens and the new earth in such a way that we shall most distinctly recognize God everywhere present and governing all things, material as well as spiritual, and shall see Him . . . by means of the bodies we shall wear and which we shall see wherever we turn our eyes . . . we shall look with those spiritual eyes of our future, we shall then, too, by means of bodily substances behold God, through a spirit, ruling all things.[74]

Margaret Miles thus notes that according to Augustine, "spiritual vision ultimately includes seeing with the eyes of the body."[75] In

---

[71] See Augustine, Gen lit 12.36.69 (PL 34:484).

[72] Augustine, Gen lit 12.36.69 (PL 34:484); Kruger, *Dreaming in the Middle Ages*, 42. See also Augustine, Civ Dei 22.17 (PL 41:778–79).

[73] See Augustine, Civ Dei 22.24 (PL 41:788–92).

[74] Augustine, Civ Dei 22.29 (PL 41:800); Augustine, *The City of God*, 863.

[75] Margaret R. Miles, "Vision. The Eye of the Body and the Eye of the Mind in Saint Augustine's *De Trinitate* and *Confessions*," *Journal of Religion* 63, no. 2 (1983): 139. See also Miles, *Augustine on the Body*, 110–11.

contrast to Origen, he maintains that in this life the body will be continuous with the one in the next life; rather than being entirely shed, the mortal body will be transformed into a spiritual body.[76] In a similar vein, Augustine teaches that the biblical *face-to-face* vision of God[77] of the next life may be perceived, albeit imperfectly and briefly, in this life: "the image which is being renewed day by day in the spirit of the mind and in the knowledge of God, not outwardly but inwardly, will be perfected by the very vision which then will be face to face, but is making progress towards it now through a mirror in an enigma."[78] This earthly participation in the heavenly vision of God, he maintains, gives human beings an appetite (*appetitus*) for the timeless gaze. It thereby tempers the desires of the flesh and assists the person in making spiritual progress.

While Origen understands the relationship between the corporeal and spiritual senses to be one of radical opposition, Augustine understands the relationship to be one of transformative evolution. According to Augustine, it is possible to sublimate the fleshly corporeal desires of the outer person to the spiritual and intellectual goals of the inner person, because of Christ's redemption and his promise of the person's renewal in God's image and likeness. In *On the Trinity*, writing about the *visio Dei*,

---

[76] Scholars have customarily noted Augustine's move from an earlier position, which stresses the difference of the angelic body from the earthly one, to a later, more materialistic position, to which I refer here. See for example John A. Mourant, *Augustine on Immortality* (Villanova, PA: Augustinian Institute, Villanova University, 1969); Joanne E. McWilliam Dewart, *Death and Resurrection* (Wilmington, DE: Michael Glazier, 1986), 164–88; Henri Marrou and A.-M. Bonnardière, "Le dogme de la résurrection des corps et la théologie des valeurs humaines selon l'enseignement de saint Augustin," *Revue des études augustiniennes* 12, nos. 1–2 (1966): 111–36; Gerald Watson, "St. Augustine, the Platonists, and the Resurrection Body: Augustine's Use of a Fragment from Porphyry," *Irish Theological Quarterly* 50 (1983/1984): 222–32; Caroline Walker Bynum, *The Resurrection of the Body in Western Christianity, 200–1336* (New York: Columbia University Press, 1995), 95, n. 132. For an extensive discussion of the "body" in Augustine, see Brown, *Body and Society*, 387–427; Miles, *Augustine on the Body*.

[77] 1 Cor 13:12.

[78] Augustine, De Trin 14.19.25 (PL 42:1054).

Augustine asserts, "Wherefore, since we have found . . . so great an unlikeness to God and the Word of God, wherein yet there was found before some likeness, this too, must be admitted, that even when we shall be like Him, when 'we shall see Him as He is' . . . not even then shall we be equal to him in nature."[79]

Indeed, Augustine teaches that the incarnation provides a bridge across the great metaphysical gap between God and fallen humanity, and between spirit and sinful flesh. Jesus Christ, the Mediator, restores our likeness to God by taking on and thus redeeming us from our sinful flesh:

> He offered himself to men [*hominibus*], when He sent bread from heaven and gave his Son, who is equal to Him and who is what He is himself, to be made man and to be killed for men, that through that which you are [*ut per hoc quod tu es*], you might taste that which you are not [*gustes quod non es*]. Indeed, it was a great thing for you to taste the sweetness of God [*gustare suavitatem Dei*], that sweetness so distant and exceedingly high, when you were cast down so low and lying in the utmost depths. Into this great separation you were sent a Mediator. . . . He himself is the Mediator, and thus he was made sweet [*inde factus est suavis*].[80]

Augustine explains that this Mediator tastes "sweet" (*suavis*, *dulcis*), because he freed us from the bitter (*amarus*) taste of our fleshly, fallen selves. As Augustine says in a sermon on Psalm 33:9, "Listen to the psalm: *taste and see that the Lord is sweet.* He was made sweet [*suavis*] to you because he liberated you. You had been bitter [*amarus*] to yourself when you were occupied only with yourself. Drink the sweetness [*dulcedinem*]; accept the pledge from so great a granary."[81] Jesus Christ became that which we

---

[79] Augustine, De Trin 15.16.26 (PL 42:1079); Augustine, *The Trinity*, 491.

[80] Augustine, En in Ps 134.5 (PL 37:1741–42); Fulton, "Taste and See," 177. See also Augustine, Conf 7.10.16 (PL 32:742).

[81] Augustine, S 145.5 (PL 38:794); Fulton, "Taste and See," 182. See also Augustine, En in Ps 134.5 (PL 37:1741–42). On Augustine's use of *sweetness*, see John C. Cavadini, "The Sweetness of the Word: Salvation and Rhetoric in Augustine's *De doctrina christiana*," in *De doctrina christiana: A Classic of*

are (humanity), so that we might taste that which we are not (divinity). Moreover, in becoming that which we are, he assumed a human body and soul, which also again made possible the proper order and harmony between them:

> For as the soul makes use of the body in a single person to form a man, so God makes use of man in a single person to form Christ. In the former person there is a mingling of soul and body; in the latter Person there is a mingling of God and man. . . . Therefore, the person of man is a mingling of soul and body, but the Person of Christ is a mingling of God and man, for, when the Word of God is joined to a soul which has a body, it takes on both the soul and the body at once. The one process happens daily in order to beget men; the other happens once to set men free.[82]

For Augustine, then, the relationship between Christ's humanity and his divinity—i.e., his two natures—is the hope of humankind. Christ's taking on the human soul and body "happens daily," because the person finds in it a model for the proper relationship between soul and body to strive for every day, in this life. Yet Christ's joining of divinity to humanity happened once, to set free humankind for eternity.

Augustine discusses this daily process explicitly in his *Eighty-Three Different Questions*, when in quoting Paul, he says, "if our outer man is corrupted, nevertheless our *inner man is renewed from day to day*."[83] Augustine then identifies the outer man with Adam and the inner man with Christ: "Again, the outer man and the inner man are so named by the Apostle, that he speaks of one as the 'old man' whom we must strip off and the other as the 'new

---

Western Culture, ed. Duane W. H. Arnold and Pamela Bright (Notre Dame: University of Notre Dame Press, 1995), 164–81; Franz Posset, "*Christi Dulcedo*: The 'Sweetness of Christ' in Western Christian Thought," CSQ 30, no. 3 (1995): 143–78, esp. 147–55; Fulton, "Taste and See," 169–204; Rosemary Drag Hale, "Taste and See," 3–14.

[82] Augustine, Ep 137.3.11 (PL 33:520); Miles, *Augustine on the Body*, 94–95.
[83] 2 Cor 4:16.

man' who must be put on."[84] Unlike Origen, Augustine thus teaches that it is possible to sublimate the corporeal desires of the outer person to the spiritual and intellectual goals of the inner person, because of Christ's redemption and his promise of the person's renewal in God's image and likeness. Indeed, as his original ideas about the middle position of spiritual vision demonstrate, he maintains that it is even possible for the body to reach across to the spirit.

Yet in his language of taste and touch Augustine is less affirmative than he is in his language of sight of the body's role in the spiritual life. An example of his gustatory imagery is seen above when he states that by taking on fallen humanity Christ allows persons to taste the sweetness of that which they are not, divinity. In other places, Augustine employs language of taste similarly to say that the Eucharist allows fallen humanity to taste divinity every day, in "daily bread."[85] But he identifies no middle ground between the intellect and body in his rhetoric of taste, as he does in his rhetoric of sight. When he uses gustatory images, he often issues a caveat restricting the qualities of taste to things that are perceived through the intellect or mind, not the body or the spirit. For example, in *On Free Choice*, he uses the etymological connection between *sapere* ("to taste") and *sapientia* ("wisdom") to make his point: "O wisdom [*sapientia*], most sweet [*suavissima*] light of the purified mind [*mentis*]!"[86] Here he associates the taste of sweetness with the mind, and by adding the imagery of light to this exclamation, he sublimates the sense of taste altogether to the sense of sight.

Augustine makes a similar move in Sermon 127 when he declares, "*We know that when he shall appear, we shall be like him, for*

[84] Augustine, Div qu 51.1 (PL 40:32); Saint Augustine, *Eight-Three Different Questions*, trans. David L. Mosher, The Fathers of the Church, vol. 70 (Washington, DC: The Catholic University of America Press, 2002), 85. Here Augustine makes another Pauline reference, this time to Col 3:9-10.

[85] See for instance Augustine, S 61 (PL 38:381).

[86] *O suavissima lux purgatae mentis sapientia!* (Augustine, Lib arb 2.16.43 [PL 32:1264]). See also Conf 9.10.24 (PL 32:774). Augustine associates sweetness with *Sapientia* in his prayers to her in his *Confessions*. See for example Augustine, Conf 1.4.4; 3.8.16; 7.3.5; 9.1.1 (PL 32:663, 690, 735, 763).

we shall see him as he is.[87] Behold, understand what you will be nourished on and how you will receive what nourishes you by eating. Thus: that what is eaten is not diminished, but whoever eats it is supported in life. For now food maintains us by eating, but the food that is eaten is diminished. When however we begin to feed on justice, to eat wisdom, to taste that immortal food, we will be supported in life and the food will not be diminished."[88] Here again he uses taste to refer to "wisdom" or "immortal food," and he is clear that the experience of it is sublimated to sight in the *visio Dei*.

Augustine insists that tasting and eating will disappear once the body is transformed. For him, eating food is a sign of the fallen body's mutability and corruption, which will disappear in the afterlife, when it will no longer be necessary.[89] So persons are supposed to taste, to eat, and to be nourished by the Eucharist in the life, in order to be led into the heavenly experience of non-eating or non-consumption in the next life.

Why is taste lost in the resurrected body for Augustine, but sight is not? The answer lies in his ranking of sight as the most superior of senses, because of its close association with truth. Smell, taste, and touch, all of which are involved in eating, are at the lower end of the hierarchy of corporeal sensation because they are more associated with bodily things, which, although they are essentially good, are still marked by the heavy price they paid for the Fall. In addition, Augustine believes that spiritual progress entails sublimating the corporeal desires of the outer man to the spiritual and intellectual goals of the inner man. The outer man is the "earthly man" or the "old man," Adam, whom one must strip off, in order to put on the inner man, the "heavenly man," the "new man," Christ. The outer man is associated with the bodily senses and is perishable. The inner man is associated with

---

[87] 1 John 3.2.

[88] Augustine, S 127.5.6 (PL 38:709); translation my own, assisted by the translation in Bynum, *The Resurrection of the Body*, 102.

[89] Bynum, *The Resurrection of the Body*, 97. For instance, Augustine says: "Take away death [i.e., in this context, corruption or decay] and the body is good." Augustine, S 155.14 (PL 38:849).

the spirit and the mind or intellect. As Biernoff puts it, Augustine believes that, "To live according to the inner man does not require the renunciation of the body, or of sensation, but their subjuga-tion—or perhaps sublimation—to intellectual and spiritual goals." So taste, and touch and smell, should not be understood in Augustine's thought as being cast off or shed, as Origen would have it, but rather subjugated or sublimated to sight, which is most closely associated with the mind and intellect. As Augustine teaches, "For so far as the world is known to us at all, it is known through sight."[90]

In sum, the relationship Augustine understands between the corporeal and spiritual senses is one of transformative evolution. Influenced as he is by his Neo-Platonic training, Augustine uses the binary categories of the inner and outer man and couples them with reason and sensation, or more generally with heaven and earth, spirit and matter. But his binary categories are not mutually exclusive alternatives, as they are for Origen. Indeed, in Augustine's language of sensation, particularly in his discussion of the three kinds of vision, he articulates a tripartite model where spiritual vision mediates between corporeal and intellectual vision. This view allows corporeal sensation to move from the lowest rung on the ladder to the highest one of reason. Augustine's polarity between the corporeal and spiritual senses is thus mediated and redeemed. When it comes to what he calls the lower senses of taste and touch (and even smell), however, Augustine witnesses a binary rather than a tripartite conception of knowledge, with taste sublimated or subjugated to sight, so that its bodily connota-tions are similarly sublimated or subjugated to more spiritual or intellectual ones.

The emphasis Augustine places on the body as necessary and essential to personhood, as well as the possibility he articulates for the corporeal senses to reach across to the spiritual senses at

[90] Augustine, De Trin 13.1.4 (PL 42:1015). As David Chidester points out, Augustine makes use of the fact that sight connotes a continuous union be-tween the seer and the thing that is seen. This is also why Augustine prefers this sense above the others to discuss how the human person knows and unites the self to God (Chidester, *Word and Light*, 59–97). See also Paul Ludwig, "Les sens spirituels chez Saint Augustin," *Dieu Vivant* 11 (1948): 81–105.

least as regards sight, becomes an important source later for Gertrude to use differently. Gertrude articulates an intermediary position for taste, but not sight. In so doing, she also draws upon Bernard's extensive use of the language of taste and touch to discuss how the person knows and achieves union with God.

Bernard's Predilection for the Language of Taste and Touch

Although Bernard's writings do not theorize about the doctrine of the spiritual senses in any kind of systematic way, he frequently use sensory language from the Bible to discuss the encounter with God, especially in his well-known commentary on the Song of Songs.[91] Bernard was certainly familiar with the tradition of the spiritual senses, including the thought of Origen and Augustine.[92]

---

[91] Several scholars have noted the concept of spiritual senses within Bernard's writings. See Jean Mouroux, "Sur les critères de l'expérience spirituelle d'aprés les Sermons sur le Cantique de Cantiques," in *Saint Bernard Théologien, Analecta Cisterciensia* (Rome: Editiones Cistercienses, 1953), 251–67; Jean Leclercq, "De quelques procédés du style biblique du S. Bernard," in *Recueil d'études sur saint Bernard et ses écrits*, ed. Jean Leclercq (Rome: Edizioni di storia et letteratura, 1962), 260–63; Michael Casey, *A Thirst for God: Spiritual Desire in Bernard of Clairvaux's Sermons on the Song of Songs*, CS 77 (Kalamazoo, MI: Cistercian Publications, 1988), 231–34, 296–98; Rudy, *Mystical Language of Sensation*, 45–65.

[92] On Bernard's use of and familiarity with Origen and Augustine, see Jean Leclercq, "Aux sources des sermons sur les Cantiques," in *Recueil d'études sur saint Bernard et ses écrits* (Rome: Edizioni di storia et letteratura, 1962–1969), 275–319, esp. 281–83; Rudy, *Mystical Language of Sensation*, 140–41, n. 1; Jean Prosper Theodorus Deroy, *Bernardus en Origenes: Enkele opmerkingen over de invloed van Origenes op Sint Bernardus' Sermones super Cantica canticorum* (Haarlem: De Toorts, 1963). Jean Leclercq shows that Origen's corpus was held and diffused at Clairvaux, Signy, Pontigny, and Saint-Thierry during the thirteenth centuries; thus Bernard would have certainly known it (Jean Leclercq, "Origène au XII siècle," *Irenikon* 24 [1951]: 425–39). According to Bernard, Gregory the Great was also familiar with the doctrine of the spiritual senses. McGinn shows some important continuous elements between Bernard's concept of the spiritual senses and Gregory the Great's (Bernard McGinn, *The Growth of Mysticism*, 185–90). On Bernard's written sources in general, see Casey, *A Thirst for God*, 22–32.

He repeats the established association of the spiritual and corporeal senses with Paul's inner and outer persons.[93] Like Augustine, he reproduces Origen's Platonic assumption that God is best perceived by the part of the person—the inner person—which, like God, is also immaterial spirit. In Sermon 31 on the Song, for instance, Bernard says, "My opinion is that of the Apostle, who said that *he who is united to the Lord becomes one spirit with him.* . . . *God is spirit,* who is lovingly drawn by the beauty of that soul whom he perceives to be guided by the Spirit, and devoid of any desire to submit to the ways of the flesh, especially if he sees that it burns with love for himself."[94]

Here Bernard follows Augustine's pattern of associating sight with reason, intellect, and truth.[95] He also maintains Augustine's teaching that the flesh obscures the person's sight of truth.[96] Indeed Bernard is concerned, as Augustine is, about the way the body and its senses are stained by death and sin as a result of the Fall: "As long as we are in the body, we are in exile from God," Bernard teaches, "not indeed that this is the body's fault, but it is the fault of the fact that it is still a body of death, or rather that *the flesh is the body of sin* in which good does not exist but rather the law of sin."[97] For Bernard, it is as if the innocent body that God created were now draped with another body, the fleshly one of sin and death.[98] Thus, like Augustine, he is quick to caution

---

[93] Bernard, Div 116.13–16 (SBOp 6/1:393). See also Bernard, Div 10 (SBOp 6/1:121–24).

[94] Quoting 1 Cor 6:17; John 4:24. Bernard, SC 31.6 (SBOp 1:223); Bernard, *On the Song of Songs I,* trans. Kilian J. Walsh, CF 4 (Kalamazoo, MI: Cistercian Publications, 1976), 129.

[95] See Bernard, SC 28.4–5; 41.3; 45.5–6 (SBOp 1:198–201; 2:30; 2:54–56); Bernard, Div 116 (SBOp 6/1:393–94).

[96] See Bernard, Conv 17.30 (SBOp 4:106).

[97] Bernard, Conv 17.30 (SBOp 4:106); McGinn, *The Growth of Mysticism,* 173. See also Bernard, SC 56.3 (SBOp 2:117–19). For a succinct summary of Bernard's doctrine of creation and the fall, see G. R. Evans, *Bernard of Clairvaux,* Great Medieval Thinkers Series (New York: Oxford University Press, 2000), 79–81. On the effects of the Fall in Bernard's anthropology, see Julia Kristeva, "Ego affectus est. Bernard of Clairvaux: Affect, Desire, Love," in *Tales of Love,* trans. Leon S. Roudiez (New York: Columbia University Press, 1987), 159.

[98] Biernoff, *Sight and Embodiment,* 34.

against the fleshly temptations of *concupiscentia* and *curiositas*.[99] Bernard teaches that we must be vigilant about the permeability of the flesh and the incessant cravings of the fleshly senses for things of the passing world.[100] This is why he warns readers of his *Sermons on the Song of Songs*, "Be careful, however, not to conclude that I see something corporeal or perceptible to the senses in this union between the Word and the soul."[101]

Similarly to Augustine, Bernard locates corporeal sensation as the place in which sin enters the body. For example, in commenting on the phrase, *His left hand is beneath my head and his right hand embraces me,*[102] Bernard preaches, "Rightly then is the left hand of the Bridegroom under the Bride's head, upon which he supports her leaning head. This leaning is the intention of her mind, and he supports it so that it may not bend or incline toward fleshly and worldly desires.[103] For the body, which is corruptible, weighs down the soul, and the earthly dwelling of the soul hems it in and keeps it preoccupied with many thoughts."[104]

As Bernard sees it, the fallen body is animated by fleshly desires that the senses insatiably crave. He places the blame of the Fall on the will, as does Augustine, not on the body or its senses.

---

[99] Bernard's understanding of *concupiscentia* and notion of *curiositas* are slightly different from Augustine's, in that they are linked principally with pride rather than lust. See Bernard, Hum 10.28; 22.57 (SBOp 3:38, 58–59); Bernard, Asc 4.4 (SBOp 5:140–41); Bernard, SC 25.9 (SBOp 1:168–69). For secondary scholarship, see Luke Anderson, "The Rhetorical Epistemology in Saint Bernard's *Super Cantica*," in *Bernardus Magister: Papers Presented at the Nonacentenary Celebration of the Birth of Saint Bernard of Clairvaux, Kalamazoo, Michigan, Sponsored by the Institute of Cistercian Studies, Western Michigan University, 10–13 May 1990,* ed. John R. Sommerfeldt, CS 135 (Spencer, MA: Cistercian Publications, 1992), 95–128; John R. Sommerfeldt, "The Intellectual Life According to St. Bernard," *Cîteaux: commentarii cistercienses* 25 (1974): 249–56; John R. Sommerfeldt, "Bernard on Charismatic Knowledge: the Truth as Gift," CSQ 32, no. 3 (1997): 295–301.

[100] Bernard, Conv 5.7; 6.11 (CF 25:39–41; 44–45; SBOp 4:78–79, 84–85); Biernoff, *Sight and Embodiment*, 54, 122.

[101] Bernard, SC 31.6 (CF 4:128–29; SBOp 1:223). See also Bernard, SC 1.11; 43.3–4; 70.2 (SBOp 1:7–8; 2:42–43; 2:209); Bernard, Asc 3.3; 6.11 (SBOp 5:133, 156); Bernard, Div 29.2–3 (SBOp 6/1:211–12).

[102] Song 2:6.

[103] Gal 5:16; 2 Tim 2:12.

[104] Wis 9:15; Bernard, SC 31.6 (CF 4:128–29; SBOp 1:223).

Bernard teaches this position vividly in his sermon *On Conversion*, when he portrays fallen humanity with an allegorical personification of Mistress Will's berating her mate, Master Reason: "I am voluptuous. I am curious. I am ambitious. There is not part of me which is free from this threefold ulcer, from the soles of my feet to the top of my head. My gullet and the shameful parts of my body are given up to pleasure; we must name them afresh, one by one. The wandering foot and the undisciplined eye are slaves to curiosity. Ear and tongue serve vanity."[105] The flesh is now the experience of the embodied person, because the will gave in to carnal pleasure over reason.[106]

Yet Bernard is clear, as Augustine is, that the flesh is redeemed by Christ. Bernard too understands the union of divinity and humanity in Jesus Christ's twofold nature to restore the soul-flesh relationship in humanity: "I say that in Christ, the Word, soul and flesh are one person, without a confusion of essences, and that they remain distinct in their number, without prejudice to the unity of his person. I would not deny that this pertains to that kind of unity by which soul and flesh is one man."[107] Like Augustine, then, Bernard understands the human to be a body-soul composite.[108] He even refers to the body as the "faithful partner of the soul."[109]

[105] Bernard, Conv 6.10 (SBOp 4:83); *Bernard of Clairvaux, Selected Works*, trans. G. R. Evans, Classics of Western Spirituality Series (New York: Paulist Press, 1987), 74.

[106] Bernard thus refigures the standard Neoplatonic opposition of matter and spirit as a battle between reason and sensuality (Janet Coleman, *Ancient and Medieval Memories: Studies in the Reconstruction of the Past* [Cambridge: Cambridge University Press, 1992], 195, 198).

[107] Bernard, Csi 5.21 (SBOp 3:484). See also Bernard, Nat 1 and 2 (SBOp 4:250–54); Bernard, Csi 2.9.18 (SBOp 3:425–26). For secondary scholarship, see John R. Sommerfeldt, *The Spiritual Teachings of Bernard of Clairvaux*, CF 125 (Kalamazoo, MI: Cistercian Publications, 1991), 3; Endre von Ivánka, "L'union à Dieu: La structure de l'âme selon S. Bernard," in *Saint Bernard Théologien*, ed. Jean Leclercq, *Analecta Cisterciensia* (Rome: Editiones cistercienses, 1953), 206.

[108] Bernard, Csi 5.20 (SBOp 3:483–84).

[109] Bernard, Dil 11.31 (SBOp 3:145–46). This is true of the body in the after-life as well as in this life for Bernard. On Bernard's anthropology, see Bernard

For Bernard, bodily processes (*observationes corporeas*) cannot be rejected in favor of spiritual ones, even if the latter go beyond the former. They are not mutually exclusive, as Origen understands them. Rather, Bernard asserts that external things are the primary means through which we know anything spiritual at all.[110] Commenting on the Pauline declaration, *The invisible things of God are understood through the things he has made,*[111] Bernard asserts, "All created things, which are corporeal and visible, can be understood by our minds only through the body's instrumentality. Therefore, our souls have need of a body. Without it we cannot attain to that form of knowledge by which alone we are elevated toward the contemplation of truths essential to happiness."[112]

According to Bernard, the human body is the vehicle for salvation, not the obstacle to it, because Christ redeemed the flesh of fallen humanity in the incarnation, through a human body and its senses: "On being made man . . . he has used our bodily feelings and senses as openings or windows, so that he would know by experience the miseries of men and might become merciful. These were things he already knew but in a different way. . . .

McGinn, "Freedom, Formation and Reformation: The Anthropological Roots of Saint Bernard's Spiritual Teaching," in *La dottrina della vita spirituale nelle opere di San Bernardo di Clairvaux: Atti del Convegno Internazionale. Rome, 11–15 settembre 1990, Analecta Cisterciensia* 46 (Rome: Editiones Cistercienses, 1990), 91–114.

[110] Bernard's support of corporeal knowledge as a means to obtain spiritual knowledge is also illustrated in his insistence that divine union manifests itself in love of neighbor, corporate works, a life of virtue, and *caritas*. See for example Bernard, SC 4.5; 46.7 (SBOp 1:20–21; 2:54); Bernard Dil 12.34 (SBOp 3:148–49); Brian Stock, "Experience, Praxis, Work and Planning in Bernard of Clairvaux: Observations on the *Sermones in Cantica,*" in *The Cultural Context of Medieval Learning: Proceedings of the First International Colloquium on Philosophy, Science, and Theology in the Middle Ages, September 1973,* ed. John Emory Murdoch, Boston Studies in the Philosophy of Science, vol. 26 (Dordrecht, The Netherlands: D. Reidel, 1973), 219–61; Bernardo Oliviera, "Aspects of Love of Neighbor in the Spiritual Doctrine of St. Bernard (1)," CSQ 26, no. 2 (1991): 114.

[111] Rom 1:20.

[112] Bernard, SC 5.1 (CF 4:25; SBOp 1:21–22). See also Bernard, SC 2.8; 74.2 (SBOp 1:12–13; 2:240); Bernard, Csi 5.3 (SBOp 3:468–69).

Do you see him becoming what he [already] was, and learning what he [already] knew, seeking in our midst openings and windows by which to search more attentively into our misfortunes?"[113] In the same physical way, Bernard instructs, persons should know God in return: "I do not mean . . . these external things should be neglected or that he who has not employed himself in these matters may soon thereby become spiritual. Rather, spiritual things, inasmuch as they are better, may not be acquired or obtained either with difficulty or not at all, except through these: as it is written, *It is not the spiritual which is first, but that which pertains to the physical, and then the spiritual.*[114] Indeed, the best man is he who performs discreetly and harmoniously both the one and the other."[115]

Because Christ knew humankind in and through the body and senses, this is the way humankind should know him in return. This is the way to gain wisdom. To articulate this teaching, Bernard weaves a net of puns between the words *sapor* (to taste), *sapere* (to know), and *sapientia* (wisdom)—the same word-play Augustine uses.[116] But whereas Augustine downplays the connotations of the physical experience of taste, Bernard exploits them in order

[113] Bernard, SC 56.1 (SBOp 2:114–15); Bernard, *On the Song of Songs II*, trans. Kilian J. Walsh, CS 7 (Kalamazoo, MI: Cistercian Publications, 1976), 88 (translator's emendations). See also Bernard, Gra 2.3; 6.17 (SBOp 3:18, 29).

[114] 1 Cor 15.46.

[115] Bernard, Apo 7.14 (SBOp 3:93–94; translation my own, assisted by the translation in Jennifer A. Harris, "The Fate of Place in the Twelfth Century: Creation, Restoration, and Body in the Writing of Bernard of Clairvaux," *Viator* 30, no. 2 [2008]: 130). This *Apology*, written in support of Cluniac reformers, is often noted for championing imageless devotion. Yet Bernard, in this passage, significantly teaches the contrary. On this point, see Ann W. Astell, " 'Hidden Manna': Bernard of Clairvaux, Gertrude of Helfta, and the Monastic Art of Humility," in *Eating Beauty: The Eucharist and the Spiritual Arts of the Middle Ages* (Ithaca, NY: Cornell University Press, 2006), 62–66.

[116] Bernard, SC 49 and 50 (SBOp 2:73–83). On this and other instances of this word play in Bernard's writings, see Bernard, SC 23.14; 67.6 (SBOp 1:145–48; 2:192); Bernard, Sent 3.96 (SBOp 6/2:154). For secondary scholarship on this topic, see Jean Leclercq, "Sur le caractère littéraire des sermons de S. Bernard," in *Receuil d'études sur saint Bernard et ses écrits* (Rome: Edizioni di storia et letteratura, 1962), 163–210; Casey, *A Thirst for God*, 297–98.

to articulate his ideas effectively. In the incarnation, he says, God "took on flesh for those who know [*sapientibus*] the flesh," so they are able "to taste and know [*sapere*] the Spirit."[117] For Bernard, the way God knows humankind, and the way humankind knows God, is analogous to the way something is known by tasting it.[118] For in tasting something, one must take the substance into the mouth and touch it, even absorbing something of it with the membranes of the epithelial cells in the tongue. One knows something's taste only by directly touching its essence—i.e., the essence of something other than oneself.[119] In Bernard's eighty-fifth sermon on the Song, he describes the way humanity tastes wisdom:

> I think it would be permissible to define wisdom [*sapientiam*] as a taste for goodness [*saporem boni*]. We lost this taste almost from the creation of our human race. When the old serpent's poison infected the palate of our heart [*cordis palatum*], because the fleshly sense [*sensu carnis*] prevailed, the soul began to lose its taste for goodness, and a noxious taste crept in. . . . When wisdom [*sapientia*] enters, it makes the carnal sense [*sensum carnis*] taste flat; it purifies the understanding, cleanses and heals the palate of the heart [*cordis palatum*]. When the palate is healed, it then tastes the good; wisdom itself has a taste [*sapit ipsa sapientia*], and there is nothing better.[120]

After having eaten the serpent's rotten fruit, the palate of the fleshly senses needs to be rebalanced and cleansed. Wisdom does

---

[117] *Obtulit carnem sapientibus carnem, per quam discerent sapere et spiritum* (Bernard, SC 6.3 [SBOp 1:27]).

[118] See Casey, *A Thirst for God*, 297–98.

[119] On this notion in the medieval monastic milieu, see Fulton, "Taste and See," 170.

[120] *Nec duxerim reprehendendum, si quis sapientiam saporem boni diffiniat. Hunc saporem perdidimus, ab ipso pene exortu generis nostri. Ex quo cordis palatum, sensu carnis praevalente, infecit virus serpentis antiqui, coepit animae non sapere bonum, ac sapor noxius subintrare. . . . Intrans sapientia, dum sensum carnis infatuat, purificat intellectum, cordis palatum sanat et reparat. Sano palato sapit iam bonum, sapit ipsa sapientia, qua in bonis nullum melius* (SC 85.8 [SBOP 2:312–13]). See also Bernard, Ep 111:3 (SBOp 7:283–85).

this, Bernard teaches, by making the "carnal sense taste flat." The experience (*experientia*) of the taste (*sapere*) of God's wisdom (*sapientia*), according to him, puts an end to the fleshly senses' incessant cravings, cleanses the heart's palate, and purifies the mind's understanding: "Perhaps" this is why "*sapientia*, that is 'wisdom,' is derived from *sapor*, which is 'taste.' Because when "'wisdom' [*sapientia*] is added to virtue, like some seasoning [*condimentum*], it adds taste [*sapidam*] to something which by itself is tasteless [*insulsa*] and bitter [*aspera*]."[121]

Bernard writes about the taste of wisdom again in *On Conversion*: "*The Spirit alone reveals it*:[122] you will consult books to no purpose; you need experience [*experimentum*] instead. It is wisdom [*Sapientia*], and man does not know its price. It is drawn from hidden places, and this sweetness is found in the land of those who live sweetly.[123] Of course the Lord is sweetness, but unless you have tasted, you will not see [*nisi gustaveris, non videbis*]. Not learning, but anointing teaches it; not knowledge [*Scientia*], but conscience [*conscientia*] grasps it."[124] Indeed, Bernard often interprets *Taste and see that the Lord is sweet*[125] to mean that the taste of wisdom is necessary in order to enjoy the sight of God in the next life. For instance, in Sermon thirty-one on the Song, he writes, "There will be fulfillment; here there is a taste. Therefore, taste and see that the Lord is sweet."[126] Bernard's belief here is like Augustine's, that persons may perceive the heavenly, *face-to-face* vision of God,[127] albeit imperfectly and briefly, in this life, in the body.[128] However, while Augustine tends to subordinate taste to

[121] Bernard, SC 85.8 (SBOp 2:312).
[122] 1 Cor 2:10.
[123] Job 28:12-13.
[124] Bernard, Conv 13.25 (SBOp 4:99–100).
[125] Ps 33:9.
[126] Bernard, Div 41.12 (SBOp 6/1:253). See also Bernard, Dil 9.26; 15.39 (SBOp 3:140–41; 152–53); Bernard, SC 19.3.7; 50.8 (SBOp 1:112–13; 2:83); Bernard, Sent 3:22 (SBOp 6/2:80).
[127] 1 Cor 13:12.
[128] Bernard, SC 31.1–2; 52.5–6; 62.7 (SBOp 1:219–20; 2:93, 159). See also Bernard, Csi 5.27 (SBOp 3:490); Bernard, SC 48.8 (SBOp 2:72); Bernard, Div 3.1 (SBOp 6/1:86–87). Moreover, for Bernard as for Augustine, the face-to-face

sight, Bernard prioritizes taste,[129] emphasizing the verb *to taste* (*gustare*) of Psalm 33:9 more than *to see* (*videre*), and in other places as well. For example, in *On Conversion*, he says, "Unless you have tasted, you will not see."[130] He even omits *videre* in an echo of 1 Peter 2:3, *gustatis quoniam dulcis est Deus*, and replaces it with *sentire*, in his nineteenth sermon on the Song, speaking of the maidens: "the odor of the spouse's outpoured oil rouses them *to taste and feel [gustare et sentire] that the Lord is sweet.*"[131] Bernard therefore makes an innovative epistemological point: knowledge of God in this life is tasted rather than seen, insofar as God is beyond rational knowing.

Bernard here uses the different modes in which the corporeal senses of taste and sight perceive things as analogues for the different ways in which persons are able to know God. In tasting, the object perceived is mediated by the taster's touching it directly or immediately, while in seeing, the object perceived is at a distance from the one who sees.[132] Analogously, for Bernard, taste signifies that knowing God in this life is immediate and mediated by the body, while sight connotes knowing God in an unmediated, spiritual way, in the remote life to come.[133]

---

visio Dei necessarily entails a certain likeness between the human person and God; see Bernard, SC 38.5; 69.7 (SBOp 2:17–18, 206) Bernard, Div 123 (SBOp 6/1:400–402).

[129] Gordon Rudy points out Bernard's departure from the traditional hierarchy of the spiritual senses, though he draws a greater distinction between Augustine and Bernard, whereas I am attempting to point out the subtle continuities and differences between the two authors' works (see Rudy, *Mystical Language of Sensation*, 1–7, 65).

[130] Bernard, Conv 13.25 (SBOp 4:99); Rudy, *Mystical Language*, 62.

[131] Ps 33:9: *Habet oleum effusum sponsa, ad cuius illae excitantur odorem, gustare et sentire quam suavis est Dominus* (SC 19.7 [SBOp 1:112]). See also Bernard, SC 50.4 (SBOp 2:80); Rudy, *Mystical Language*, 62, 146, n. 37.

[132] See Rudy, *Mystical Language*, 8; Hans Jonas, "The Nobility of Sight: A Study in the Phenomenology of the Senses," in *Phenomenon of Life: Toward a Philosophical Biology* (Chicago: University of Chicago Press, 1982), 135–56. That taste is both "immediate" and "mediated" is not a contradiction in terms; rather, it points out two different qualities of the knowledge derived from taste.

[133] See Bernard, SC 9.8; 9.10; 67.4–8 (SBOp 1:47, 47–48; 2:190–94).

Bernard uses this analogy again in the tenth of his *Sermons on Different Topics*. He orders the senses according to how distant the objects they perceive are from the sense organs. He begins with touch and taste, which perceive objects immediate to their sense faculties, and then moves to smell and hearing and then sight, which are able to perceive things farther away from the sense organs. All of this is analogous, he says, to the different ways persons love:

> touch corresponds to love of parents [*tactui comparatur amor parentum*]; taste corresponds to love of brothers or fraternal love [*gustui comparatur amor socialis, amor fratrum*]; smell corresponds to natural love [*odoratui comparatur amor naturalis*]; hearing corresponds to spiritual love [*auditui comparatur amor spiritualis*], and sight corresponds to love of God [*visui comparatur amor divinis*].[134]

Bernard's logic governing this hierarchy of senses is thus as follows: touching and tasting connote the love of parents, siblings, and friends—the love that we know most immediately, because it is closest to us—whereas smelling, hearing, and seeing connote the love we know more abstractly, the love that is more remote from us. Here Bernard still ranks sight as the highest sense, associating it with the love of God. But again, taste and touch precede sight in order to illustrate how the love of God is known in this life: God's love is remote, as in the experience of sight, but it is also mediated in this life, as in the senses of taste and touch.

Likewise, in *On Loving God* Bernard teaches that it is "by tasting" God's "sweetness" that persons attain the highest level of love on this side of heaven, that is, loving God for God's own sake.[135] This taste prepares persons for the life to come, which includes the *visio Dei*. Again, making use of Psalm 33:9, he declares, "Of course the Lord is sweetness, but unless you have tasted, you will not see [*nisi gustaveris, non videbis*]."[136] Bernard

---

[134] Bernard, Div 10 (SBOp 6/1:109–10). Bernard offers the same ranking, based on the same criterion in Sent 3.73 (SBOp 6/2:112).

[135] Bernard, Dil 9.26 (SBOp 3:140). See also Bernard, Dil 15.39 (SBOp 3:152–53); Bernard, SC 50.4 (SBOp 2:80).

[136] Bernard, Conv 13.25 (SBOp 4:99); Rudy, *Mystical Language*, 63.

emphasizes the necessity of tasting wisdom before seeing God, because he promotes an experiential way of knowing God that begins with the bodily senses and emotions. This way of knowing God, as denoted by the bodily implications of taste imagery, is a foundational step for a kind of higher knowledge that is associated with sight, as in seeing God *face to face*. He instructs accordingly, "For it is said, 'Taste and see that the Lord is sweet.' This is hidden manna, it is the new name which no one knows except him who receives it."[137]

Noteworthy about Bernard's teaching, here—especially given the pride of place he assigns to language of touch and taste—is that the corporeal sense of taste plays no real role in the kind of experiential wisdom he promotes. It remains an analogy for the spiritual sense. Rather than physically tasting the manna of the Eucharist, Bernard tends to talk about eating the spiritual manna in the Bible. This metaphor of eating the Scriptures was commonplace in medieval monastic literature, often used to express the practice of *lectio divina*, the recitation of the Divine Office, and the rumination on Scripture passages throughout the daily monastic routine.[138] Bernard uses the metaphor to teach that persons taste that which is sweet and good—i.e., wisdom—by unpacking the meaning of the words on the *sacra pagina*.[139] For example, he says, "Solomon has bread to give that is splendid and delicious, the bread of that book called the Song of Songs. Let us bring it forth then if you please, and break it."[140] In addition, he teaches, "As food is sweet to the palate, so does a psalm delight the heart. But the soul that is sincere and wise will not fail to chew the psalm

---

[137] Bernard, Conv 13.25 (SBOp 4:99); Rudy, *Mystical Language*, 63.

[138] Carruthers, *The Book of Memory*, 44, 161, 167.

[139] Bernard's use of eating as instruction in SC 23 closely follows Origen's use of the same metaphor. See Rudy, *Mystical Language*, 146, n. 42.

[140] Bernard, SC 1.1 (CF 4:1; SBOp 1:3). Later in his *Sermons on the Song of Songs*, Bernard tempers the idea of transformation, specifying that the mutual eating of the Bride and Bridegroom does not signify total assimilation into one substance or nature; the engulfing is more discrete. He wants to make clear that the bride and the Bridegroom [i.e., the human person and God], like the Father and the Son, "are capable of containing each other without being divisible, and of being contained without being divided" (Bernard, SC 71.7 [SBOp 2:218–19]; Rudy, *Mystical Language*, 65).

with the teeth as it were of the mind, because if he swallows it in a lump, without proper mastication, the palate will be cheated of the delicious flavor, sweeter even than honey that drips from the comb.[141] Let us with the Apostles offer a honey comb at the table of the Lord in the heavenly banquet."[142] Bernard thus instructs that wisdom (*sapientia*), or experiential knowledge of God, is gained by spiritually tasting Christ through the incarnate Word made flesh in the Bible.[143]

Curiously, for Bernard, it is not the physical sense of taste that leads to this spiritual taste of experiential wisdom, but rather the physical sense of sight. As Ann Astell notes, it is the "The scriptural images" that "fire the imagination, stimulate meditation, enrich the memory, provide passionate strength for the will to do good and to avoid evil."[144]

This tendency to associate corporeal sight with the spiritual taste of wisdom is illustrated again in Bernard's own mystical encounters with God. For example, Bernard's first mystical vision, as recorded in William of Saint-Thierry's Book One of the *Vita prima sancti Bernardi*, came to him as a young man, in the church of Châtillon-sur-Saône, during the Christmas Eve solemn Night Office.[145] As William relates it, Bernard had fallen asleep while waiting for the celebration to begin: "Then it happened that the child Jesus revealed himself in his Holy Nativity to the little boy, awakening in him the beginnings of divine contemplation and increasing his tender faith. Jesus appeared to him *like the spouse*

---

[141] Ps 18:11.

[142] Luke 24:42; SC 7.5 (SBOp 1:34; CF 4:41–42). See also Renée Bennet, "The Song of Wisdom in Bernard's *Sermones Super Cantica Canticorum*," CSQ 30, no. 2 (1995): 151.

[143] See Edith Scholl, "Sweetness of the Lord: Dulcis and Suavis." CSQ 27, no. 4 (1992): 362–63.

[144] Astell, "*Hidden Manna*," 75.

[145] *Vita prima Bernardi*, 1.4 (CCCM 89B:35–36; William of Saint-Thierry, Arnold of Bonneval, and Geoffrey of Auxerre, *The First Life of Bernard of Clairvaux*, trans. Hilary Costello, CF 76 [Collegeville, MN: Cistercian Publications, 2015], 7). This first book was composed by William of Saint-Thierry during Bernard's lifetime, with a view to his canonization. On the authorship and history of the *Vita Prima*, see Marsha L. Dutton, "A Case for Canonization: The Argument of the *Vita Prima Sancti Bernardi*," CSQ 52, no. 2 (2017):132–35.

coming forth from his chamber. He appeared to him before his very eyes as the wordless Word was being born from his mother's womb, *more beautiful than all the children of men,* from the womb of the virgin mother."[146] As William narrates it, Bernard experiences the "beginnings of divine contemplation" through corporeally seeing the Word made flesh, in the image from the Psalm.

While Bernard's sensory vocabulary is replete with the bodily images—a vocabulary that includes and even, at times, prioritizes the experience of taste over sight—in the final analysis, these images remain no more than analogies. According to Bernard, corporeal sight, rather than taste, is what leads to the sweet taste of wisdom and hidden manna. This subordination of taste to sight is similar to what is present in Augustine's sensory language. Even though Bernard's emphasis on experience tends to emphasize the critical role the body and the senses play in the way persons know and return to God, Bernard still maintains the traditional ranking of the corporeal senses, which harks back all the way to Origen and recognizes corporeal sight as the superior sense, because of its association with reason and truth.[147]

This aspect of Bernard's teaching is critical for Gertrude's. As Astell points out, Gertrude knows Bernard's *Vita prima,* and she uses the visionary accounts therein to articulate her own.[148] She brings "to the fore what he kept in the background" and "reads the Eucharist as if it were a text."[149] Put differently, Gertrude understands the Eucharist as a visible sign, something that she

---

[146] Pss 18:6; 44:3. *Vita prima Bernardi* 1.4 (CCCM 89B:35); *The First Life of Bernard of Clairvaux,* 7.

[147] Bernard also maintains the traditional doctrine that the most immediate union the soul can enjoy is the heavenly *visio Dei.* He says that this kind of union is reserved for the pure of heart, like the angels, who have laid aside the body (Bernard, SC 52.5–6 [SBOp 2:92–93]). See also Bernard, SC 38.3 (SBOp 2:16), saying that even the most devout souls on earth are not ready for a vision of God's inaccessible brightness.

[148] Astell, "Hidden Manna," 90–91.

[149] Astell, "Hidden Manna," 67. Bynum also notes that Bernard's eating imagery paved the way for the eucharistic devotion that would come after him in the later Middle Ages (Caroline Walker Bynum, *Holy Feast and Holy Fast: The Religious Significance of Food to Medieval Women* [Berkeley: University of California Press, 1987], 94).

can also taste and eat corporeally. Gertrude also promotes the experience of the taste of wisdom before sight. But taste for her finds its expression in actually eating and tasting the Word made flesh—not as in seeing a biblical image, but as in tasting the eucharistic wafer itself.

In her doctrine of the spiritual senses, Gertrude skillfully intertwines chosen themes from the established tradition with themes of her own. She leaves behind the dualist and Origenist aspects of the doctrine of the senses, while reclaiming and reinterpreting some of Augustine's and Bernard's more holistic concepts. Gertrude thus puts forth her own theory that the person experiences a foretaste of the *visio Dei*, particularly in the liturgy, by means of both the corporeal and spiritual senses of taste. In order to enunciate this teaching, Gertrude draws from Augustine's conception of the three kinds of vision and picks up where Bernard left off in his emphasis on the critical role of tasting wisdom in order to see God.

CHAPTER FOUR

Gertrude's Doctrine of the Spiritual Senses

The first chapter of Book One of Gertrude's *Herald* begins with an elaborate defense of the use of sensory language in theological discourse.

> Since the unseen and the spiritual can never be expressed
> for human understanding other than through analogy with
> the physical and the visible, we have to suggest them by
> means of human and material images. Master Hugh attests
> this in his discourse *On the Inner Man*, Chapter Sixteen:
> "Holy Scripture, in order to engage the speculative powers
> of lower beings, and to come down to the level of human
> frailty, describes invisible reality by means of the forms of
> visible things, and impresses their memory on our minds
> by the beauty of outward forms which arouse our desire.
> This is why it speaks sometimes of a land flowing with milk
> and honey, sometimes of flowers, sometimes of perfumes;
> sometimes the singing of people, the chorus of birds, sym-
> bolize the harmony of celestial joys." Read the Revelation
> of John and you will find Jerusalem variously described as
> decorated with gold and silver and pearls, and various other
> gems. We know, of course, that none of them is there, where
> all the same, nothing can be altogether lacking, for nothing
> of that kind is there by substance, but all of them are present
> by analogy.[1]

---

[1] Gertrude, *Herald* 1.1.4 (CF 35:41; SCh 139:124).

In this passage, the author of Book One, an anonymous sister or group of sisters at Helfta, cites Scripture and an authoritative Victorine text to justify the material and bodily imagery used throughout the book. However, the authors do not get their Victorine reference quite right. The quotation is actually from chapter fifteen of Richard of St. Victor's *The Book of the Twelve Patriarchs* (sometimes called *Benjamin minor*).[2] Furthermore, in the quotation, Richard is describing visible things to discuss "invisible realties" as a condescension to "human frailty." Physical, visible images, he says, are necessary to arouse our desire and thus direct our minds to the beauty of invisible reality. Yet this passage in the *Herald* describes the use of "human and material images" as a fact, or a requisite of analogy. The difference is subtle, but nonetheless important. As Jeffrey Hamburger notes, "What for Richard represents but one rung of a ladder that leads gradually to the heights of contemplation (and a low rung at that), represents in the Helfta corpus, not a propaedeutic, but the platform on which Gertrude rests."[3]

The error in the Victorine citation should not be understood as a misreading of the idea contained therein; rather, Gertrude and her collaborators are adapting the passage to validate the meaning of their own different perspective on the matter. Gertrude's collaborators admitted in the *Herald*'s Prologue that they had difficulty providing accurate references for the numerous biblical passages and theological authors Gertrude referred to in her discussions with them. For this reason, they invited future readers to revise their original citations. In addition, the words of the passage and the idea they express are correct, even if the title they cite is not. As one of the most extensive discussions of speculation

---

[2] Richard of Saint Victor, *Les douze patriarches, ou, Beniamin minor. Texte critique et traduction*, ed. Jean Châtillon and Monique Duchet-Suchaux, SCh 419 (Paris: Les Éditions du Cerf, 1997), 128–30.

[3] Jeffrey S. Hamburger, "Speculations on Speculation: Vision and Perception in the Theory and Practice of Mystical Devotion," in *Deutsche mystik im abendlandischen Zusammenhang: Neu erschlossene Texte, neue methodische Ansätze, neue theoretische Konzepte. Kolloquium Kloster Fischingen 1998*, ed. Walter Haug and Wolfram Schneider-Lastin (Tübingen: Max Niemeyer Verlag, 2000), 389.

in the Middle Ages, *The Book of the Twelve Patriarchs* served as an essential source for many medieval spiritual writers.[4] Gertrude and the nuns at Helfta would therefore have certainly known about the book's influential instructions on spiritual analogy. So the way they adapted the book's ideas, even while getting its title wrong, indicates that Gertrude and her sisters are suggesting a change in course for the entire direction of the meaning of sensory language in medieval spiritual discourse. They are teaching that physical and material images are indispensable tools in theological and spiritual writing, since sensory experience is the primary means for divine knowledge.

The passage quoted above from Book One of the *Herald* is characteristic of the way Gertrude engages with the reception history (*Wirkungsgeschichte*) of the tradition on the doctrine of the spiritual senses. She does not simply reproduce or uncritically assume the ideas passed down to her; rather, like any good scholar, she is selective, choosing the sources that will serve her best. She accepts some ideas, and she challenges others by moving beyond them. When she makes an innovative move, she adapts ideas from authoritative sources to support her own theories effectively.

Gertrude develops her sophisticated doctrine of the spiritual senses by placing the language of sight against the backdrop of the ancient association between seeing and the intellect or reason. Her discussion of vision departs sharply from Origen's by using some of the innovations made by Augustine's and Bernard's treatments, particularly Augustine's threefold theory of vision. In addition, Gertrude's original ranking of the five spiritual senses inverts Origen's as subsequently echoed by Augustine and Bernard. The distinction between Gertrude's rhetoric of taste and touch and Bernard's treatment of such language accents her development. She places taste and touch as the highest modes of knowing God in this life because, according to her, when people eat the wafer

---

[4] The treatise was important for Bonaventure, for example. See Robert Javelet, "Saint Bonaventure et Richard de Saint Victor," in *Bonaventuriana: Miscellanea in onore di Jacques Guy Bougerol, OFM*, ed. Francisco de Asis Chavero Blanco (Rome: Edizioni Antonianum, 1988), 63–96; Hamburger, "Speculations on Speculation," 389, n. 140.

in eucharistic communion, they taste and touch Jesus' humanity with their corporeal senses, and by way of the union of his twofold nature, they taste and touch his divinity with their spiritual senses at the same time.

Gertrude's Language of Seeing and Knowing

Like the tradition she inherits, Gertrude seems to favor the language of sight when speaking of God in sensory terms. This approach is evident in her referring to *sight* (*videre*/*visus*) and *eye* (*oculus*) in her *Exercitia* more often than to any other sensory activity or faculty.[5] In addition, in at least one instance in her writings, she implies that sight is not just the highest but the only spiritual sense capable of perceiving God. She shows this in one of her prayers: "O love, Rabbi, my Lord, more sublime than the heavens and deeper than the abyss, whose wondrous wisdom [*sapienta*] blesses all things by sight alone [*solo visu*]."[6]

Gertrude's regard for sight as the superior sense seems to come from her belief in the traditional association of sight with truth and reason. For example, she uses *seeing* as a metaphor for being enlightened by God, or for knowing and learning about the divine attributes. In one prayer from her *Exercises*, she writes, "O imperial morning star, fulgent with divine brightness [*claritate divina*]. Oh when will your presence enlighten [*illustrabit*] me?"[7] "[L]et me, in truth, with the clean eye of my heart [*in veritate mundo cordis oculo*], scrutinize and examine, learn more [*addiscam*], know [*sciam*] and recognize them [i.e., the divine attributes] as wholly as is lawful in this life."[8]

In addition, Gertrude's privileging of sight reflects her identification of the *summum bonum* as the biblical description of seeing

---

[5] The word index of the English translation easily makes this point (see Gertrude, *Exercises* [CF 49:152–65]). I am grateful to Gertrud Jaron Lewis for sharing with me her translation notes and indices, which also make this point for Gertrude's original Latin.

[6] Gertrude, *Exercises* 5.299–300 (CF 49:83; SCh 127:180).

[7] Gertrude, *Exercises* 5.43–46 (CF 49:74; SCh 127:160).

[8] Gertrude, *Exercises* 5.346–48 (CF 49:85; SCh 127:182).

God *face to face*.[9] Several of the petitions of her *Exercises* yearn for this final goal, for instance, "When, oh when may I come to that place where you are, God, true light, God and Lamb? I know that I will at last see you with my eyes [*te videbo meis oculis*], O Jesus, my saving God."[10] "Thus, what I now believe in hope, I may gladly see with my eyes in reality [*oculis meis laeta videam in re*]. Let me see you as you are [*videam te sicuti es*]; let me see you face to face [*videam te facie ad faciem*]."[11]

For Gertrude, this face-to-face heavenly vision of God is the goal of human striving. She writes numerous prayers, again found in her *Exercises*, that long for this experience of being able to see God directly, "without mediation": "My God, my very bright inheritance, oh when, after the snares of this death have been destroyed, will I personally see you without mediation [*sine medio*] and praise?"[12] "When, oh when will I be held tight in your blessed arms and behold you, O God of my heart, without mediation [*sine medio*]? Ah! Quickly, quickly, let me be snatched from this exile, and in jubilation see your mellifluous face! Amen."[13] According to Gertrude, this experience characterizes the afterlife. She is clear: the boundary that separates the human person from knowing God in this kind of unmediated way, in this life, is the body. She even refers to the body as a "wall," which blocks the face-to-face sight of God in this life and which will only disappear after the body's death. She writes, "Oh, who will free me from the exile of this pilgrimage? Oh, who will snatch me from the snares of this age? Oh, when will I leave behind this miserable body [*corpus hoc miserum*] in order to see you without mediation [*sine medio*], O God, love, star of stars? In you, O dear love, I will be snatched from the temptation of this death. Unworried and exultant, stepping over the wall [*murum*] of my body into you, God, my lover, I will see

[9] 1 Cor 13:12.

[10] Gertrude, *Exercises* 5.469–70 (CF 49:90; SCh 127:192).

[11] Gertrude, *Exercises* 1.229–30 (CF 49:31; SCh 127:76). See also Gertrud Jaron Lewis, "Introduction," in Gertrude, *Exercises* (CF 49:8).

[12] Gertrude, *Exercises* 6.323–25 (CF 49:105; SCh 127:224).

[13] Gertrude, *Exercises* 5.490–93 (CF 49:91; SCh 127:194).

you there in truth, face to face, without any obscurity [*sine aenigmate*]."[14]

Up to this point, Gertrude's ideas on sight keep with the established tradition, even all the way back to Origen. What she accepts and reproduces from the tradition before her forms the basis for her subsequent nuance. Indeed, when she declares that the face-to-face *visio Dei* may be perceived to some degree in this life, in the body, she begins to depart from Origen, while more closely following Augustine and Bernard. Praising God, she asserts, "You are the very bright mirror of the holy Trinity, which *there* one is permitted to look at face to face through the eye of a clean heart, but *here* only obscurely [*aenigmate*]."[15] For Gertrude, then, it is not that the body entirely prevents the human person from seeing God, but that one's sight of God here is not as clear as it will be there, when God will be seen without mediation. She thus creates a tension in her prayers between the mediated and unmediated vision of God, a tension that corresponds to the here and there and the now and then. The English translator of the *Exercises* explains, "Gertrud defines human life backwards, so to speak. . . . Life on earth is represented in the traditional image of a pilgrimage whose destination is our ultimate home. As this image suggests, life is anything but static."[16] Gertrude emphasizes the necessity of spiritual growth and constant renewal when she prays,

> Oh, how happy, how blessed [is the one] whose sojourn ends in you. Alas, for me, alas for me, how long will it be extended? Oh what a *then* it will be when that very pleasant and lovely *now* arrives; when the glory of my God, my king, and my spouse is manifested and appears to me [offering] endless fruition and sempiternal gladness; when in truth, I

[14] Gertrude, *Exercises* 5.279–85 (CF 49:83; SCh 127:178) with my minor emendation. See also Gertrude, *Exercises* 6.612 (CF 49:115; SCh 127:244), distinguishing between the "spirit" (*spiritum*) and the "rotten body" (*corpus putridum*).

[15] Gertrude, *Exercises* 5.55–56 (CF 49:75; SCh 127:160) (translator's emphasis).

[16] Lewis, "Introduction," in Gertrude, *Exercises* (CF 49:9).

contemplate and see this desirable, this wished-for and this lovable face of my Jesus for which my soul has so long thirsted and whose radiance it has yearned for. Surely *then* I will be satisfied and filled by the torrent of his voluptuousness, which, locked away for so long now, lies hidden for me in the storeroom house of divinity. *Then* I will see and contemplate my God, my dearest love, in whom my spirit and my heart *now* grow faint.[17]

Significantly, twice in the *Exercises* Gertrude reconciles the tension between now and then, or collapses the boundary between them; both are within a eucharistic context.[18] The first, in Exercise Three, celebrates the anniversary of the monastic consecration. It occurs when Gertrude refers to the ritual responsorial verse "his blood has adorned my cheeks," sung after communion during the Mass of the "Rite of the consecration of virgins."[19] She tells her readers repeatedly to claim, "*Already* his body is in companionship with my body, and his blood has adorned my cheeks."[20] In this passage, when now and then are reconciled, soul and body seem to be as well—i.e., Gertrude is declaring a direct or immediate experience of God while still in the body. What is also significant is that Gertrude uses *rose-colored* (*rosa, rosues*) throughout her writings as the symbolic color for Christ's human and divine or twofold nature.[21] Therefore, when she writes that Christ's "blood

---

[17] Gertrude, *Exercises* 5.254–66 (CF 49:82; SCh 127:176). Translator's gloss and translator's emphasis in the first two instances; my emphasis in last three instances.

[18] My discussion of these two instances are from the following article, used with permission: Ella Johnson, "Liturgical Opportunities for 'Deep Crying unto Deep': The Rhetorical Function of Now/Then Dualities in Gertrud of Helfta," *Medieval Mystical Theology* 24, no. 1 (2015): 45–58.

[19] For the liturgy of the Consecration see *Pontificale romanum* (Mechliniae: H. Dessain, 1873), 126–40. See also Lewis, "Introduction," in Gertrude, *Exercises* (CF 49:13–14). See also the tenth-century Pontifical from Germany, which the Helfta nuns are likely to have known (*Le pontifical romano-germanique du dixième siècle I: Le texte 1* [Città del Vaticano: Bibl. Apostolica Vaticana, 1963]).

[20] Gertrude, *Exercises* 3.291–92 (CF 49:53; SCh 127:114). My emphasis.

[21] Gertrude, *Exercises* 3.13; 4.222; 4.237 (CF 49:41, 65, 65; SCh 127:92, 140). Lewis makes this point in Gertrude, *Exercises* (CF 49:30, n. 56). In addition,

has adorned my cheeks" in this liturgically based passage, she is basing her reconciliation of the already/not yet on her eucharistic union with Christ's humanity and divinity.

In the second instance, in Exercise Five, Gertrude similarly employs the rose-colored symbolism by describing Christ's cheeks as flushed and his eyes as glowing red. She does so to teach about the special kind of union with Christ, whom she refers to as the "*Omega* and *Alpha*," that is possible in eucharistic communion with him in the here and now: "Ah! Show me your face and make me contemplate [*contemplari*] your radiance. Lo, your face, which the most beautiful dawn of divinity illuminates, is pleasant and comely. Miraculously your cheeks blush [*rubet*] with *Omega* and *Alpha*. Very bright eternity burns inextinguishably in your eyes. There God's salvation glows as red [*rutilat*] for me as a lamp. There radiant charity sports merrily with luminous truth."[22] By reversing the biblical *Alpha* and *Omega*,[23] Gertrude makes her point: the union between Christ's humanity and divinity, made fully present to the human person's body and soul in eucharistic communion, allows for the wall of the body and the boundary between the now and then to be crossed in the here and now. She thus claims that in eucharistic communion the human person can enjoy an experience akin to the face-to-face vision of God.

Gertrude argues that when people receive the Host they make physical contact with Christ's humanity, concomitantly making spiritual contact with his divinity. She grounds this teaching on her assertion that the "fullness of the divine dwells bodily" [*habitat corporaliter omnis plenitudo divinitatis*] in the sacred Host.[24] In this aspect of her eucharistic understanding, she alludes to the doctrine of the hypostatic union of Christ's two natures and the related

---

the *Herald* details that on one occasion, after receiving eucharistic communion, Gertrude "saw the Lord Jesus dip the host which he held in his hand as it were in the heart of God the Father and bring it out tinted a rosy red [*roseam*], as if reddened [*rubricatam*] by blood" (Gertrude, *Herald* 3.17.1 [CF 63:66; SCh 143:74]).

[22] Gertrude, *Exercises* 5.66–73 (CF 49:75; SCh 127:162).
[23] Rev 1:8. Lewis highlights this point in Gertrude, *Exercises* (CF 49:75, n. 21).
[24] Gertrude, *Herald* 2.7.1 (CF 35:119–20; SCh 139:260).

notion of *communicatio idiomatum*—that is, while Christ's divine attributes are communicated to his humanity, his human properties are communicated to his divinity. As Gertrude explains it, because the eucharistic Host really is Christ, it contains his human and divine natures. In addition, because Christ's two natures are conjoined and their corresponding properties communicate with one another, humans encounter both properties in their reception of the Eucharist. Christ himself asks her in Book Three of the *Herald*, "Does not the catholic faith hold that anyone who receives communion on a single occasion, to him I give myself for his salvation with all the benefits contained in the treasuries of my divine and human natures alike? And the more often, however, a person has received communion, the more greatly the accumulation of his blessedness is increased and multiplied."[25] On the authority of her hearing of Christ himself, Gertrude thus teaches that when someone eats the sacred communion wafer, that person becomes united to Christ's *humanitas* in the body, and through this bodily union, that person also becomes united to his *divinitas* in the spirit.

This position occurs in a different account from Book Three of the *Herald*, which describes Gertrude's union with Christ's humanity and divinity within the liturgy of the Eucharist:

> One day during Mass at the elevation of the host [*elevationis Hostiae inter Missam*], while she was offering that most sacred host to God the Father as worthy reparation for all sinners and as compensation for all her own acts of neglect, she perceived that her soul was brought before the gaze of divine majesty [*conspectui divinae majestatis praesentatam*] in that good pleasure in which Christ Jesus, splendor and image of the glory of his Father, Lamb of God without spot, offered himself at the same time on the altar to God the Father for the salvation of the world. For God the Father saw her through the most blameless human nature of Jesus Christ as purified from all sin and spotless, and saw her through his most excellent divine nature as enriched and adorned with

[25] Gertrude, *Herald* 3.54.2 (CF 63:164; SCh 143:234).

every sort of virtue with which that glorious divine nature
flowered through his most holy nature.[26]

Here the *Herald* reports that through Gertrude's physical gaze
upon the elevated Host, she was brought before God's gaze. It is
as if she experienced a face-to-face vision of God. Through the
testimony of her experience, Gertrude teaches again that within
the Mass, especially in eucharistic communion, the tension between the now and then passes away. Even though she is physically gazing at the Host rather than eating it, she is united with
the Lamb of God. God the Father sees her in her body as united
to Christ's humanity, and thus, in her soul, she is united to his
divinity. Both her body and soul can have such an experience of
divine union, because both Christ's humanity and divinity are
made truly present to her in the Eucharist, and her body and soul
unite respectively to his humanity and divinity.

In an autobiographical account from Book Two of the *Herald*,
Gertrude describes her experience of the unmediated *visio Dei*, in
the eucharistic here and now. This account is especially significant
because she refers explicitly to the biblical face-to-face vision of
God[27] and quotes from Bernard's thirty-first sermon on the Song
of Songs for authority:

> On the second Sunday in Lent, while they were singing at
> Mass before the procession the responsory beginning *I have
> seen the Lord face to face*, my soul was illuminated by a mi-
> raculous and priceless flash. In the light of divine revelation,
> I saw what seemed to be a face, right up against my own, as
> described by Bernard: "Not the recipient but the giver of
> form, not affecting the eyes of the body [*non perstringens ocu-
> los corporis*] but rejoicing the face of the heart, pleasing not
> by its outward appearance but by its gift of love." In this
> vision, flowing with honey, I saw your eyes which are like
> suns directly opposite my own and I saw how you, my sweet
> darling, were then acting not on my soul alone but also on

---

[26] Gertrude, *Herald* 3.18.7 (CF 63:73; SCh 143:86). See also Gertrude, *Herald*
3.18.5–6 (CF 63:71–73; SCh 143:82, 84, 86).

[27] As in Exod 40:33.

my heart and all the parts of my body [*affeceris non solum animam meam, verum etiam cor meum cum omnibus membris*], as you alone know how.[28]

Gertrude begins this account by quoting Bernard, to describe her vision as "not affecting the eyes of the body."[29] This description is consistent with her belief that the clear and direct *visio Dei* will only be experienced after death, when the human person has stepped over the wall of the body. But then, at the end of the passage, she describes the vision as affecting not just her soul, but also her heart and her whole body. The key to unlocking Gertrude's apparent self-contradiction in this passage is its liturgical context.[30] She here again demonstrates her view that within the Mass, especially when one receives eucharistic communion, the tension between now and then passes away. She depicts being united with Christ's humanity in her body and being united to his divinity in her soul. In case anyone might regard her position as an unwarranted extension of traditional thought, Gertrude cites Bernard as an authority and then moves beyond him. She is not misreading Bernard. Rather, she here again refers to him as an authority in order to highlight and support the difference between her own original position and his.

Gertrude also appears to be seizing upon Augustine's understanding of the relationship between Christ's humanity and his divinity—i.e., his two natures—as the hope of humankind. He teaches that when divinity joined to humanity in the incarnation, humankind was redeemed. But he also taught that in Christ, in the relationship between his human soul and body, humankind

---

[28] Gertrude, *Herald* 2.21.1 (CF 35:157; SCh 139:322).

[29] Bernard's sermon reads, *nec dubium quin eo iucundiorem, quo intus, non foris. Verbum nempe est, non sonans, sed penetrans; non loquax, sed efficax; non obstrepens auribus, sed affectibus blandiens. Facies est non formata, sed formans; non pestringens oculos corporis, sed faciem cordis laetificans: grata quippe amoris munere, non colore"* (Bernard, SC 31.6 [SBOp 1:223]).

[30] Hamburger comments on Gertrude's use of Bernard in this passage, but in a slightly different way; Jeffrey F. Hamburger, *The Visual and the Visionary: Art and Female Spirituality in Late Medieval Germany* (New York: Zone Books, 1998), 146–47.

is offered a model of redemption, that is, a model for the proper relationship between body and soul to strive for every day, in this life. Such a model, for example, teaches how the three kinds of vision—corporeal, spiritual, and intellectual—should be properly ordered in this life, until they are finally reconciled and held in unity in the *visio Dei*. Gertrude agrees with Augustine on both counts about humankind's being redeemed and finding a model for living in Christ's joining of humanity and divinity. But she puts her own spin on things when teaching her eucharistic understanding of knowing God. She holds that when receiving the Eucharist, persons do not have to worry about proper order, because the body and soul are already properly ordered in the here and now.

Gertrude's development of Augustine's teaching becomes particularly evident in the juxtaposition of two vignettes from her *Herald*. The first comes from the Prologue. Like the passage quoted at the opening of this chapter, it appears to provide a justification for the corporeal images throughout the book. Yet it does so by using Augustine's distinctions between the corporeal, spiritual, and intellectual kinds of vision. The *Herald* calls attention to Gertrude's own experience of these three kinds of vision: "And although the loving Lord, on both ordinary and feast days, continuously and impartially poured out his grace on her, through visions of physical likenesses [*imaginationes corporearum similitudinum*] as well as through purer enlightenments of her thoughts [*illuminationes cognitionum*], all the same he wished to have described in this little book visions of physical likenesses [*imaginationibus corporearum similitudinum*], for human understanding."[31] Here the Helfta nuns appear to be ranking Gertrude's visions according to Augustine's threefold schema. Like him they are stressing the middleness of spiritual vision—i.e., that it occupies a realm between that of corporeal vision and intellectual vision and functions as the intermediary between the dichotomous extremes of sensual involvement in corporeality and the intellectual consideration of an idea. Similarly, in this passage the Helfta nuns

---

[31] Gertrude, *Herald* 1 Prol.6 (CF 35:34; SCh 139:114).

describe the "enlightenments of her [i.e., Gertrude's] thoughts" as "purer" than her "visions of physical likeness."

However, the second vignette, an autobiographical and eucharistic account from Book Two of the *Herald*, collapses this ranking. Given Gertrude's understanding of human-divine union within liturgical context, this reconsideration of Augustine's position should come as no surprise. She recounts that one day, after receiving communion and returning to her choir stall, she gazed at the image of Christ in her prayer book and saw a ray of light, like an arrow, entering and repeatedly withdrawing from Christ's wounded side. She says that she understood the ray of light to be an invitation for union with Christ: "For when I had received the life-giving sacrament, and had returned to my place in choir, it seemed to me as if something like a ray of the sun came out from the right-hand side of the crucified Christ painted on the page [*depicti in folio*], that is, from the wound in the side. It had a sharp point like an arrow and, astonishingly, it stretched forward and, lingering thus for a while, it gently elicited my love."[32]

According to Augustine's theory, the three kinds of vision Gertrude experiences here may be distinguished as follows: her sight of the painted image of the crucified Christ on the page is corporeal, because it is perceived through her body and presented to the senses of her body; her vision of the arrow entering and withdrawing from Christ's wound is spiritual, since it is the image of an absent body, and it is perceived not by Gertrude's body but by her soul; and her understanding of the arrow as eliciting her love is intellectual, because the arrow's meaning is known by her

[32] Gertrude, *Herald* 2.5.2 (CF 35:113; SCh 139:248, 250). Again, Hamburger's reading of this passage is different from but complementary to this reading (Hamburger, *The Visual and the Visionary*, 125–27). For the Helfta nuns' use of hand-held books during liturgical ceremonies, see Bruce W. Holsinger, *Music, Body, and Desire in Medieval Culture: Hildegard of Bingen to Chaucer* (Stanford, CA: Stanford University Press, 2001), 251. On the themes of Christ's wound and arrows in late medieval art and devotional practice, see Barbara Newman, "Love's Arrows: Christ as Cupid in Late Medieval Art and Devotion," in *The Mind's Eye: Art and Theological Argument in the Middle Ages*, ed. Jeffrey F. Hamburger and Anne-Marie Bouché (Princeton: Princeton University Press, 2006), 263–86.

intellect. What is particularly striking in this account, in light of Augustine's threefold theory of vision, is Gertrude's claim that the three kinds of visions interact with one another. After she receives the Eucharist, she says that she simultaneously experiences a corporeal and spiritual vision of Christ. As she puts it, "a ray of the sun" proceeded from Christ, who was "painted on the page."[33] Furthermore, she says that she has an intellectual vision or understanding from her spiritual vision of the ray, protruding from the corporeal vision of the book; that is, she understands from the ray that Christ is eliciting her love. Only at the end of time, according to Augustine, when matter and spirit are reconciled, will the three kinds of vision be held in unity and will spiritual vision include seeing with the eyes of the body. Yet for Gertrude, the boundaries of space and time and matter and spirit disappear in the context of the liturgy. So whereas Augustine maintains the eventual reconciliation of the three different types of vision in heaven, Gertrude uses his theory and goes beyond it to assert the possibility of their reconciliation in the here and now, in the liturgy.[34]

---

[33] Gertrude's affirmation of the value of physical vision and corporeal images also contradicts Bernard's cautious provisos about corporeal imagery and visionary experience. As Ann Astell notes, "The role of . . . visual artwork in triggering Gertrude's visions is what distinguishes them most clearly from St. Bernard's" (Ann Astell, "Hidden Manna": Bernard of Clairvaux, Gertrude of Helfta, and the Monastic Art of Humility," in *Eating Beauty: the Eucharist and the Spiritual Arts of the Middle Ages* [Ithaca and London: Cornell University Press, 2006], 96). Hamburger suggests that Bernard's exhortation to his monks to use a visual imagination, "while a contradiction of his iconoclastic stance in the *Apologia*," seems to have actually "open[ed] the door to the visual arts" in monasteries like Helfta (Hamburger, *The Visual and the Visionary*, 105). See Astell, "Hidden Manna," 86.

[34] Gertrude also describes the simultaneous activity of the three kinds of visions in the liturgy in the first of her *Exercises*. Drawing from the liturgy for the sacrament of baptism, she uses the corporeal vision of a lighted candle to represent and encourage her readers' intellectual vision or "inner enlightenment" (*illuminatione interiori*). At the same time, Gertrude's language prompts her readers to experience a spiritual vision of the "burning lamp [*lampadem ardentem*]" of divine charity within their souls: "In receiving the light [*lumen*], you will pray for inner enlightenment ([*Illuminatione interiori*].

Thus Gertrude uses Augustine's and Bernard's ideas about sight as both source and authority for her own. She draws from their thought to claim that sight is the superior spiritual sense, inasmuch as it connotes the heavenly goal of the spiritual life: the face-to-face vision of God. Like Augustine and Bernard, she claims that the human person can know something of this experience, in this life. In particular, the sight of God in the here and now is obscure, whereas then it will be clear and direct. But Gertrude strikes out on her own when she discusses the *visio Dei* in a specifically eucharistic context. When the human person receives communion, she maintains that the face-to-face vision of God now, in this life, is reconciled, as it will be then in the next life; the vision of God here and now is not obscure, but direct, as it is there and then. Because the tensions between the now/then, here/now, and body/soul are overcome in eucharistic communion, the sight of God, according to Gertrude, is clear and immediate.

Gertrude to some extent agrees with Augustine and Bernard in the need to be cautious about corporeal sense perception because of the body's fallenness. She too says that the senses are "fleshly" as a result of the Fall, and that they are continuously tempted to seek transitory things over God.[35] Yet rather than merely warning about such temptation, she stresses that Christ's

---

Ah Jesus, inextinguishable light [*lumen inextinguibile*], kindle the burning lamp [*lampadem ardentem*] of your charity within me inextinguishably [*inextinguibiliter*], and teach me to guard my baptism without blame. Then, when called, I come to your nuptials, being prepared I may deserve to enter into the delights of eternal life to see you, the true light [*visura te verum lumen*], and the mellifluous face of your divinity. Amen (Gertrude, *Exercises* 1.171–77 [CF 49:28; SCh 127:72]).

[35] Like Augustine and Bernard, Gertrude upholds the notions of *concupiscentia* and *curiositas*, and she locates them in the will, not the flesh. See for example, her discussion of the will and its tendency to seek transitory over divine things: Gertrude, *Herald* 3.4.1 (CF 63:33–34; SCh 143:22, 24). See also Doyère, "Sainte Gertrude et les sens spirituels," 433–34. For her use of "temptation" (*tentatio*), see Gertrude, *Exercises* 1.38; 1.45–46; 4.94; 5.283; 5.402–5; 6.732; 7.194 (CF 49:22, 23, 61, 83, 87, 119, 128; SCh 127:58, 60, 130, 178, 188, 252, 272). Generally, on Gertrude's notion of sin, especially as evident in the *Exercises*, see Hildegard Gosebrink, "In der Sinne Achtsamkeit—Leib und Sinne in Gertruds 'Exercitia spiritualia,'" in *In Aufbruch neuer Gottesrede: Die*

incarnation redeems it. She teaches that Christ took upon himself "the bodily substance of our earth" (*substantiam corporis de terra nostra*) in order "to supply" (*suppletio*) for the sinfulness of humanity.[36] Such unity of humanity with divinity, as she depicts it, results from Christ's suprarational love for humankind and his overwhelming desire to be in communion with us: "In your madness you united two such total opposites. Or, to phrase it with greater dignity, the innate, natural loveliness of your goodness . . . whose more natural flow you directed toward the salvation of humanity, persuaded you to summon the farthest-flung, most miserable specimen of the human race . . . from the far reaches of her complete worthlessness to keep company with royal—no, divine—grandeur, so that every creature living on earth might grow in confidence."[37] For Gertrude, it is marvelously astonishing that divinity was united to humanity in the salvific, hypostatic union of Jesus Christ incarnate, but she finds it even more astonishing that this kind of saving unity is still present to humankind every day in the Eucharist.[38]

Gertrude goes so far as to teach that such union with God in the Eucharist purifies the "flesh" and effectively restores the image and likeness of God in which the human person was originally created. As this account of Christ's "madness" continues, she depicts her own experience of eucharistic purification and restoration by employing the image of hot wax, an image commonly

---

Mystik der Gertrud von Helfta, ed. Siegfried Ringler (Ostfildern: Grünewald, 2008), 76–92. Gertrude, *Exercises* 1.190–95 (CF 49:25; SCh 127:72, 74).

[36] Gertrude, *Exercises* 3.103 (CF 49:44; SCh 127:100). On the theme of *suppletio* in Gertrude's writings, see Cyprian Vaggagini, "The Example of a Mystic: St. Gertrude and Liturgical Spirituality," in *Theological Dimensions of the Liturgy* (Collegeville, MN: Liturgical Press, 1976), 758–59.

[37] Gertrude, *Herald* 2.8.3 (CF 35:122; SCh 139:264, 266).

[38] Gertrud Lewis notes in relation to this point, "The human nature of Christ as one with the Spirit and as part of the Trinity, while 'still in the substance of my flesh' (VI, 107, 180, 418), represents the pivotal point of Gertrud's mystical life" (Gertrud Jaron Lewis, "Introduction," in Gertrude, *Exercises* [CF 49:7]). See also André Rayez, "La Mystique féminine et l'humanité du Christ," *Dictionnaire de spiritualité ascétique et mystique, doctrine et histoire*, ed. Marcel Villler, et al. (Paris: Beauchesne, 1937), 7/1:1088.

used in medieval eucharistic debates and discussions of the *imago Dei*:[39]

> the Lord made his appearance in that part of his blessed breast in which he had, at Candlemas, received my soul like wax carefully softened in the fire. [My soul] was covered with little beads of sweat breaking out on it, as if the substance of that wax, shown to me earlier, had melted and liquefied because of the excessive heat hidden within. But the divine treasure-chest, by some supernatural but indescribable, or rather unthinkable, power was absorbing these apparent beads of moisture, so that the love there possessed was fully revealed where so great and impenetrable a secret was unlocked.[40]

In its traditional usage the hot wax metaphor stressed the fundamental disparity between the *imago Dei* in the human person and that in Christ, the true *imago Dei*, that is, it was used to suggest a resemblance that is merely formal in nature. The imprint of the seal's shape, in this usage, would not impart any of its matter on the hot wax.[41] Yet Gertrude uses the metaphor to stress the likeness

---

[39] Hamburger, "Speculations on Speculation," 385, nn. 123–24. Hamburger notes the many references listed under *cire* (wax) in the index to Robert Javelet, *Image et ressemblance au douzième siécle: de saint Anselme á Alain de Lille*, 2 vols. (Paris: Letouzey et Ané, 1967), 2:346. For applications of the wax metaphor in spiritual works, see Siegfried Ringler, *Viten- und Offenbarungsliteratur in Frauenklöstern des Mittelalters: Quellen und Studien*, Münchener Texte und Untersuchungen zur deutschen Literatur des Mittelalters, Bd. 72 (Munich: Artemis Verlag, 1980), 275–76. Hamburger also notes that the metaphor of hot wax originates in Aristotle's *De Anima* (424a, 17–21): "In general, with regard to all perception, we must take it that the sense is that which can receive perceptible forms without their matter, as wax receives the imprint of the ring without the iron or gold, and takes the imprint which is only gold or bronze, but not qua gold or bronze" (trans. in Stephen Everson, *Aristotle on Perception* [Oxford: Clarendon Press, 1997], 57–58).

[40] Gertrude, *Herald* 2.8.4 (CF 35:122–23; SCh 139:266).

[41] The twelfth-century text that Javelet cites says, *Tanta differentia est inter imaginem quae est Filius et imaginem quae est homo (comme entre Raison et raison), quanta differentia est inter filium regis et formam sigilli impressam, immo multo major est differentia* (Javelet, *Image et ressemblance*, 2:142, n. 26).

between God and the human person—particularly corporeal likeness, which is quite different from a formal resemblance. Christ
absorbs the "beads of moisture" from her heart, which is liquefied
by the fire of his own. In other words, after she is purified in eucharistic communion by way of union with his humanity, her
image and likeness to him in her body are restored—so much so
that he assumes her bodily form.[42]

Another account of Gertrude's liturgical experience affirms
this teaching. It tells of one occasion, during the community's
celebration of the Mass, when Gertrude was complaining to God
about the fact that she had to miss the liturgy and the chance to
receive communion, because she was ill. Christ then embraced
her and chanted, *"Truly, man was made in the image of God.*[43] And
thus, showering kisses on her eyes and ears, her mouth and her
heart, her hands and her feet, and at each one repeating the same
words, sweetly chanting them, through those very words he most
courteously renewed in her soul his divine *image and likeness."*[44]
Even then, when Gertrude could not receive communion physically, Christ imparted on her the blessing she would have obtained
from it. He gave each of her body's members—including her
sensory organs—a benediction that effectively restored her body
to the image and likeness of his humanity.

That Gertrude believes such an experience is available to anyone who receives the sacred Host is evident in the prayers she
prescribes for others in her *Exercises*. On the theme of following
Christ, in Exercise Four, for instance, Gertrude writes the following petitions: "I offer to you the marrow of my forces and of my
senses as a holocaust of new praise and intimate thanksgiving";[45]

---

[42] On the exchange between Gertrude's heart and Christ's Sacred Heart,
see Barbara Newman, "Iam cor meum non sit suum: Exchanging Hearts from
Heloise to Helfta," in *From Knowledge to Beatitude: St. Victor, Twelfth-Century
Scholars, and Beyond: Essays in Honor of Grover A. Zinn, Jr.*, ed. E. Ann Matter
and Lesley Smith (Notre Dame, IN: University of Notre Dame Press, 2013),
281–99 at 290–92.

[43] Gen 1:26.

[44] Gertrude, *Herald* 4.14.7 (CF 85:85; SCh 255:162).

[45] Gertrude, *Exercises* 6.206–8 (CF 49:101; SCh 127:216).

"Make my conduct like yours. . . . Enclose my senses in the light of your charity so that you alone may teach, guide, and instruct me within the penetralia of my heart";[46] "Ah! O love, dip my senses in the marrow of your charity so that through you I may become a gifted child and you yourself may be, in truth, my Father, teacher, and master."[47] In addition, later in her *Exercises*, Gertrude encourages her readers to pray the following: "Oil and anoint my senses with the blood streaming from that most glorious head, with the pain of [those] venerable senses that by that balsamy savor I may be altogether transformed. . . . Ah, my most dulcet Jesus, may the actions of your holiest senses totally conceal my guilt and make amends for all my thoughtlessness,"[48] and "My king and my God, abide in the substance of my flesh [*meae carnis substantia*]."[49]

Gertrude's teaching that the Eucharist is the most effective vehicle for restoring the human person to the image of God's likeness is further demonstrated in the account of her own conversion experience. As the first Book of the *Herald* reports it, with Augustinian language, "she had been far from God, in a land of unlikeness [*regione dissimilitudinis*] . . . while clinging too closely to the liberal arts." Then "she put off her old nature with its deeds and put on the new nature which is created after God's likeness in true righteousness and holiness."[50] Later, years after her conversion, while thanking God on the day after having received

[46] Gertrude, *Exercises* 4.238–40 (CF 49:65–66; SCh 27:140).

[47] Gertrude, *Exercises* 5.322–24 (CF 49:84; SCh 127:180). For more on Gertrude's references to Christ as teacher and her embodied learning from him, see Alexandra Barratt, "Infancy and Education in the Writings of Gertrud the Great of Helfta," *Magistra* 6, no. 2 (Winter 2000): 17–30.

[48] Gertrude, *Exercises* 7.183–85; 188–90 (CF 49:128; SCh 127:272). The gloss is my own, which emends the translator's.

[49] Gertrude, *Exercises* 6.107 (CF 49:97; SCh 127:208).

[50] Gertrude, *Herald* 1.1.2 (CF 35:38–39; SCh 139:120). It is noteworthy that Gertrude's conversion differs significantly from Augustine's in that it is not a turn away from dramatic sensual, bodily temptations, like lust, but rather from spiritual and intellectual inattention to God. See Laura Grimes, " 'Theology as Conversation': Gertrude of Helfta and her Sisters as Readers of Augustine," Ph.D. dissertation, University of Notre Dame, 2004, 22.

communion, she gained the understanding that the most effective
way for this re-creation and restoration to occur is through receiving the Eucharist with heartfelt devotion. Her religious sisters
explain that God imparted this wisdom to her:

> as often as someone attends Mass with devotion, concentrat-
> ing on God who there offers himself in the sacrament for the
> common salvation of the whole world, he is truly seen by
> God the Father as with the same good pleasure as God looks
> on the sacred host that is offered to him. It is like someone
> who steps from darkness into the radiance of the sunlight
> and is at once completely flooded with light. Then she asked
> the Lord, "My Lord, does someone who falls into sin im-
> mediately lose this blessedness, just as someone who retreats
> from the light of the sun into the dark loses the welcome
> brightness of light?" The Lord replied, "No, for although in
> sinning to a certain extent he obscures the light of the divine
> favor from himself, none the less my loving-kindness always
> keeps the trace of that blessedness in that man for eternal
> life: he multiplies this blessedness as often as he strives with
> devotion to attend the sacraments."[51]

For Gertrude, sin is what obscures the sight of or experience of
God, in the body, in the here and now. Put differently, the body
is a wall between the human person and God in this life, but only
inasmuch as it carries the mark of sin. But God is clear with
Gertrude in this passage that when a person receives the Eucharist
with appropriate devotion and intention, the image and likeness
of God will be restored to the fallen body and soul of that person.
Once purified as such, the person may see God clearly in body
and soul.

Gertrude thus presents an important and innovative epistemology in light of the tradition of the spiritual senses before her.
She argues that God may be known in and through the human
body and its senses in this life, after having been purified and
restored to God's image and likeness by way of eucharistic com-

---

[51] Gertrude, *Herald* 3.18.8 (CF 63:73–74; SCh 143:86, 88).

munion. Stemming from this belief is her reorientation and elaboration of the corporeal sense of sight. Because of the claim she makes for the body and its senses' restoration, she is able to release corporeal images, which had been absorbed into the mechanism of allegory alone, from their uplifting function. This is perhaps why Gertrude opens the account in which she describes her eucharistic communion with God with the metaphor of hot wax, by quoting Romans 1:20: *the invisible realities of God can be expressed to the outer understanding through created beings.*[52] Whereas corporeal vision had been denigrated by the established tradition, by understanding it as evoking contemplation of an invisible creator, or sometimes redirected by channeling it up the appropriate ladder of perception, Gertrude indicates that God can be seen and known corporeally.[53]

Moreover, the other corporeal senses besides sight, even those that the tradition regards as lower and bodily, have value for Gertrude. As she sees it, all of the corporeal senses work together with their spiritual analogues as partners in knowing and loving God. Indeed, in her *Exercises*, she instructs her readers to pray for God's descent upon their bodily sense organs, so that their spiritual senses can perceive God more clearly: "Signing your ears and nose with the sign of the holy cross, you will pray to the Lord that he himself open wide the ears of your heart to his law and fill all that is within you with the scent of his fame."[54] Gertrude does not leave out taste and its correlative sense of touch here, because she regards them as too bodily to perceive the immaterial God; rather, she singles them out for a longer, special benediction of their own. In Gertrude's thought, these two senses are privileged to know God in this life because of their special role in perceiving Christ in the eucharistic Host.

[52] Gertrude, *Herald* 2.8.4 (CF 35:122; SCh 139:266).

[53] In general this transition occurs in the thirteenth century in discussions of vision. See Suzannah Biernoff, *Sight and Embodiment in the Middle Ages* (Basingstoke, UK: Palgrave Macmillan, 2002), 163.

[54] Gertrude, *Exercises* 1.87–88, 95–98 (CF 49:25l; SCh 127:64).

To Taste (*Sapor, Sapere*) Wisdom (*Sapientia*) in the Eucharist

Several times in her *Exercises* Gertrude follows Bernard by prioritizing taste over sight in the approach to God.[55] Her reason for doing so, like his, seems to be based on the immediate and mediated characteristics of taste. Bernard sometimes emphasizes the verb *gustare* and omits the verb *videre* from Psalm 33:9 (*gustate et videte quoniam suavis est Deus*). Gertrude also emphasizes taste before sight, yet with a slightly different technique. In an intriguing passage in her *Exercises*, she quotes the alliterative combination of *vacare et videre* ("be still and see") from Psalm 46:10 and then supplements it with the sense of *gustare* ("taste") as given in Psalm 33:9, *gustate et videte* ("taste and see"). Gertrude makes these changes in order to place the immediate sense of taste before the more remote sense of sight, which she anaphorically exploits in the following lines.[56]

> Be at leisure [*vaca*] now; taste and see [*gusta et vide*] how dulcet and how remarkable is the spouse whom you have chosen above thousands.
>
> See what and how great is that glory for which you have condemned the world.
>
> See what the good is like for which you have waited.
>
> See what the homeland is like for which you have sighed.
>
> See what the prize is like for which you have labored.
>
> See who your God is, what he is like and how great he is, whom you have cherished, whom you have adored and for whom you have always wished.[57]

---

[55] The following pages in this chapter are based on the following article, reprinted here with permission from *Viator*: Ella Johnson, "To Taste (*Sapere*) Wisdom (*Sapientia*): Eucharistic Devotion in the Writings of Gertrude of Helfta," *Viator* 44, no. 2 (2013): 175–99, esp. 185–99.

[56] Gertrude, *Exercises* (CF 49:95, n. 18).

[57] Gertrude, *Exercises* 6.58–65 (CF 49:95–96; SCh 127:204). In a prayer in the first of her *Exercises*, Gertrude again links the idea of tasting to its delay until the next life: "Make me taste [*degustare*] the sweetness of your Spirit," "make

Following in Bernard's footsteps again, in another place in her *Exercises* Gertrude uses Psalm 33:9 to articulate the way that the immediate and mediated taste of union with God in this life precedes and anticipates something of the immediate sight of God in the next life.[58] Her prayer calls out to God, "O most lovable radiance, when will you satisfy me with yourself? If only I might here perceive the fine rays of your Venus-like beauty for a little while and at least be permitted to anticipate your gentleness for a short time and sweetly beforehand to taste [*praegustare*] you, my best share."[59]

In these passages, Gertrude's language of sight communicates the idea that God is always to some extent distant from persons in this life and beyond rational knowing, while her language of taste teaches that the Eucharist is an opportunity for persons to make immediate contact with and know God in the here and now. For in tasting God in the Eucharist, one immediately touches the body of God as mediated in the consecrated Host and is able to enjoy an earthly "taste" or "foretaste" (*praegustatio/praegustare*) of the heavenly sight of God. As her religious sisters report in the *Herald*, Gertrude learns from Christ that one receives divine knowledge more directly and immediately by tasting the Host rather than by seeing it:

> Another time, during the distribution of the sacrament, she strongly desired to see the host and was prevented from doing so by the crowds of those approaching the altar. She understood that the Lord was gently inviting her and saying, "The sweet secret that concerns us must be unknown to those who are far from me. But you—if it pleases you to know—

---

me run to pastures of eternal life, where I can be at leisure for eternity and see that you, my Lord, are truly sweet" (Gertrude, *Exercises* 1.92; 1.102–3, 1.125 [adapted from my translation in the article] [SCh 127:64, 66]).

[58] Gertrude also juxtaposes the faculties of sight and taste with synesthesia. In a few places she uses gustatory language for the biblical sight of God (e.g., God's "mellifluous face") (Gertrude, *Exercises* 1.84; 5.271 [CF 49:25, 82; SCh 127:64, 176]).

[59] Gertrude, *Exercises* 5.47–51 (CF 49:75; SCh 127:160). For *foretaste* (*praegustatio/praegustare*), see e.g., Gertrude, *Exercises* 5.345; 6.502 (CF 49:85, 111; SCh 127:182, 236).

draw near and experience the taste of that hidden manna, not by seeing but by eating [*accede et non videndo sed gustando experire quid sapiat illud absconditum manna*].[60]

In this account, Gertrude learns that she may come closer to the "hidden manna" in the here and now, "not by seeing but by eating." Like Bernard, she underlines the immediate quality of taste. But she does so for a different reason: to teach that the physical sense of taste makes direct contact with the body of Christ in the consecrated Host.

Because of the immediacy of taste, Gertrude even explicitly inverts the traditional sensory hierarchy. Gertrude presents her alternative schema in Exercise five. The schema begins with the lowest, corporeal sense of sight, which perceives God at a distance in this life, and it ascends to the highest, corporeal senses of taste and touch, which perceive God immediately in the here and now. Finally, it culminates with a request for the *summum bonum*, the experience of the biblical seeing God face to face in the next life. Her unique ordering appears within a benediction she prescribes for both the corporeal and spiritual senses:

> [W]hen you are at leisure for love (for the kindling of your senses by the true sun, who is God, so that your love may never be extinguished but may grow from day to day) assiduously reflect on one of these verses:
> Blessed the eyes that see you, O God, love.
> When, oh when may I come to that place where you are, God, true light, God and Lamb? I know that I will at last see you with my eyes, O Jesus, my saving God.
> Blessed are the ears that hear you, O God, love, Word of life.

[60] Gertrude, *Herald* 3.18.18 (CF 63:77; SCh 143:96). The historical context of this passage is important. As Caroline Walker Bynum points out, medieval Christians were peculiarly prone to conflate the experience of receiving the eucharistic host on their tongues with seeing, because they thought tasting it physically did not really matter (Bynum, *Holy Feast and Holy Fast: The Religious Significance of Food to Medieval Women* [Berkeley: University of California Press, 1988], 60–61). See also my discussion of this point in chapter one.

When, oh when will your voice full of mellifluous pleasantness console me, calling me to you?

Ah! Let me not fear hearing evil, but let me quickly hear
the glory of your voice. Amen.

Blessed the nose that breathes you, O God, love, life's most
dulcet aroma.

When, oh when will the fragrance of your mellifluous
divinity breathe upon me?

Ah! Let me come quickly to the fat and lovely pastures of
sempiternal vision of you. Amen.

Blessed the mouth that tastes, O God, love, the words of
your consolation, sweeter than honey and the honeycomb.

When, oh when will my soul be filled again out of the
cream of your divinity and become inebriated with your
plentiful voluptuousness?

Ah! Let me taste you thus *here*, my Lord, for you are sweet,
that *there* I may for eternity happily and thoroughly enjoy
you, O God of my life. Amen.

Blessed the soul that clings inseparably to you in an embrace of love and blessed the heart that senses the kiss of
your heart, O God, love, entering with you into a contract
of friendship that cannot be dissolved.

When, oh when will I be held tight in your blessed arms
and behold you, O God of my heart, without mediation?

Ah! Quickly, quickly, let me, snatched from this exile, in
jubilation see your mellifluous face! Amen.[61]

Gertrude charts out this *via mystica*, with its summit in taste and
touch in this life, because it is through these senses that the human
person directly perceives Christ, the Mediator, in the here and
now, as mediated through the communion Host. As she puts it,
"Ah! Let me taste you thus *here*, my Lord, for you are sweet, that
there I may for eternity happily and thoroughly enjoy you, O God
of my life. Amen."[62]

[61] Gertrude, *Exercises* 5.464–493 (CF 49:90–91; SCh 127, 192, 194) (with
adaptations from my own translation); translator's emphasis.
[62] For a similar pattern of ordering, see Gertrude, *Herald* 2.24.1 (CF 35:172–
73; SCh 139:350, 352). In his reading of the *Herald*, Olivier Quenardel suggests
that Gertrude takes for the basis of her structure of sensation the order of

Moreover, because of her beliefs in the restoration and renewal of the human person that are possible by way of eucharistic communion, Gertrude honors the senses of taste and touch as the privileged means by which the human person may become deified in this life. For instance, she writes in her *Exercises*, "In tasting [*degustatione*] your pleasantness, I am alive."[63] "May the faithful God, the true Amen, who does not grow faint, make me thirst fervently for the dear Amen with which he himself affects [the soul]; taste [*gustare*] with pleasure the dulcet Amen with which he himself refreshes [the soul]; be consummated in happiness by that saving Amen with which he himself perfects [the soul]."[64]

Gertrude juxtaposes both the immediate and the mediated characteristics of taste, as well as its corporeal and spiritual senses. She teaches that the person makes immediate physical contact and mediated spiritual contact with Christ, the Mediator between the here/there and then/now in the consecrated Host. According to her, in eucharistic communion, as the physical sense of taste and touch directly contact the body of God in the consecrated Host, concomitantly the spiritual senses of taste and touch contact the divine nature of Christ, which is present there in heaven but also here within, as mediated by the communion wafer.

Gertrude's ideas about the way the corporeal and spiritual senses of taste work in tandem are evident in the first of the *Spiritual Exercises* in a prayer "For receiving communion of the life-giving body and the blood of the spotless Lamb, Jesus Christ." She instructs her readers to pray,

---

Christian pedagogy and the order of the eucharistic liturgy. In both cases, he says, "Le large embrassement de la vision doit passer par l'étreinte resserrée de la manducation pour que l'homme puisse voir Dieu comme Dieu veut être vu." He argues, "La logique de cette pédagogie sensorielle, apostolique et non sans rapport à la mystagogie, qui trouve son apogée dans la communion eucharistique, débouche sur une mise en disponibilité de l'homme pour Dieu, à la manière de Marie. C'est la visée ultime de la *pietas Dei*: faire de l'*Ecclesia* tout entière, et chacun de ses membres, le Temple où Dieu vient prendre sa joie" (Olivier Quenardel, *La communion eucharistique dans le* Héraut *de l'amour divin de Sainte Gertrude d'Helfta: situation, acteurs et mise en scène de la divina pietas* [Brepols: Turnhout, 1997], 141–42).

[63] Gertrude, *Exercises* 4.356–57 (CF 49:70; SCh 127:150).
[64] Gertrude, *Exercises* 1.234–38 (CF 49:32; SCh 127:76, 78).

O most dulcet guest of my soul, my Jesus very close to my heart,
let your pleasant embodiment [*incorporatio*] be for me today . . .
eternal salvation,
the healing of soul and body, . . .
and the enclosing [*conclusio*] of my life sempiternally in you.[65]

With the phrase "let your pleasant embodiment be for me today,"
Gertrude again implies that the human person makes direct, immediate contact with the body of Christ in receiving the eucharistic Host. Yet the tomorrow of eternal salvation is also found in
the Eucharist today, by way of Christ's "pleasant embodiment."
The spiritual sense of taste allows for this opportunity by way of
its contact with the divine nature of Christ, mediated by the consecrated Host. That the spiritual and physical senses of taste and
touch make contact with Christ in eucharistic union is further
illustrated by Gertrude's prayer: "Let it be for me . . . the healing
of soul and body."

Gertrude's understanding of the Eucharist as integrative of body
and soul is additionally seen in her original structure of sensation
in the benediction considered above. In the tradition of the doctrine of the spiritual senses, writers generally view the spiritual
and physical senses as having an inverse order. The physical
senses ascend from touch to sight, while the spiritual senses ascend from sight to touch. Yet Gertrude pictures both the physical
and spiritual senses as ascending from sight to touch, so that the
physical senses have the same order as the traditional order of
the spiritual senses. For Gertrude, the spiritual order is the arche-
type for the physical order. This idea seems to be based on her
belief that eucharistic union with Christ, the Mediator, suspends
the boundaries between space and time and humanity and divinity. When she explicitly ranks the senses, she refers at once to the
physical and spiritual analogues as operating simultaneously.

Indeed, in two other places in her writings, Gertrude explicitly
ranks the senses from sight to touch, and she aligns the physical
senses with their spiritual analogues to present them as working

---

[65] Gertrude, *Exercises* 1.178–79; 189–90; 193–95 (CF 49:29–30; SCh 127:72,
74).

in tandem. First, in the fifth of her *Spiritual Exercises*, Gertrude writes a series of benedictions that progress through the physical and spiritual sensory faculties together in this order: from the eyes to the ears, then to the nose, and finally to the mouth: "Blessed the eyes that see you, O God, love, . . . Blessed are the ears that hear you, O God, love, Word of life. . . . Blessed the nose that breathes you, O God, love, life's most dulcet aroma. . . . Blessed the mouth that tastes, O God, love, the words of your consolation, sweeter than honey and the honeycomb. . . . Blessed the soul that clings inseparably to you in an embrace of love."[66] In the second instance, in her spiritual autobiography in Book Two of the *Herald*, Gertrude reproduces this ranking of the physical and spiritual senses, from sight to hearing and smelling up to taste and touch. Again, she refers to the physical and spiritual faculties as acting together simultaneously. After receiving the Eucharist one day, she exclaims, "What sights, what sounds, what scents, what delicious savors, what sensations! . . . For even if the combined abilities of human beings and angels could be concentrated into a single moment of worthy knowledge, it would not be adequate fully to express even a single word by which one could in the least degree aspire to the sublimity of such great excellence."[67]

Gertrude offers more insight into her sensory schema in the first of her *Spiritual Exercises*, which calls to mind the baptismal rite. She speaks of the "salt of wisdom," thereby making a reference to blessed salt typically eaten by catechumens in the preliminary rites of baptism.[68] Patristic authors like Augustine associated

---

[66] Gertrude, *Exercises* 5.468–87 (CF 49:90–91; SCh 127:192, 194).

[67] Gertrude, *Herald* 2.8.5 (CF 35:123; SCh 139:268).

[68] Robin Jensen explains the role of salt in the baptismal rites of the early church: "In some sense the salt was a substitute sacramental sign, given to those not yet eligible to receive the Eucharist. . . . Salt also had the particular benefits of warding off demons and strengthening the purpose of those who received it, perhaps in the same way that salt serves to preserve and flavor food" (Robin M. Jensen, *Baptismal Imagery in Early Christianity: Ritual, Visual, and Theological Dimensions* [Grand Rapids, MI: Baker Academic, 2012], 35).

salt with strengthening the mind and receiving wisdom.[69] With this phrase, then, Gertrude stands within the tradition. Yet she refers to both the corporeal and spiritual senses of tasting salt and wisdom respectively, and implies that they function concomitantly: "At this point, you will pray that your mouth be filled with the salt of wisdom [*sapientiae*] that you may be able to savor the taste [*sapere*] of faith in the Holy Spirit. Most dulcet Jesus, let me receive from you the salt of wisdom and the spirit of understanding favorable to eternal life. . . . Make me taste [*degustare*] the pleasantness of your Spirit."[70]

Also, noteworthy about this passage is the way that Gertrude, like Augustine and Bernard, uses the etymological association of taste (*sapere*) and wisdom (*sapientia*). Yet in another place where she discusses the taste of wisdom, she moves beyond their teaching. She claims that significant divine learning occurs when the human person tastes the eucharistic Host *physically and spiritually*.[71] In her spiritual autobiography, she cries out to God,

> Hail, my salvation and the light of my soul! May all that is encompassed by the path of heaven, the circle of the earth and the deep abyss give you thanks for the extraordinary grace with which you led my soul to experience and ponder the innermost recesses of my heart. . . . you endowed me with a clearer light of knowledge of you. . . . I do not remember . . . having ever enjoyed such fulfillment except on the days when you invited me to taste the delights of your royal table. Whether your wise providence ordered this, or my assiduous neglect brought it about, is not clear to me.[72]

---

[69] See, for instance, Augustine, Conf 1.11.17 (PL 32:669); Jensen, *Baptismal Imagery*, 35.

[70] Gertrude, *Exercises* 1.87–90 (CF 49:25; SCh 127:64).

[71] As Caroline Bynum explains, "almost all medieval mystics sometimes speak of 'tasting God,' and the verb itself is a kind of bridge between the physical act of eating the host and the inner experience of resting in the sweetness (*fruitio*) of mystical union" (Bynum, *Holy Feast and Holy Fast*, 151).

[72] Gertrude, *Herald* 2.2.1–2 (CF 35:103–4; SCh 139:232, 234).

Gertrude certainly agrees with Bernard that to touch or to taste God is not to know but to "experience."[73] But in her language of taste and touch, Gertrude emphasizes the physical role in knowing God. She is firm in her belief that Christ is made flesh in the Eucharist and is thus perceptible to the corporeal as well as spiritual senses of taste and touch. Her religious sisters report that Gertrude reflects on the importance of the mouth as the most important part of the body, because it receives the Eucharist directly:

> After receiving communion, one day while she was meditating with what great care one should guard the mouth, as it in particular among the other parts of the body is the receptacle of the precious mysteries of Christ, she was instructed by this analogy: if someone does not guard the mouth from idle, untruthful, ugly, slanderous words and so on, she comes impenitent to holy communion and in such fashion receives Christ—as far as she can—like someone who buries a visitor on his arrival by piling up stones on the doorstep, or hits him on the head with a hard crow-bar![74]

Gertrude even asks God on another occasion, "what glory does your divinity delight to gain from my chewing your spotless sacraments with my unworthy teeth?"[75]

At another time, her sisters report that Gertrude understands her corporeal chewing of the host as breaking apart and distributing food to the Mystical Body of Christ: "whenever at the reception of the sacrament she longed that the Lord would grant her as many souls from purgatory as the number of parts into which the host was broken in her mouth, and consequently tried to break it up into very many parts, the Lord said to her, 'That you may understand that the effects of my mercy are more than all my works and that there is no one who can exhaust the abyss of my loving-kindness, look, I grant that by the ransom of this life-giving

---

[73] Rebecca Stephens, "The Word Translated: Incarnation and Carnality in Gertrude the Great," *Magistra* 7, no. 1 (Summer 2001): 83–84.

[74] Gertrude, *Herald* 3.18.9 (CF 63:74; SCh 143:88).

[75] Gertrude, *Herald* 3.18.17 (CF 63:77; SCh 143:96).

sacrament you shall receive much more than you venture to pray for.' "⁷⁶ Such metaphors of bodily encounter—conjuring up as they do the person's mouth and its teeth chewing and swallowing Jesus' flesh so that it may restore the Mystical Body—reveal Gertrude's understanding that the God who is infinite and beyond all rational knowing is also fleshly humanity—a humanity that feeds and physically encounters persons.

Gertrude's sisters describe her eucharistic repose on Christ's breast in similar physical terms:

> Another day when about to communicate she withdrew herself from it even more than usual because of her unworthiness. She implored the Lord to receive that holy Host on her behalf in his own person and incorporate [*incorporaret*] it within himself and then breathe into her out of the noble respiration of his most delightful breath. . . . Thence when she had rested for awhile in the bosom of the Lord as it were beneath the shadow of his arms, in such a way that her left side seemed to lean against the blessed right side of the Lord, a little later she raised herself up and perceived that from the loving wound in the Lord's most holy side she had contracted a pink [*roseam*] scar on her left side. After this when she was approaching to receive the body of Christ, the Lord seemed to receive that sacred host in him with his divine mouth. Passing through her inmost being it emerged from the wound in Christ's most holy side and, like a dressing, fitted itself over that same life-giving wound. Then the Lord said to her, "See how this host unites you to me in such a way that it covers up your scar from one side and my wound from the other, and becomes a dressing for both of us."⁷⁷

In this account, Gertrude's sisters report her understanding that the physical process of eating the Eucharist is mutual, involving both her body and Christ's humanity. She asks Christ to take the Host into himself, and she understands that she is conformed to

---

⁷⁶ Gertrude, *Herald* 3.18.26 (CF 63:80–81; SCh 143:102).

⁷⁷ Gertrude, *Herald* 3.18.27 (CF 63:81; SCh 143:104). On the traditions of Christ's wounds and sacred heart, as well as Gertrude's engagement with it, see nn. 32 and 42 above.

him when the scar forms on her side. Yet Gertrude's communion affects Christ as well. The Host covers up his wound, just as it covers up her scar; indeed, it dresses their common wounds at once.

By suggesting such mutual assimilation, Gertrude's language of taste and touch moves beyond even the most body-affirming aspects of Augustine's and Bernard's language. They frequently qualify their language of eating, tasting, touching so as not to endorse the lower, more bodily ways of knowing God. Indeed, when Bernard speaks of leaning on the wounded side of Christ, he is explicit that such union is spiritual only. In his fifty-first Sermon on the Song, for instance, Bernard evokes the biblical image of John leaning on Jesus' breast at the Last Supper: "Happy the soul who reclines on the breast of Christ and rests between the arms of the Word!"[78] Such tactile imagery in Bernard's writing operates solely as an allegory of union between the soul and the Word, making nothing of the carnal implications of the imagery.[79]

Gertrude, by contrast, is concerned to draw attention to the possibility of the human person's intermingling with or even being transformed into Christ in both body and soul. This teaching is based upon her fundamental belief that when human persons perceive Christ's humanity in eucharistic communion in their corporeal senses, they perceive his divinity in their spiritual senses as well. In her spiritual autobiography, she recounts her experience of being transformed by a eucharistic encounter with the humanity and divinity of the Christ child:

> As in a moment of revelation my soul realized that it had been offered, and had received, in place of its heart so to speak, a tender little boy. In him there lay hidden the gift of

[78] Bernard of Clairvaux, *On the Song of Songs*, S 51.5.5 (CF 31:44; SBOp 2:87).
[79] As Caroline Walker Bynum notes, among twelfth-century Cistercians like Bernard, "the heart—which is already the sweetness John tasted on Jesus' breast and the cleft in the rocks where the Apostle hides—is primarily God's love. Although feeding imagery and images of refuge surround it, it is not explicitly a symbol of the Eucharist. . . . By Gertrude's day . . . devotion to the sacred heart is an explicitly Eucharistic devotion" (Bynum, *Jesus as Mother*, 192–93).

complete perfection, which is truly the best endowment. When my soul cradled him within itself it suddenly seemed to be completely changed into the same color as him—if that can be called a "color," which cannot be compared with any visible quality.

Then my soul perceived a meaning that defies explication in the sweet words, *God shall be all in all*.[80] It felt that it held within itself the Beloved, installed in the heart, and it rejoiced that it was not without the welcome presence of its Spouse, with his most enjoyable caresses. Offered the honeyed draughts of the following divinely inspired words, it drank them in with a thirst that could not be satisfied: "Just as I bear the stamp of the substance of God the Father[81] in regard to my divine nature, so you bear the stamp of my substance in regard to my human nature, for you receive in your deified soul the outpourings of my divine nature, just as the air receives the sun's rays. Penetrated to the very marrow by this unifying force, you become fit for a more intimate union with me."[82]

For Gertrude, the language of sweetness and caressing is more than an allegory. She emphasizes the physical connotations of the imagery of taste and touch, because it is actually in physically perceiving the humanity of Christ in the Eucharist with these two senses that the body and soul of the human person will be deified and restored to the image and likeness of God.

It is for this reason that Gertrude exploits the tactile implications of eucharistic devotion instead of avoiding them as do Augustine and Bernard. She even describes her own physical union with God in the Eucharist in terms of mutual intimacy (*mutuae familiaritatis*) and exchange. She counts as her most treasured eucharistic experiences Christ's wounding of her heart and his exchange of her heart with his: "Among all these pleasures I have two favorites: that you imprinted on my heart the brilliant necklace of your most saving wounds; and that you fixed the wound of love so plainly

[80] Heb 1:3.
[81] Heb 1:3.
[82] Gertrude, *Herald* 2.6.2 (CF 35:117; SCh 139:258).

and so effectually in my heart. . . . You also bestowed on me the added intimacy of your priceless friendship, by offering in many different ways that most noble ark of godhead, your deified Heart, to increase all my delights, sometimes giving it freely, sometimes as a great sign of our mutual intimacy [*mutuae familiaritatis*], exchanging it for mine."[83]

Even more than Bernard, Gertrude stresses that the human person is integrated equally in soul and body; both parts of the human person, then, can be simultaneously united to God, even in this life. According to her, the human person can achieve an immediate relation to God in the here and now, in body and soul, especially in eucharistic communion. The corporeal senses of taste and touch in the Eucharist are the gateway to union with God in the soul.

---

[83] Gertrude, *Herald* 2.23.7–8 (CF 35:165–66; SCh 139:336, 338). See also Gertrude, *Herald* 2.6–8 (CF 35:116–123; SCh 139:256–68). On the traditions of Christ's wounds and Sacred Heart, as well as Gertrude's engagement with it, see nn. 32 and 42 above. On the comparison between Gertrude's and Bernard's devotions to Christ's wounds, see Sheryl Frances Chen, "Bernard's Prayer Before the Crucifix that Embraced Him: Cistercians and Devotion to the Wounds of Christ," CSQ 29, no. 1 (1994): 47–51. As Laura Grimes has made clear, Gertrude was also working with the Augustinian notion of "heart," the "mens" in its highest act by which intellect and affect combine in the act of *caritas*. For instance, in the *Herald*, Gertrude relates to God, "Suddenly you were there unexpectedly, opening a wound in my heart [*infigens vulnus cordis meo*] with these words, 'May all your affections [*affectionum tuarum*] come together in this place; that is may the sum total of your delight, hope, joy, sorrow, fear and your other affections [*affectionum tuarum*] be fixed firmly in my love [*stabiliantur in amore meo*]' " (Gertrude, *Herald* 2.5.2 [CF 35:113; SCh 139:250]). At first blush, this understanding of *heart* does not seem to reveal a physical kind of union with God, as seen elsewhere. However, it is important to note that Gertrude's union with Christ, as this passage relates it, occurs in a eucharistic and communal context. Along with her sisters, after Mass, Gertrude is taking part in a devotion that honors the incarnation. The context, as Grimes notes, emphasizes the ongoing incarnation of Christ in his mystical body, the community of Christians, of which Gertrude is a corporate member and through which she receives Christ's mercy and grace. Thus the union of her heart with Christ's is body-dependent and should be viewed as body-to-body. See Grimes, "Theology as Conversation," 118–19.

Even in the liturgical context in which Bernard's visions occur, Bernard uses taste to refer to the sweetness of the spiritual taste of true doctrine in the Scriptures, the "living bread" and the "hidden manna," instead of the corporeal taste of the eucharistic Host in the liturgy; he emphasizes Christ, the incarnate Word made flesh in the Scriptures, rather than Christ made flesh in the eucharistic Host. At times, undeniably, Gertrude's language corresponds to Bernard's rhetoric. She too says that the words of the Bible are "honeyed and honey-sweet [*super mel et favum*]."[84] Moreover, she suggests that the words she writes, because they are so based in Scripture, are *sweeter than the honeycomb (favo mellis dulciores)*.[85] Yet Gertrude goes farther than Bernard when she associates the "sweetness" of her own words with the "sweetness" of the Eucharist. For instance, she reports that Christ tells her the following about her *Herald*: "I have placed this book thus upon My Heart, that every word contained therein may be penetrated with divine sweetness, even as honey penetrates bread."[86] Indeed, in the same account we are told that once the manuscript had been completed, one of Helfta nuns hid the work in the sleeve of her habit when she communicated, and the book received the same benediction that effectively transubstantiates bread and wine for the salvation of all.[87] As Ann Astell argues, "Whereas Bernard eats the sacred scriptures as if they were Eucharist, Gertrude reads the Eucharist as if it were text."[88]

---

[84] Gertrude, *Herald* 3.18.17 (CF 35:77; SCh 143:96).

[85] Ps 18:11; Gertrude, *Herald* 1.1.2 (CF 35:39; SCh 139:122). In fact, Gertrude's *Exercises* are so saturated with the words for sweetness that the translators of the English edition, Gertrude Lewis and Jack Lewis, took special lexical efforts to avoid an "untruthful impression of saccharinity" in their English translation of the text. "To guard against such cloying sweetness," they explain, "we have taken these steps: *dulcis* is represented by its English cognate 'dulcet' and *mellifluous* by its cognate 'mellifluous.' *Suavis* has become 'pleasant' " (Gertrude, *Exercises*, CF 49:32, n. 63).

[86] Gertrude, *Herald* 5.33.1 (SCh 331:264, 266). Translation my own.

[87] Gertrude, *Herald* 5.33.1 (SCh 331:264). See my discussion in chapter one.

[88] Moreover, Astell says, "Gertrude did not in fact misread Bernard; rather she complements him, bringing to the fore what he kept in the background" (Astell, "Hidden Manna," 67).

Taste and touch are certainly central metaphors in Gertrude's writings, not merely because the Eucharist is the place in Christian ritual in which God is most intimately received, but also because taste and touch express the way the human person makes immediate physical contact and mediated spiritual contact with Christ, the Mediator between the here and there, in the consecrated Host. According to Gertrude, as the physical senses of taste and touch directly contact the human nature of Christ in the consecrated Host, the spiritual senses of taste and touch contact the divine nature of Christ, present *there in heaven, but also here* within and mediated by the communion wafer. To be sure, the corporeality of Gertrude's language of taste and touch is justified by her position that in the Liturgy, bodily sensation can and does cross the times and spaces that separate human and divine lives.

Conclusion

Gertrude employs the senses actually and figuratively—corporeally and spiritually. Her recitation of specific psalms and aspects of the traditional rhetoric of the spiritual senses, as well as her justification of the use of images, indicates a working knowledge of sensory language used by Augustine and especially Bernard. But more than her sources, Gertrude uses the physical senses—in particular sight, taste, and touch—to help activate the spiritual senses in approaching divine union. Her gustatory language implies that because of their direct physical contact with the body of God and mediated spiritual contact with Christ's divine nature in eucharistic communion, the senses of taste and touch, including both the physical senses and their spiritual analogues, are privileged as the gateways to union with God in this life. Rather than sight, as the tradition would have it, taste is the instrument *par excellence* for apprehending divine grace and for growth in God. The overall impression of the spiritual senses left by Gertrude's writings is that the soul joins with the body when the physical and spiritual senses are together applied in liturgically based exercises. According to Gertrude, liturgical sensory piety has as its *telos* the culmination and expectation of the divine-human encounter.

Gertrude's spiritual instructions in her *Exercises* and her visionary accounts in the *Herald*, therefore, seek to cultivate in others a
piety that is both sensorially rich and self-aware. Liturgical tropes
and rituals intermingle with instructions for personal piety in
ways that engage her readers in practices that include both
physical and spiritual sensory experience as an essential component. Through liturgical rituals and also through her instructions
based on them, Gertrude grants value to the physical and spiritual
senses as channels through which believers can approach and
encounter the divine. As she is a frequent recipient of eucharistic
communion, she encourages others to follow her, against the
devotional trend of the time. Of course Gertrude is predisposed
to such an integrated understanding of mind-body-spirit in the
Cistercian-Benedictine traditions of prayer, manual labor, and
corporal works of charity. But more is at stake in Gertrude's writing than engagement of the spiritual and physical senses in the
process of human-divine interaction. She understands the body
and its senses, as well as the soul and its senses, in their concomitant experience of perception as yielding knowledge of God. The
liturgy becomes a school in which both physical and spiritual
senses are open to divine presence and trained to perceive its teaching.[89] Baptism in the incarnate Christ and ongoing eucharistic
communion with him recreates the body and soul of the human
person, and liturgy guides the person's experience. Because Christ

---

[89] To provide just one example of how she charges the stuff of liturgical
worship with meaning, in Exercise one, Gertrude invites her readers to remember various stages of the corporeal experience of the rite of baptism: the
sight of the lighted candle, the smell of the chrism oil, the sound of the reading of the Creed and formula of the exorcism, the taste of baptismal salt, and
the touch of baptismal water and white gown. See especially Gertrude, *Exercises* (CF 49:1.51–177, 22–23, 25–28; SCh 127:60–72). For the various stages of
the baptismal rite that Gertrude draws from, see Lewis, "Introduction," in
Gertrude, *Exercises* (CF 49:11–12). Grimes also analyzes the meaning of Gertrude's use of liturgical sources, primarily in the *Exercitia*, to articulate a
theology of baptism. See Laura M. Grimes, "Bedeutung der Liturgie im Werk
Gertrudes von Helfta," in *"Vor dir steht die leere Schale meiner Sehnsucht":
Die Mystik der Frauen von Helfta*, ed. Michael Bangert and Hildegund Keul
(Leipzig: Benno, 1998), 68–80.

himself approaches humankind through corporeality in the incarnation and the Eucharist, she argues that humankind should approach God corporeally as well as spiritually.

CHAPTER FIVE

"Do This in Memory of Me":
Ritual, Re-Membering, and Reading

In his *Meditations on Prayer*, Gertrude's Cistercian predecessor, William of Saint-Thierry, associates meditative reading or *lectio* with the Eucharist by using the image of sweetness:

> As your clean beasts, we there regurgitate the sweet things [*dulcedine*] stored within our memory, and chew them in our mouths like cud for the renewed and ceaseless work of our salvation. That done, we put away again in that same memory what you have done, what you have suffered for our sake. When you say to the longing soul, "open your mouth wide, and I will fill it," and she tastes and sees your sweetness [*gustans et uidens suauitatem*] in the great Sacrament that surpasses understanding [*incomprehensibili*], then she is made that which she eats, bone of your bone, and flesh of your flesh.[1]

William juxtaposes the sweet taste of *lectio* with the sweet taste of the Eucharist, as Bernard does. But William goes farther than Bernard in his use of "sweetness," by making the point that the

---

[1] William of Saint Thierry, *Meditations*, trans. Sister Penelope, CF 3 (Kalamazoo, MI: Cistercian Publications, 1977), 8.7.7–8, p. 142; Guillaume de Saint-Thierry, *Oraisons méditatives*, trans. Jacques Hourlier, SCh 324 (Paris: Éditions du Cerf, 1985), 140. Edith Scholl discusses use of *dulcis* and *suavis* in the Cistercian tradition, noting its roots in the Bible and patristic writings (Edith Scholl, "Sweetness of the Lord: Dulcis and Suavis," CSQ 27, no. 4 [1992]: 359–66; Edith Scholl, "The Sweetness of the Lord," in Edith Scholl, *Words for the Journey: A Monastic Vocabulary*, MW 21 [Collegeville, MN: Cistercian Publications, 2009], 133–41).

Word made Flesh is present in both the Word of God and the Eucharist. For William, when one ruminates on the words and images of the Bible and commits them to memory, one is united to God in the flesh, as in eucharistic communion.[2]

Gertrude, however, takes Bernard's use of sweetness one step further than William, exploiting Bernard's beliefs by associating her own words—not just those of Sacred Scripture—with the sweetness of God in the Eucharist. Like William, she claims that one can experience the kind of sweetness attained in eucharistic communion by meditating on biblical images and words. But, as she sees it, this principle extends to her words. She promises her readers the experience of the sweetness otherwise reserved to eucharistic communion and scriptural meditation.

So, for instance, when Gertrude instructs people to read her *Herald*, she says they should follow the same steps as they do in reading the Bible, steps that in the monastic tradition entail *lectio*, *meditatio*, and *contemplatio*. The effect of such reading, she claims, is that her readers will be able "to taste for themselves how sweet is the Lord."[3] Indeed, at the conclusion of her *Herald*, she asserts, "the more simple readers of this book, who are not capable of swimming by themselves in the ocean of divine mercy, place themselves at least on course by using this means, and launched by the delight of the good offices which have been done toward neighbor, they can give themselves to reading [*lectionibus*], to meditation [*meditationibus*], to contemplation [*contemplationibus*], and thus commence finally to taste [*gustare*] for themselves how sweet [*dulcis*] is the Lord, and how really fortunate is one who hopes in Him and who devotes to Him his every thought."[4]

---

[2] On this comparison, see Marsha L. Dutton, "Eat, Drink, and Be Merry: The Eucharistic Spirituality of the Cistercian Fathers," in *Erudition at God's Service: Studies in Medieval Cistercian History XI*, ed. John R. Sommerfeldt, CS 98 (Kalamazoo, MI: Cistercian Publications, 1987), 6–9. See also Marsha L. Dutton, "Intimacy and Imitation: The Humanity of Christ in Cistercian Spirituality," in *Erudition at God's Service*, CS 98:40–42, 50.

[3] Cyprian Vaggagini, "The Example of a Mystic: St. Gertrude and Liturgical Spirituality," in *Theological Dimensions of the Liturgy* (Collegeville, MN: Liturgical Press, 1976), 750.

[4] Gertrude, *Herald* 5.36.1 (SCh 331:274). Translation my own.

Gertrude frequently uses the imagery of taste and sweetness to articulate her teaching that eucharistic communion entails union between Christ, in both his humanity and his divinity, and the human person, in both body and soul. The question remains, then, as to whether Gertrude is explicitly claiming that the experience of sweetness offered by her words includes union with Christ's humanity and divinity, in one's body and soul, as does the sweetness of eucharistic communion.

Because of its genre of devotional instruction, in her *Spiritual Exercises* Gertrude is even more explicit than in her *Herald* about mapping a way for her readers to taste for themselves divine sweetness. Along with images and schemes taken from tradition of the doctrine of the spiritual senses, she laces her words with liturgical tropes. Moreover, each of the seven exercises is based on a different liturgical rite. Exercise one, for example, draws from the sacrament of baptism, while Exercises two to four recall aspects of rituals that constitute a day in the life of a cloistered nun—respectively, the rituals of clothing, consecration, and profession. Exercises five and seven make free use of the seven canonical hours of the Divine Office, while Exercise six is based in the rite of eucharistic communion.[5] Furthermore, Gertrude begins three of her seven exercises by citing the biblical verse of Jesus' command to his disciples in the rite of the Last Supper: *Do this in memory of me.*[6] In Gertrude's Latin use, the trope *In mei memoriam facietis* also calls to mind the liturgical formula for the consecration of bread and wine in the Roman Rite Canon of the Mass.[7]

---

[5] Gertrud Jaron Lewis, "Introduction," in Gertrude, *Exercises* (CF 49:11–18). Lewis regards Exercise six as being relatively free from the influence of liturgical ritual or Scripture, instead combining bridal imagery with a musical theme. However, my reading of Exercise six agrees more with that of Claire Taylor Jones's theory that it is based on eucharistic communion (Claire Taylor Jones, "*Hostia jubilationis*: Psalm Citation, Eucharistic Prayer, and Mystical Union in Gertrude of Helfta's *Exercitia spiritualia*," *Speculum* 89, no. 4 [October 2014]: 1032).

[6] Luke 22:19; Gertrude, *Exercises* 1.5 (CF 49:21; SCh 127:56); Gertrude, *Exercises* 2.1 (CF 49:34; SCh 127:80); Gertrude, *Exercises* 6.6 (CF 49:93; SCh 127:200).

[7] On the medieval history of the consecratory formula, see Francis J. Wengier, *The Eucharist-Sacrifice* (Milwaukee, WI: The Bruce Publishing Co., 1955), 173–85. The first section of my chapter here has been reprinted, with slight

In her *Exercises*, Gertrude intimately braids the eucharistic connotations of *In mei memoriam facietis* with two other tropes from
the monastic tradition in order to build a close association between the Eucharist and the Memory of God (*memoria Dei*), an
association that is in fact a critical motif within the text. Gertrude
also employs other images from the biblical, monastic, and theological traditions to further bolster the eucharistic framework she
constructs in and claims for her *Exercises*: she argues that reading
her words is an extension of union between the person's body
and soul and Christ's humanity-divinity, otherwise reserved to
eucharistic communion.

"Do this in memory of me": Remembering Ritual in Gertrude's *Spiritual Exercises*

By peppering her *Exercises* with seemingly familiar liturgical
tropes, like "Do this in memory of me," Gertrude is following a
fairly common rhetorical principle in medieval meditative writing. As the work of literary historian Mary Carruthers has shown,
the construction of memory inventories was central to medieval
religious authorship. Carruthers calls "meditation" a "craft of
thinking" because it entails more than "mental contemplation"
but, in fact, involves "tools . . . made of language and image,
primarily the tropes and figures and schemes discovered in the
Bible, the liturgy, and the arts."[8] Far from using these inventories

---

emendations, and with permission, from Ella Johnson, " '*In mei memoriam
facietis*': Remembering Ritual and Refiguring 'Woman' in Gertrud the Great
of Helfta's Spiritualia Exercitia," in *Inventing Identities: Re-examining the Use
of Memory, Imitation, and Imagination in the Texts of Medieval Religious Women*,
ed. Bradley Herzog and Margaret Cotter-Lynch (New York: Palgrave Macmillan, 2012), 165–86. Much scholarship has noted the liturgical quality of Gertrude's writings. See the discussion in chapter one above.

[8] Mary Carruthers, *The Craft of Thought: Meditation, Rhetoric, and the Making
of Images, 400–1200*, Cambridge Studies in Medieval Literature 70 (Cambridge,
UK: Cambridge University Press, 2000), 3–5. See also Mary Carruthers, *The
Book of Memory: A Study of Memory in Medieval Culture*, 2nd ed., Cambridge
Studies in Medieval Literature (Cambridge, UK: Cambridge University Press,
2008); Mary Carruthers and Jan M. Ziolkowski, eds., *The Medieval Craft of*

merely for routine memorization, medieval writers employed them as sites of rhetorical invention for imaginatively and creatively composing texts and meditations. This practice demonstrates, she says, that the cognitive procedures involved in traditional rhetoric or literary invention (*inventio*) require a memory store or inventory (*inventio*): "Some type of locational structure is a prerequisite for any inventive thinking at all." In the idiom of medieval monasticism, she says, people do not "have" ideas; they "make" them.[9]

Carruthers points out that for medieval religious authors, "The routes of the liturgy and the routes of a mind meditating its way through the sites (and 'sights') of Scripture became . . . their essential conception of Invention, the mind thinking":[10] "This assumption leads . . . to the need for 'place,' because remembering is a task of 'finding' and of 'getting from one place to another' in your thinking mind."[11] Carruthers thus shows that medieval meditation was conceived of as a way that was mapped out by biblical images and tropes: "If we adopt for a moment the central figure in the rhetorical *ductus*—that of flow and movement, as through an aqueduct—we can think of ornaments of composition as causing varieties of movement: steady, slow, fast, turn, back up. . . . Compositional *ductus*, moving in colors and modes, varies in both direction and in pace, after it takes off from its particular beginning (the all-important point 'where' one starts) towards its target (*skopos*)."[12]

Carruthers' work thus shows that the biblical-liturgical trope *In mei memoriam facietis*, in particular, is central to the rhetorical strategy Gertrude employs in the construction of her *Exercises*. Because she begins three of her seven exercises with the trope, Gertrude seems to have chosen it as the starting point to direct the way her readers' meditations should proceed. Moreover,

---

Memory: An Anthology of Texts and Pictures (Philadelphia, PA: University of Pennsylvania Press, 2002).

[9] Carruthers, *The Craft of Thought*, 11–12.

[10] Carruthers, *The Craft of Thought*, 61.

[11] Carruthers, *The Craft of Thought*, 23.

[12] Carruthers, *The Craft of Thought*, 116.

significantly, from this starting point she generates two other tropes: the "remember the future" injunction and the "place of the tabernacle" image.

Carruthers clearly demonstrates that the "remember the future" injunction, which Gertrude employs, is commonplace in the tradition of monastic writing. It harks back to the theme underlying Augustine's *City of God*. In addition, Carruthers says, the Augustinian idiom eventually evolved into the fundamental model for monastic life in the Middle Ages.[13] She explains the regular monastic conceptualization: "Remember Jerusalem . . . is a call not to preserve but to act—in the present, for the future. The matters memory presents are used to persuade and motivate, to create emotion and stir the will. And the 'accuracy' or 'authenticity' of these memories—their simulation of an actual past—is of far less importance . . . than their use to motivate the present and to affect the future."[14] Carruthers identifies an important idea implicated in this understanding: humans are able to "remember the future," because that by which we comprehend time—*memoria*—allows us to recall things past, contemplate things present, and ponder things future *"through their likeness to past things."*[15]

Gertrude certainly espouses the belief Carruthers pinpoints. Confident in the ability of the human faculty of memory to comprehend simultaneously all time—i.e., past, present, and future—she thinks persons in this life should strive to continually contemplate the next life. To assist with this continual contemplation, she composes her prayer to Christ in Exercise one, which anticipates the future end of the present life: "so that while I am on this pilgrimage set up in body alone, my memory [*memoria*] may always abide in avid thought there where you are, my best share . . . so that, at the termination of my life . . . I may come

---

[13] Carruthers, *The Craft of Thought*, 66–69. On Augustine's notion of memory and its influence on later writers, see Patrick J. Geary, *Phantoms of Remembrance: Memory and Oblivion at the End of the First Millennium* (Princeton, NJ: Princeton University Press, 1994), 17–19.

[14] Carruthers, *The Craft of Thought*, 67.

[15] Carruthers, *The Craft of Thought*, 69. Carruthers' emphasis. Carruthers illustrates this idea with the work of Boncompagno da Signa, a rhetoric professor at Bologna in 1235.

to that most dulcet kernel [*dulcissimam nucem*], where, in the new star of your glorified humanity [*in glorificatae humanitatis*], I may see the very brightest light of your very outstanding divinity."[16] Indeed, for Gertrude, memory is the capacity in time that gives the human person access to past, present, and future. Yet in addition to the temporal metaphors within this passage, Gertrude also uses spatial ones to build a tension between the *here*, where the human person is on pilgrimage, and the *there*, where Christ resides *in glorificatae humanitatis*. She does so again, more explicitly, in the sixth exercise: "Then, as if you were somewhat refreshed [*refecta*] by praising your God, your king, who is in the sanctuary, rise up now with heart wide open to delight [*deliciandum*] in God, your lover, throwing into him all the love of your heart so that *here* he may nourish [*enutriat*] you with the blessing of his gentleness and *there* may lead you to the blessing of his plentitude of fruition [*fruitionis*] forever."[17]

Gertrude thus clearly ties her here/there spatial metaphors to the conception of the "way" of monastic meditation. As Carruthers has argued, "the rhetorical concept of *ductus* emphasizes way-finding by organizing the structure of any composition as a journey through a linked series of stages, each of which has its own characteristic flow (its 'mode' or 'color'), but which also moves the whole composition along. . . . For a person following the *ductus*, the 'colors' act as stages of the way or ways through to the *skopos* or destination."[18] It becomes evident, then, that Gertrude's use of "here" and "there" refers not so much to actual places or spaces as to mental positions, serving both as a habitation for the mind and a direction for meditation.

---

[16] Gertrude, *Exercises* 1.205–10 (CF 49:41; SCh 127:74). In another place in the same exercise, Gertrude similarly writes, "O most dulcet guest of my soul, my Jesus very close to my heart, let your pleasant embodiment be for me today the remission of all my sins . . . so that, while I am on this pilgrimage set up in body alone, my memory may always abide in avid thought where you are, my best share" (Gertrude, *Exercises* 1.189–90 (CF 49:29; SCh 127:72–74).

[17] Gertrude, *Exercises* 6.490–95 (CF 49:111; SCh 127:236). Translator's emphasis.

[18] Carruthers, *The Craft of Thought*, 80–81.

Likewise, Gertrude teaches that by the recollection of the heavenly banquet, her readers will experience a "foretaste" (*praegustatio/praegustare*) *here* of the "most dulcet kernel [*dulcissimam nucem*]" they will ultimately taste *there*: "If the memory of your praise [*laudis memoria*] is so dulcet [*dulcis*] in this misery, what will it be like, my God, when in the splendor of your divinity your glory appears? If the small drops of this foretaste [*praegustationis*] of you are so refreshing [*reficunt*], what will it be like, my holy dulcet [*dulcedo*] one, when you are given to me copiously? If you console me here by fulfilling my desire with good things [*bonis*], what will it be like, O God of my salvation, when you absorb my spirit in you?"[19] The *there* and *skopos* of this passage refer to the *then* of the world made right—i.e., the new heaven and the new earth. This *then* is beyond the future of this life. Moreover, because this *then* is beyond time, it is also beyond the capacity of memory, which can only remember temporal past, present, and future. With eucharistic imagery, Gertrude teaches that the memory of God (*memoria Dei*) evokes for her readers the experience of the refreshment, delight, nourishment, and fruition found both in the eschatological banquet and in the glorified Christ in the Christian life today. In the passages quoted above, Gertrude calls her readers to remember that even before the Eschaton, through the Memory of God, as in the Eucharist, the human person is nourished by the foretaste (*praegustationis*) and fruition (*fruitionis*) of the next life. For Gertrude, the *memoria Dei*, like the Eucharist, transcends time.

Indeed, the biblical command to repeat *in mei memoriam facietis* itself connotes the transcendence of time. As philosopher Catherine Pickstock observes, "it is a present imperative, a recall that is anticipated, a detour not by the past but by the future, when after is before, and before is after, and where isolating an homogenous thread of time becomes a delicate task."[20] It is thus fitting for Gertrude to designate *in mei memoriam facietis* as the starting point for her *Exercises*, since she intends her book to continually

[19] Gertrude, *Exercises* 6.500–505 (CF 49:111; SCh 127:236).
[20] Catherine Pickstock, *After Writing: On the Liturgical Consummation of Philosophy* (Oxford: Blackwell Publishers, 1998), 223.

renew persons' attention to the activity of the grace of God present from baptism up to preparation for death. Her text instructs persons in the memory of God, which for Gertrude (re-)creates or (re-)invents a channel by means of which the human person may transcend time and directly encounter Christ in the here and now, the Mediator between the *then* and *now*, the human and the divine.

The connection Gertrude makes between the "remember the future" trope and the Eucharist is also based on her belief that the memory of God, like the communion Host, includes the real presence of Christ, the Mediator between divinity and humanity, the *here* and *there*, and the *then* and *now*. Gertrude's reasoning is especially evident in a passage from her fifth exercise. She prescribes a meditation on Christ's presence in the Eucharist that reverses the biblical Alpha and Omega from Revelation 1:8: "Lo, your face, which the most beautiful dawn of divinity illuminates, is pleasant and comely. Miraculously your cheeks blush [*rubet*] with *omega* and *alpha*. Very bright eternity burns inextinguishably in your eyes. There God's salvation glows as red [*rutilat*] for me as a lamp. There radiant charity sports merrily with luminous truth. . . . Honey and milk drip down from your mouth to me."[21] Gertrude here again, as throughout her works, uses "rose-colored" (*rosa, rosues*) as the symbolic color for Christ's human-divine nature.[22] In this passage, therefore, when she describes Christ's

---

[21] Gertrude, *Exercises* 5.69–73 (CF 49:75; SCh 127:162). Indeed, only about fifty years before Gertrude's birth, the Fourth Lateran Council (1215) officially used the term *transubstantiation* for the first time to define the physical presence of Christ in the Eucharist: "One indeed is the universal Church of the faithful, outside which no one at all is saved, in which the priest himself is the sacrifice, Jesus Christ, whose body and blood are truly contained in the sacrament of the altar under the species of bread and wine; the bread (changed) into his body by the divine power of transubstantiation, and the wine into the blood [*transubstantiatis pane in corpus et uino in sanguinem potestate diuina*], so that to accomplish the mystery of unity we ourselves receive from his (nature) what he himself received from ours" (quoted in Michael O'Carroll, *"Corpus Christi": An Encyclopedia of the Eucharist* [Wilmington, DE: Michael Glazier Books, 1988], 196). O'Carroll's emendations and my gloss.

[22] See Gertrude, *Exercises* (CF 49:30, n. 56).

cheeks as flushed and his salvation as glowing red, she implies that the already/not yet dichotomy is overcome in the memory of God, as in the Eucharist, because of the humanity-divinity union in Christ made fully present there. So she situates her readers' minds between their own future and past in the glorified Christ, the *omega* and *alpha*, because in this way they encounter the presence of Christ in his humanity and divinity, through the *memoria Dei* today.

The way Gertrude uses the "remember the future" trope in the construction of her text demonstrates her desire to associate the memory of God with the Eucharist. In fact, in several instances, Gertrude composes a single verse that employs both the trope and her liturgical starting point, "Do this in memory of me." For instance, in the first exercise, Gertrude tells readers to celebrate the memory (*memoriam*) of their baptism so they will have the opportunity to be pure and restored in body and soul at the end of their lives: "Be zealous . . . in celebrating the memory [*memoriam*] of your baptism," she says, in order to remember the future, "to be in the condition, at the end of your life, of presenting to the Lord the spotless garment of your baptismal innocence and the whole and undefiled seal of your Christian faith."[23]

This rhetorical strategy recurs in Exercise four. There Gertrude combines the traditional monastic trope "remember the future" with the liturgical trope "Do this in memory of me," by instructing her readers to celebrate the memory of their future celestial home: "Celebrate the memory [*memoriam*] of that radiant praise with which you will be jubilant to the Lord for eternity, when you will be satisfied fully by the presence of the Lord; and your soul will be filled with the glory of the Lord."[24] So, in an effort to stir her readers further toward their heavenly aim, she combines the two tropes. In doing so, she makes clear to her readers that the memory of God, like the consecratory formula, (re-)creates a channel through which the human person may directly encounter and experience Christ, the Mediator between the *then* and *now*.

[23] Gertrude, *Exercises* 1.1 (CF 49:21; SCh 127:56).
[24] Gertrude, *Exercises* 6.5–8 (CF 49:93; SCh 127:200).

The relationship Gertrude constructs between the Eucharist and *memoria Dei* further appears in her use of another particularly rich monastic trope, the "place of the Tabernacle." Carruthers explains that in its medieval rhetorical use, this trope too connotes the transcendence of time. The trope brings together the future, the present, and the past by simultaneously conjuring up images of the Heavenly Citadel, the eucharistic tabernacle, and Ezekiel's Temple.[25] Gertrude stands in line with the monastic tradition in this regard, using the Heavenly City/Tabernacle/Temple trope to arrange and link up the future and past in the minds and lives of her readers in the present. Two prayers from Exercise six show her innovative use of the monastic schema. She first evokes the image of the past tabernacle: "May that wonderful tabernacle [*tabernaculum*][26] of your glory, which alone has ministered to you worthily as a holy dwelling-place and through which you can best make amends for me to yourself for the due measure of praise and glory that I owe you, be jubilant to you."[27] Then she brings to mind an image of the Heavenly City: "my soul . . . groaning because I am delayed by my sojourn, mentally follows you into the sanctuary [*sancta*] where you yourself, my king and my God, abide in the substance of my flesh. Oh, how blessed are those who dwell in your house."[28] It becomes evident, then, that Gertrude understands the *memoria Dei* to entail a eucharistic kind of union with Christ, physically manifest in the past Tabernacle of the Covenant, in the present Tabernacle of the Eucharist, and in the future Heavenly City. In rhetorical terms, the reader will know this happy collation of the images of the Heavenly City, Tabernacle, and Temple by the experience of the *templum Dei* of 1 Corinthians 3:16-17, that *templum* that is inside each person.

In this way, Gertrude adds the image of the heart to the Heavenly City/Tabernacle/Temple trope, doing so in terms reminiscent of John Cassian's counsel to "build in your heart the sacred

---

[25] For more on this theme generally in medieval monastic rhetoric, see Carruthers, *The Craft of Thought*, 221–76, esp. 269–71.

[26] Pss 41:5; 42–43:4.

[27] Gertrude, *Exercises* 6.451–54 (CF 49:109; SCh 127:232).

[28] Gertrude, *Exercises* 6.105–7 (CF 49:97; SCh 127:208).

tabernacle of spiritual knowledge" (*si scientiae spiritalis sacrum in corde uestro uultis tabernaculum praeparare*).[29] In the *Herald* she describes both God's deified heart and her own heart as a tabernacle or ark of divine presence and truth, and as a sign of the Ark of the Covenant. On one occasion she reports to Christ, "Your most compliant sweetness kindly promised. . . . 'Come and receive the official confirmation of my covenant [*pacti*] with you.' . . . I saw you open up as if with both hands that ark [*arcam*] of divine constancy and infallible truth [*divinae fidelitatis atque infallibilis veritatis*], that is, your deified Heart [*deificatum Cor*]. I saw you commanding me . . . to place my right hand within it. Then you shut the opening up, with my hand caught inside it, saying 'There! I promise to maintain in their integrity the gifts I have conferred on you.' "[30] In addition, she reflects, "For although I wavered mentally and enjoyed certain dangerous pleasures, when I returned to my heart [*cor*]—after hours and even after days, alas, and after weeks, I fear to my great sorrow—I always found you there."[31] Moreover, Gertrude explicitly relates her heart to the eucharistic banquet. She praises God in another passage from the *Herald*: "Hail, my salvation and the light of my soul! May all that is encompassed by the path of heaven, the circle of the earth and the deep abyss give you thanks for the extraordinary grace with which you led my soul to experience and ponder the innermost recesses of my heart . . . you endowed me with a clearer light of knowledge of you. . . . I do not remember . . . having ever enjoyed such fulfillment except on the days when you invited me to taste the delights of your royal table."[32] Gertrude's experience leads her to believe that the presence of God found in the Ark of the Covenant, the Heavenly City, and the Eucharist may also be found within the human heart. One has only to be attentive to it.

[29] Quoted in Carruthers, *The Craft of Thought*, 270, 358, n. 110.

[30] Gertrude, *Herald* 2.20.14 (CF 35:155; SCh 139:318).

[31] Gertrude, *Herald* 2.3.3 (CF 35:106; SCh 139:238). Indeed, Gertrude testifies that on only one occasion, as the result of a worldly conversation, could she not feel the presence of God when she evoked the *memoria Dei*. See Gertrude, *Herald* 2.3.3 (CF 35:106–7; SCh 139:238, 240); Gertrude, *Herald* 2.23.2–3 (CF 35:163; SCh 139:330, 332).

[32] Gertrude, *Herald* 2.2.1–2 (CF 35:103–4; SCh 139:234).

Thus Gertrude conceives of the role of the liturgical trope "Do this in memory of me" in meditative memory work as providing a eucharistic framework and map for the entire meditative text she constructs in her *Spiritual Exercises*. Gertrude uses this trope in close connection to other significant ideas in the rhetorical tradition to create for her readers a locational structure that centers on one main idea: the relationship between the memory of God and the Eucharist. Because the formula "Do this in memory of me" concludes the consecration of the Host in the liturgy of the Eucharist, for Gertrude it is a channel that allows the human person to transcend time through an encounter with the Mediator between divinity and humanity, then and now, and already and not yet.

Meditative Reading as Eucharistic

Categories of medieval piety developed by Leonard Boyle help to explain Gertrude's association of meditative reading with the Eucharist. In fact, these categories draw attention to the tendency in medieval Christianity to associate all kinds of popular expressions of piety with the Eucharist. Boyle explains that in the Middle Ages, all embodied forms of Christian devotion are understood to be "like the Eucharist itself," in that "they are simply extensions of faith to things to which, at human level, a person of faith may relate easily."[33] He explains that the Eucharist exploits embodied devotion in the "grossest form imaginable" in its physical remembrance of Christ's words: "Eat my body. Drink my blood." As he says, "This is an invitation to an act of piety on the bodily level of food and drink, a level common to all. It is a divine acknowledgement of the human need for bodily expression as well as spiritual expression of faith and thanksgiving."[34] Boyle thus contends that "there is no real room for two 'tiers' of mediaeval or other piety, one 'learned,' the other 'popular.' All again are expressions of one,

[33] Leonard E. Boyle, "Popular Piety in the Middle Ages: What is Popular?" *Florilegium: Carleton University Annual Papers on Classical Antiquity and the Middle Ages* 4 (1982): 190.
[34] Boyle, "Popular Piety," 187.

single object of belief, and all the expressions, in relation to the incomprehensibility of the object, are in the long run 'popular.' All are equally inadequate expressions of gratitude on the part of believers for the mysterious gift of faith, on to which they hold with the help of the giver."[35] He explains, "those who engage in acts of piety are, without distinction, simply returning thanks, each in his or her own way, to God. . . . And this piety, at its most general level, takes the form of obedience to his commandments, and, at its more specific Christian level, takes on as well the singular form of Thanksgiving proposed by his Son: the Eucharist."[36]

On the basis of this association, Boyle categorizes the various forms of piety in the Middle Ages according to their relation to the Eucharist, arranging the categories concentrically around the central hub of the liturgy of the Eucharist. For example, the inmost circle contains those acts most clearly "liturgical," that is, celebration of the Eucharist and the other sacraments. The second ring, drawn outside and around the first, includes "semi-liturgical" expressions, i.e., those closely yet not intimately connected to the Eucharist, such as preaching and reading or chanting the Divine Office. The third circle consists of pious acts that Boyle calls "para-liturgical." These are devotions, like prayers for the intercession of the saints, as in the liturgical calendar, which are more remotely related to the Eucharist. The fourth circle is comprised of "non-liturgical" expressions, which are outside the boundaries of an explicitly liturgical context but are not in conflict with its meaning. All kinds of common acts of devotion that are offered in thanksgiving to God (e.g., prayers and supplications offered throughout one's daily life) belong to this category. The final and outermost circle encompasses actions that are "a-liturgical," that is, those that oppose the spirit of the Eucharist.[37]

These categories help to illustrate why Gertrude conceives almost any act of devotion as being eucharistic in its capacity for intimate union with God. For example, Gertrude's understanding of the liturgy of the Hours—an act which Boyle classifies as "semi-liturgical"—as closely related to the Eucharist is evident in her

---

[35] Boyle, "Popular Piety," 186–87.
[36] Boyle, "Popular Piety," 186–87.
[37] Boyle, "Popular Piety," 187.

report of celebrating the Divine Office. In recounting her experiences in prayer during one Feast of the Annunciation, she quotes the verse *Here I am (Ecce adsum)* in a passage in her spiritual autobiography.[38] The biblical verse from Isaiah is significant, because she would have prayed an allusion to it in Psalm 39, on the Vigil of the Annunciation that year: *Sacrifice of oblation you did not want, but ears you have perfected for me. Holocausts and offerings for sin you did not demand; then I said, behold I come.*[39] Moreover, cited in the context of the Annunciation, the verse from Isaiah also draws attention to its New Testament re-appropriation: *On entering the world he said, sacrifice and oblation you did not want, but a body you have prepared for me. Holocausts and sin offerings did not please you; then I said, Behold I come in.*[40]

Gertrude calls attention to these allusions to the verse from Isaiah in Psalm 39 and Hebrews 10 when she quotes it in a passage in her spiritual autobiography and appropriates the meanings in these Scriptures to link them to her own eucharistic practice: "But you who say 'Here I am!'[41] before you are summoned, anticipated on that day [the Feast of the Annunciation] by forestalling me, unworthy as I was, in the blessings of sweetness. . . . Giver of gifts, give me this gift: may I henceforward offer on the altar of my heart a sacrifice of joy, that by my supplication I may win for myself and all those whom you have chosen the privilege of enjoying often that sweet union and unifying sweetness, which was quite unknown to me before that hour! . . . I do not remember, however, having ever enjoyed such fulfillment except on the days when you invited me to taste the delights

---

[38] Isa 58:9; 70:24. As Cheryl Clemons points out, Psalm 39:7–8 belonged to the monastic ferial psalter for Monday Matins. In this passage, Gertrude notes that the feast day was on Monday that year (Cheryl C. Clemons, "The Relationship between Devotion to the Eucharist and Devotion to the Humanity of Jesus in the Writings of St. Gertrude of Helfta," Ph.D. dissertation, Catholic University of America, 1996, 107). She cites John Harper, Appendix II "The Psalter," in *The Forms and Orders of Western Liturgy: From the Tenth to the Eighteenth Century* (Oxford: Clarendon Press, 1991), 244.

[39] PL 29:189 as quoted and translated in Clemons, "The Relationship," 107.

[40] Heb 10:5–7. Clemons, "The Relationship" 107.

[41] Isa 58:9; 70:24.

of your royal table."[42] Indeed, Gertrude clearly sees her celebration of the Office that day as a eucharistic act of thanksgiving.

Still, the verse "Behold I am," as Gertrude uses it in this account, evokes one more meaning worthy of consideration. She echoes the teaching from the Benedictine Rule that states, "even before you ask me, I will say to you *Here I am*."[43] As quoted above, she writes, "But you who say 'Here I am!' before you are summoned, anticipated that day by forestalling me, unworthy as I was, in the blessings of sweetness."[44] Gertrude declares here that Christ proclaims "Here I am!" before he is summoned. So Gertrude insists that God has anticipated humans' need for salvation throughout human history. This anticipation is fulfilled in the incarnation, in a radical way, Gertrude says, "when you betrothed our human nature to yourself in the Virgin's womb."[45] It is also true, she testifies, in her own conversion experience. For this reason, she confidently teaches that Jesus is present to every human person before he is summoned, even outside of an explicitly liturgical context.

Gertrude returns to this point at the beginning of Exercise six, when she instructs her readers,

> Now and then, set aside for yourself a day on which, without hindrance, you can be at leisure to praise the divine and to make amends for all the praise and thanksgiving [*laudis et gratiarum*] you have neglected all the days of your life to render to God for all the good he has done. And that will be a day of praising and thanksgiving [*laudis et gratiarum*] and a day of jubilation, and you will celebrate the memory of that radiant praise [*celebrabis memoriam illius speciosae laudis*]

---

[42] Gertrude, *Herald* 2.2.2 (CF 35:104; SCh 139:234). In similar language in her *Exercises*, she encourages others often to return thanks to Christ for his eucharistic sacrifice: "Daily on the altar you offer for me such a sacrifice to God the Father, such a holocaustal incense, that it goes beyond all merit and is truly capable of paying all my debt. You present again to the Father a Son truly pleasing to him that you may placate him toward me and truly reconcile [me to him]" (Gertrude, *Exercises* 7.479–86 [CF 49:292; SCh 127:292]). Translator's emendation.

[43] Benedict, RB Prol. 18, as quoted in Clemons, "The Relationship," 106.

[44] Gertrude, *Herald* 2.2.2 (CF 35:104; SCh 139:232, 234).

[45] Gertrude, *Herald* 2.2.2 (CF 35:104; SCh 139:232).

> with which you will be jubilant to the Lord for eternity, when
> you will be satisfied fully by the presence of the Lord; and
> your soul will be filled with the glory of the Lord.[46]

This passage also seems to invoke the imagery of sin offering and oblation, as in Psalm 39 and Hebrews 10.

Furthermore, Gertrude wants her readers to appropriate the imagery personally, as she herself does, by making a sacrifice of "praise and thanksgiving" in their hearts. That she instructs them to "celebrate the memory of that radiant praise" with which they will praise God in eternity is also significant. For she is again combining the monastic trope "remember the future" with the liturgical one, "Do this in memory of me." In doing so, she reinforces her point that the *memoria Dei*, like the consecratory formula, (re-)creates a channel through which the human person may directly experience divine union with Christ, the Mediator between the *then* and *now*. Gertrude thus insists that Christ is available to those who call on him at any time.

In a passage from her *Exercises*, in Exercise five, Gertrude engages the monastic intention that the celebration of the Hours would sanctify the entire day with prayer, to make her point that even those acts that are "semi-liturgical," like praying the Divine Office, should assist one in keeping the memory of God continuously, at all times. She tells her readers to imagine themselves as pupils in the "school of love" and to make a special intention for the rest of their day at each of the seven canonical hours.

> at Lauds, pray the Lord himself, the supreme master, to teach
> you the art of love . . . at Prime, pray to the Lord to lead you
> into the school of love [*scholam amoris*] where you may learn
> further to recognize and love Jesus . . . at Terce, pray to the
> Lord to inscribe on your heart the fiery law of his divine love
> with the living letters of his Spirit that you may cling to him
> inseparably at all hours. . . . At Sext, pray to the Lord that
> you may progress so much in the art of loving him that his
> love may possess you as his own tool. . . . At None, pray
> to the Lord, the King of kings himself, that he may accept

---

[46] Gertrude, *Exercises* 6.1–7 (CF 49:93; SCh 127:200).

you in the militia of love and teach you to take upon yourself
the pleasant yoke and light burden so that you may follow
your Lord with your cross, clinging to your God with un-
divided love . . . at Vespers, march forward unworried, with
Jesus, your lover, in the armor of love against all temptation
so that in him, whose mercy always aids and consoles you,
you may be able to triumph over your flesh, the world, and
the devil, and to triumph gloriously over every temptation. . . . At Compline, earnestly wish with the cherished
one to become inebriated with the wine of love and in union
with God to become unconscious to the world.[47]

Gertrude's reference to "the school of love" alludes both to the
Prologue to the Benedictine Rule, which speaks of the monastery
as the "school of God's service," and to the common Cistercian
adaptation of the phrase, "the school of love."[48] Like the Cistercians before her, Gertrude employs the image frequently in her
Exercises to teach that the monastic person learns about Christ's
love by way of experiencing it in the day-to-day experience of
community life.[49] By using it here, Gertrude emphasizes her point
that a liturgical kind of union with God can and should be extended to everyday activities, through the practice of remembering God in doing them.[50]

[47] Gertrude, *Exercises* 5.292–435 (CF 49:83–88; SCh 127:178–90).
[48] RB Prol. 45–50. See, for example, Bernard, Ep 320.2 (SBOp 8:254); William
of St. Thierry, *The Nature and Dignity of Love*, trans. Thomas X. Davis, CF 30
(Kalamazoo, MI: Cistercian Publications, 1981), 9.26 (PL 184:396D). See also
Étienne Gilson, *The Mystical Theology of St. Bernard*, trans. A. H. C. Downes
(New York: Sheed and Ward, 1940), especially chapter 3, entitled "School of
Love."
[49] See for example Gertrude, *Exercises* 2.25–30 and 52–55 (CF 49:35–37; SCh
127:82, 84). She later uses the image once more, in a similar vein, in Exercise
five (Gertrude, *Exercises* 5.360–75 [CF 49:86; SCh 127:184]). About this passage,
Pierre Doyère remarks that Gertrude is teaching about the significance of
both the active and contemplative aspects of monastic life (Gertrude, SCh
127:184 n. 4; see Gertrude, *Exercises* [CF 49:86, n. 73]).
[50] To make a similar point, Gertrude speaks of the monastery at Helfta as
the body of Christ, designating the temple as his heart, the ambulatory as his
feet, the workshop as his hands, the parlor as his mouth, the classrooms as
his eyes, and the confessional as his ears (Gertrude, *Herald* 3.28.1 [CF 63:98–

Gertrude asserts that this continuous practice of the memory of God, as in the school of love, engenders union with God in the here and now. In Exercise five, she gives direction to her readers on how to ask for God's guidance in every moment, "Pray the Lord himself, the supreme master, to teach you the art of love by the anointing of his Spirit, taking you up as his own disciple, so that, with him as [your] teacher, you may be exercised untiringly in the virtue of charity."[51] As Gertrude sees it, Christ and the Spirit are so close to their pupils that they point out each letter of every word in every lesson. They do this in order to draw their pupils into even closer union with them:

> Oh, if you now unfolded your wondrous alphabet to me that my heart might enroll itself in the same curriculum as you. Tell me now by living experience what the glorious and foremost *alpha* of your beautiful cherishing-love is like; and do not conceal from me that fruitful *beta* which fills generations with your imperial wisdom. . . . Teach me through the co-operation of your Spirit the *tau* of supreme perfection and lead me to the *omega* of full consummation. In this life make me so perfectly learn more of your scripture, [which is] full of charity and cherishing-love that in fulfilling your charity not one *iota* in me may be idle, for thereby I might endure a delay when you, O God, love, my dulcet love, summon me to you to contemplate you yourself in yourself forever. Amen.[52]

99; SCh 143:128, 130]). In addition, Mechthild of Hackeborn once perceived Christ as walking alongside each of her religious sisters as they processed out of chapel one day after Terce (Mechthild of Hackeborn, *Liber* 1.19 [LSG 64; BSG 78]).

[51] Gertrude, *Exercises* 5.293–96 (CF 49:83; SCh 127:178). Translator's gloss. See also Gertrude, *Exercises* 4.29–36 (CF 49:58; SCh 127:126). For more on Gertrude's references to Christ as teacher and her new kind of learning, see Alexandra Barratt, "Infancy and Education in the Writings of Gertrud the Great of Helfta," *Magistra* 6, no. 2 (Winter 2000): 17–30. See also Rebecca Stephens, "The Word Translated: Incarnation and Carnality in Gertrud the Great," *Magistra* 7, no. 1 (Summer 2001): 83–84.

[52] Gertrude, *Exercises* 5.337–43, 349–55 (CF 49:85; SCh 127:182, 184). Translator's gloss. On this passage and its scriptural allusions, see Mary Forman,

Indeed, the entirety of Gertrude's *Exercises* is didactic. She offers workaday solutions for extending one's eucharistic union
with God outside of explicitly liturgical contexts. By reading her
visionary accounts and by practicing her exercises, her readers
are to learn to weave a sacrifice of praise to Christ, in thanksgiving
for and remembrance of his saving works, into the fabric of their
daily lives. For Gertrude, actions belonging to any one of Boyle's
"liturgical," "semi-liturgical," "para-liturgical," or "non-liturgical"
categories have the capacity to unite and restore persons to Christ,
just as the Eucharist does, so long as they have the intention of
keeping the memory of God continuously.

Gertrude understands the daily activities of the school of love
as having the capacity for a kind of divine union that is as radically intimate as eucharistic communion. To make a clear association between the Eucharist and the "school of love," later, in
Exercise five, she uses gustatory imagery: "Diligently and one by
one, show me with the finger of your Spirit the individual letters
[*litteras*] of your charity. Then reaching the very marrow of the
foretaste [*praegustationis*] of your gentleness, let me, in truth, with
the clean eye of my heart, scrutinize and examine, learn more,
know and recognize them as wholly as is lawful in this life."[53]
In this passage Gertrude also makes a significant allusion to 2 Corinthians 3:2-3, wherein Christ is referred to as the letter written
on human hearts: "you are a letter from Christ, sent by us, and
written not with ink, but with the Spirit of the living God, not on
tablets of stone but on fleshy tablets of the heart."[54] Here Gertrude

---

"Gertrud of Helfta's 'Herald of Divine Love': Revelations through *Lectio
Divina*," *Magistra* 3, no. 2 (Winter 1997): 8–10.

[53] Gertrude, *Exercises* 5.344–48 (CF 49:85; SCh 127:182).

[54] This is the English translation of the Vulgate: *Epistola nostra vos estis,
scripta in cordibus nostris, quae scitur, et legitur ab omnibus hominibus: manifestati
quod epistola estis Christi, ministrata a nobis, et scripta non atramento, sed Spiritu
Dei vivi: non in tabulis lapideis, sed in tabulis cordis carnalibus* (*Biblia Vulgata
iuxta Vulgatam Clementinam nova edition*, ed. Alberto Colunga and Laurentio
Turrado, Biblioteca de Autores Cristianos 14 [Madrid: La Editorial Catolica,
S. A., 1985]; quoted and translated in Forman, "Gertrud of Helfta's 'Herald
of Divine Love,' " 8, n. 7). The imagery in this account was popular throughout the later Middle Ages. See Eric Jager, "The Book of the Heart: Reading
and Writing the Medieval Subject," *Speculum* 71, no. 1 (January 1996): 1–26.

is also probably drawing from her own experience of divine union, as in her spiritual autobiography, she records Christ's writing on her heart.[55]

In one passage, Gertrude recounts that she received an interior kind of stigmata after praying for Christ to write on her heart: "Most merciful Lord, write your wounds in my heart with your precious blood, that I may read [*legam*] in them your suffering and your love alike. May the memory [*memoria*] of your wounds remain with me unceasingly in the recesses of my heart, that sorrow for your suffering may be kindled in me. Grant also that all creation may grow worthless in my eyes, and that you alone may impart your sweetness [*dilectionis*] to my heart."[56] When she wanted unceasingly to keep the memory of God and his saving love for her alive in her heart, Christ granted her desire by physically imprinting his wounds on her heart.[57]

Yet Gertrude is clear that one does not have to be a visionary or mystic to experience such union with Christ.[58] She makes this point when she prescribes a prayer similar to her own for readers of her *Exercises*: "Make the sign of the holy cross on your breast

[55] Gertrude, *Herald* 2.4–5 (CF 35:109–15; SCh 139:242–54).

[56] Gertrude, *Herald* 2.4.1 (CF 35:109; SCh 139:242), with emendations based on my translation.

[57] A eucharistic interpretation of this passage stands in line with Marsha Dutton's interpretation of Cistercian images of Christ's blood and stigmata as eucharistic. See Dutton, "Eat, Drink, and Be Merry," 1–30. Dutton's interpretations were challenged by Caroline Bynum, who views such devotions of Christ's blood not in terms of Eucharist, but of cleansing, fertility, sacrifice, and ecstasy (Caroline Walker Bynum, "The Blood of Christ in the Later Middle Ages," *Church History* 71, no. 4 [December 2002]: 685–714, especially 685–88).

[58] As Laura Grimes has demonstrated in her careful analysis of the *Herald*, Gertrude understands this experience of becoming the "book" of Christ's heart not as extraordinary and limited to a select few, but accessible to all Christian believers. Indeed, Gertrude says that she hopes that by reading her story in the *Herald*, her readers will attend to the gifts of their own hearts. She also remarks that different people should be able to find in her book things suited to their particular needs for instruction and consolation (Grimes, "Theology as Conversation: Gertrude of Helfta and her Sisters as Readers of Augustine," Ph.D. dissertation, University of Notre Dame, 2004, 188–99). In this regard, Gertrud recognizes the individuality of each of her readers in practicing the *memoria Dei*.

and your shoulder and say: For the love of your love, make me
always bear the pleasant yoke and the light burden of your pre-
cepts on my shoulders and forever wear the mystery of the sacred
faith on my breast like a bunch of myrrh. Thus, may you remain
crucified for me, always fixed within my heart. Amen."[59] By rec-
ommending this prayer, Gertrude indicates her desire for others
to have an experience of continuous divine union in their hearts
similar to her own. In this regard, it is important that she says
nothing about the stigmata in this petition; instead, she instructs
her readers to make the simple sign of the cross, asking for the
grace to "forever wear the mystery of the sacred faith."

Moreover, as Hildegund Keul notes, in this passage Gertrude
is drawing on the historical development of the word *sacrament*
from the Greek word *mysterion* and the Latin term *sacramentum.*[60]
Before the number of formally defined sacraments was set at seven
in the fifteenth century, these terms were used, as in Augustine,
to indicate any kind of visible signs of invisible realities.[61] In this
account Gertrude teaches that even the physical gesture of the Sign
of the Cross is a visible sign of one's constant memory of God.
She encourages this practice because she believes it will extend
one's union with Christ's wounds outside the moment of eucharistic communion. Accordingly, she has her readers pray that
Christ may "remain crucified for me" and be "always fixed within
my heart." Indeed, for Gertrude, the smallest bodily acts, when
coupled with the memory of God, like making the sign of the
cross, will unite the human person to God in the here and now.

---

[59] Gertrude, *Exercises* 1.160–64 (CF 49:28; SCh 127:70). For more on this
exercise that Gertrude prescribes, see Ina Eggemann, "Betende Theologie:
Beten und Beten-Lehren als Ort theologischer Erkenntnis im Exerzitienbuch
Gertruds von Helfta," *Aufbruch zu neuer Gottesrede: Die Mystick der Gertrud
von Helfta*, ed. Siegfried Ringler (Ostfildern: Matthias Grünewald, 2008),
155–56.

[60] See Hildegund Keul, "Das Sakrament des Wortes: Mystik und Seelsorge
in den Brüchen der Zeit," in *Aufbruch zu neuer Gottesrede: Die Mystik der
Gertrud von Helfta*, ed. Siegfried Ringler (Ostfildern: Grünewald, 2008), 177.

[61] Allan D. Fitzgerald, ed., *Augustine Through the Ages: An Encyclopedia*
(Grand Rapids, MI: Eerdmans, 1999), 740–43.

Such divine union, she declares, may also be attained by devoutly reading her books. In the *Herald*, she reports that Christ himself promised her this:

> If anyone wishes to read this book with a devout intention of spiritual progress, I shall draw him so closely to myself that he will read it as if my own hands were holding the book and I myself shall keep him company at the task. As when two people are reading the same page, each is aware of the other's breath, so shall I draw in the breath of his longings. This shall move my loving-kindness to have mercy on him. Moreover I shall breathe into him the breath of my divinity which, through my Spirit, will create him anew within.[62]

As Gertrude understands it, the breath inhaled and exhaled in the physical act of reading intermingles with the very breath of God.[63] Likewise, in the *Exercises*, she instructs people in their holy reading to ask God for a kind of mouth-to-mouth resuscitation: "Let my spirit be recreated and newly remade in the Spirit of his mouth so that his good Spirit may lead me onto the right ground";[64] "All holy apostles, ah! Pray that I experience the kiss of his mellifluous mouth, of the living Word of God, which you have touched."[65] Here again Gertrude is associating the words she writes with the Eucharist. Her use of *mellifluous* connotes the experience of eucharistic communion, which in the Middle Ages is so often described as "sweet." Moreover, in these passages, she suggests that Jesus Christ will be united to her readers, in both

[62] Gertrude, *Herald* 2 Prol.1 (CF 35:31; SCh 139:108, 110). See also Gertrude, *Herald* 5.36.1 (SCh 331:208).

[63] The practice of medieval meditative reading is not just an intellectual activity, but a physical one as well. As Jean Leclercq notes, "in the Middle Ages, as in antiquity, they read usually, not as today, principally with the eyes, but with the lips, pronouncing what they saw, and with the ear, listening to the words pronounced, hearing what is called the 'voices of the pages'" (Jean Leclercq, *The Love of Learning and the Desire for God: A Study of Monastic Culture* [New York: Fordham Press, 1982], 19, 66).

[64] Gertrude, *Exercises* 1.9–12 (CF 49:21–22; SCh 127:56, 58).

[65] Gertrude, *Exercises* 3.133 (CF 49:46; SCh 127:102).

his humanity and his divinity, by the very act of reading her books.

Gertrude is particularly explicit about the opportunity of body-soul union with Christ's twofold nature by way of reading in another passage from the *Herald*. It recounts her experience of chanting Vespers on the Feast of the Holy Trinity one year: "Then while the antiphon *Let him kiss me* was being sung, *a voice came from the throne saying*: 'Let *my beloved Son* approach, *in whom I am most pleased*[66] in all things, and let him offer a surpassingly sweet kiss to my delight.' Then the Son of God, stepping forward in human form [*in humana forma*], offered a most sweet kiss to his incomprehensible divine nature [*incomprehensibili divinitati*], to which his most holy human nature [*humanitas*] alone, in an inseparable bond of union, deserved to be most blessedly united."[67]

According to Gertrude, union with Christ's divinity in the human person's soul, by way of union with his humanity in the human person's body, may be experienced in the here and now, even outside of the context of eucharistic communion, by reading the words she writes. She not only makes this audacious claim but supports it in an impeccably orthodox way. She uses commonplace principles found in the liturgical, biblical, and monastic traditions.

Conclusions

Modern assumptions that reading and writing practices are timeless sometimes obscure the ideas embedded within Gertrude's writings. Carruthers' work challenges these assumptions and reveals that Gertrude consciously chooses the images in the liturgical, biblical, and monastic traditions to articulate her theory that the *memoria Dei*, like the Eucharist, transcends time and that,

[66] Song 1:1; Rev 19:5; Matt 3:17; Matt 17:5.
[67] Gertrude, *Herald* 4.41.2 (CF 85:192; SCh 255:328). As Barratt notes, the antiphon from Song 1:1 is "Not one of the antiphons for Trinity Sunday but used at various feasts of the Virgin" (CF 85:192, n. 4). For another account of her divine union in chanting the Hours, see Gertrude, *Herald* 2.21.4 (CF 35:159; SCh 139:326).

therefore, even by meditating upon the words she writes with the intention of keeping the memory of God, her readers may be united to Christ's humanity and divinity, in body and soul.

Far from understanding these "non-liturgical" acts of piety as replacements or substitutes for receiving the Eucharist, Gertrude understands them as emanating from it. Boyle's categories show that medieval persons understood that Christ himself instructed his followers to eat his body and drink his blood, re-membering him on the bodily level. They knew that all other bodily expressions of faith were related to this "singular form" of eucharistic thanksgiving.[68] Gertrude and her community demonstrate this commonplace belief. Within the context of the declining opportunity for lay people to receive the Host,[69] she presents herself as an apostolate of frequent communion. She insists that receiving the sacred Host is the ultimate opportunity for the human person's body-soul union with God's humanity-divinity in this life. By associating other pious devotions with the Eucharist, especially the act of reading her words, Gertrude seeks to extend and prolong this kind of union with God outside of the moment the human person receives the Host in the Mass.

Repeatedly Gertrude shows the effects of such divine union to be salvific and restorative. So she claims that through eucharistic communion with Christ within the liturgy or extended beyond it in the memory of God, the human person has the opportunity to transcend not just the divisions between here and there, then and now, humanity and divinity, but also the conventional assumptions about the behavior of men and women.

[68] Boyle, "Popular Piety in the Middle Ages," 186–87.
[69] See discussion in chapter 2 above.

CHAPTER SIX

"This Is My Body":
Woman as Signifying Humanity
and Divinity

As historians of the Christian Middle Ages have shown, from the twelfth century onward, ordained priests became increasingly set apart from lay persons in nearly every aspect of the religious culture. At the intellectual, social, and moral level, priests were regarded as especially privileged. Their authority was drawn from their role to be dispensers of the sacraments, particularly the Eucharist, to lay persons, who were dependent on them.[1] The sharp distinction between clergy and laity, of course, hardened the male/female divide, given the fact that women were not ordained to the priesthood. Even Hildegard of Bingen, who was a highly educated Benedictine nun and preacher, who crafted a prophetic identity for herself, and who was highly critical of the decadence and corruption of the priesthood, repeated the conventional *topos* opposing male and female as divine to human or mind and spirit to flesh: "Man . . . signifies the divinity of the Son of God and woman his humanity."[2]

---

[1] Miri Rubin, *Corpus Christi: The Eucharist in Late Medieval Culture* (Cambridge: Cambridge University Press, 1991), 51. See also John Van Engen, "The Christian Middle Ages as an Historiographical Problem," *American Historical Review* 91 (1986): 547.

[2] Hildegard of Bingen, *Liber divinorum operum*, PL 197:885. See also Caroline Walker Bynum, ". . . And Women His Humanity: Female Imagery in the Religious Writing of the Later Middle Ages," in *Gender and Religion: On the Complexity of Symbols*, ed. Caroline Walker Bynum, Steven Harrell, and Paula Richman (Boston, MA: Beacon Press, 1986), 274; Alcuin Blamires, "Paradox

As recent scholarship has revealed, medieval writings commonly demonstrate this asymmetrical evaluation of "man" and "woman" as soul/body, divinity/humanity, but also rational/ irrational and virility/weakness. The influence of these ancient dichotomies regularly appears in a variety of writings of Gertrude's day, in works of theological, philosophical, and even scientific nature.[3]

Such dichotomies, as Caroline Walker Bynum has shown, had implications for women's spirituality. In their writings and devotions, medieval women tended to emphasize Christ's humanity and their own. They focused on the incarnation of God in the physical realm, and their devotions were eucharistic and Christocentric, oriented toward encountering or assimilating with Christ's humanity, because traditional theological discussion and devotional trends taught them to associate *humanitas* with physicality and being a woman.[4]

Yet Gertrud's writings resist these simple dualisms. Gertrude crafts within her *Exercises* a female *persona* that is liberated from traditional prescriptions for women's behavior. Her images of God and self in the prose of her *Herald* are consistent with this *persona*, as they subvert the behavioral roles and traits conventionally connected with men and women.[5] Further, Gertrude's visionary

in the Medieval Gender Doctrine of Head and Body," in *Medieval Theology and the Natural Body*, ed. Peter Biller and A. J. Minnis, York Studies in Medieval Theology (York: York Medieval Press, 1997), 13–29.

[3] On this association in medieval theories of science and medicine, see Vern L. Bullough, "Medieval, Medical and Scientific Views of Women," *Viator* 4 (1973): 485–501; Joan Cadden, *Meanings of Sex Difference in the Middle Ages: Medicine, Science, and Culture*, Cambridge History of Medicine (Cambridge, UK: Cambridge University Press, 1993); Danielle Jacquart and Claude Alexandre Thomasset, ed., *Sexuality and Medicine in the Middle Ages* (Princeton, NJ: Princeton University Press, 1988).

[4] Caroline Walker Bynum, "Women Mystics and Eucharistic Devotion in the Thirteenth Century," *Women's Studies* 11 (1984): 179–214. Bynum illustrates this thesis throughout Caroline Walker Bynum, *Holy Feast and Holy Fast: The Religious Significance of Food to Medieval Women* (Berkeley: University of California Press, 1988).

[5] Because contemporary definitions of *sex, gender*, and *sex roles* vary, it is important to define my use of the terms. I use *sex* to refer to a person's

priesthood shows how Gertrude's conception of man and woman has the effect of subverting the ecclesial roles aligned with them—at least in her self-imagery. Her priestly claims—even to bind and loose souls—are also supported by her eucharistic theory, which is nuanced and highly innovative.

"Woman" as Re-Identified in Gertrude's *Exercises*

In crafting her meditative texts, Gertrude is deliberate about her use of gendered pronouns and grammatical endings. Whether she is composing prayers to God or addressing her readers, in all seven sections of her *Spiritual Exercises* Gertrude writes from the feminine perspective. In her Latin prose, she almost entirely uses feminine grammatical endings for nouns, as for example, "That in the violence of living love I may become your prisoner [*captiva*] for all time."[6] This feminine voice differs from that of the psalms and liturgical prayers, which filled Gertrude's day, addressing God from the viewpoint of a male devotee, with male pronouns.[7] Even when she refers to biblical parables with male protagonists, like the prodigal son, she replaces masculine nouns with feminine ones. For instance, she writes about the "prodigal daughter" (*prodiga filia*)[8] and the "adopted daughter" (*filiam adoptasti*).[9] She

---

biological status (typically "male" or "female," as understood in the Middle Ages). *Gender* refers to the attitudes and behaviors that the dominant culture typically associates with a person's biological sex. The phrase *sex roles* refers to the sexual behaviors and actions typically associated with being "male" or "female," defined by the dominant culture. Sex roles, therefore, reflect the interaction between biological status and the behaviors and attitudes typically associated with biological sex and reproductive anatomy. At the same time, these contemporary linguistic categories of sex and gender do not apply to thirteenth-century understandings of women and men. For that reason, in elucidating Gertrude's thought, I generally avoid these terms, which she would not recognize.

[6] Gertrude, *Exercises* 7.65 (CF 49:124; SCh 127:262).

[7] Gertrud Jaron Lewis, "Introduction," in Gertrude, *Exercises* (CF 49:6–9).

[8] Gertrude, *Exercises* 4.184 (CF 49:63; SCh 127:126).

[9] Gertrude, *Exercises* 5.510 (CF 49:91; SCh 127:196). In the *Herald*, she also replaces the popular image of John leaning on Christ's breast at the Last Supper with a young girl (*puella*). Gertrude, *Herald* 5.32.2 (SCh 331:256). See also Lewis, "Introduction," in Gertrude, *Exercises* (CF 49:6).

uses feminine pronouns as well when she refers to God. In fact, in most of Exercise seven, Gertrude personifies divine attributes as female figures (e.g., Goodness [*Bonitas*], Charity [*Caritas*], Cherishing-love [*Dilectio*], Compassion [*Misericordia*], Peace [*Pax*], Loving-kindness [*Pietas*], Wisdom [*Sapientia*], and Truth [*Veritas*]).[10] Finally, she draws from different rituals in the life of a nun, so that they may be easily remembered by her readers (i.e., the sacrament of Baptism; the rituals of clothing, consecration, and a profession of a cloistered nun; and the Divine Office).[11] In this way, the female authorial voice of the *Exercises* connects with the experience of women religious.

Yet Gertrude did not envision her *Exercises* to be read only by women. As her biographer testified in the *Herald*, Gertrude wrote "examples of spiritual exercises" (*documenta spiritualium extercitationum*) primarily for the women of the Helfta community, but also for "all those who wished to read them."[12] That she intended men as well as women to practice her exercises means that she would have anticipated that both men and women would adopt the female *persona* she maintained in composing her exercises. The feminine perspective of the *Exercises* should thus be read as a consciously created female *persona* rather than as an address to an audience comprised only of women.

Several of the prayers Gertrude composes in the feminine perspective in her *Exercises* discuss the need to renounce associations of women with sensuality, weakness, and sinfulness in order for them to be able to gain traits typically associated with men, like virility and rationality. In Exercise five, for example, she describes

---

[10] Lewis, "Introduction," in Gertrude, *Exercises* (CF 49:7). Of course the personification of these attributes as female figures is common in patristic and medieval authors. See Barbara Newman, *God and the Goddesses: Vision, Poetry, and Belief in the Middle Ages*, The Middle Ages Series (Philadelphia: University of Pennsylvania Press, 2005), 1–3.

[11] Gertrude parenthetically remarks that readers outside of the religious state of life should make the appropriation to their own life circumstances (Gertrude, *Exercises* 3.21 [CF 49:41; SCh 127:94]).

[12] Gertrude, *Herald* 1.1.2 (CF 35:39; SCh 139:135). The next section of the same chapter in the *Herald* describes Gertrude counseling several women within the Helfta community and a large number of outsiders, who included both men and women (Gertrude, *Herald* 1.1.3 [CF 35:40–41; SCh 139:136–38]).

the change in traits required for the "fragile sex" to attain divine union; she asks Jesus to replace sensuality and weakness with virility and rationality: "May all my vigor [*vires*] become so appropriated to your charity and my senses so founded and firm in you [*sensus mei in te fundati et firmati*] that, while of the fragile sex [*sexu fragili*], I may, by virtue of a virile soul and mind [*animi menteque virili*], attain to that kind of love which leads to the bridal-couch [*thalamum cubiculi*] of the interior bed-chamber of perfect union with you."[13] This exercise is replete with traditionally defined masculine and military imagery. Readers are instructed to pray,

> O queen of queens, charity [*reginarum regina charitas*], make [me], for the sake of your glory, bound to you by oath in the new warfare of cherishing you [*in nova tuae dilectionis militia*]. . . . Gird my thigh with the sword of your Spirit [*gladio spiritus*], most mighty [*potentissime*] one, and make me put on virility in my mind [*mente virum*] so that in all virtue I may act manly and energetically [*viriliter agam et strenue*]; and inseparably with you, I may persevere, well strengthened [*bene solidata*] in you, with an unconquerable mind [*invincibili mente*].[14]

Ultimately, the replacement of weak "sensuality" with "manly" strength and "virility in . . . mind" is the path Gertrude lays out toward divine union.

Because Gertrude composes this prayer from the feminine perspective, whether a man or a woman is performing the exercise, that person is praying as a woman who wants to become "manly" in mind and spirit. The inconsistency between feminine grammatical endings and conventionally associated masculine traits shows that Gertrude understands women as able to transcend the spiritual impediments typically associated with women. In other words, by the very act of praying as a woman for manly

[13] Gertrude, *Exercises* 5.394–99 (CF 49:87; SCh 127:186), with my emendation to the translation.

[14] Gertrude, *Exercises* 5.386–93 (CF 49:87; SCh 127:186). Translator's insertion; with my emendation to the translation.

traits, a real woman may liberate herself from associations with weakness. Indeed, this idea coheres with the locational structure of the *Exercises*, which emphasizes the idea that the *memoria Dei* transcends time and entails a transformative encounter with Christ, the Mediator between the already/not yet dichotomy. By performing the memory of God in Gertrude's *Exercises*, women are no longer hindered in the spiritual life by associations with sensual weakness and irrationality but are able to be strong and rational, as men are conventionally thought to be.

Yet in considering the female *persona* Gertrude's memory of God invents, it is important to distinguish between women's bodies and the behaviors typically associated with them. Gertrude does not teach that the *memoria Dei* annihilates the female sex so that a woman *becomes* a man in the body or in the soul.[15] Rather she challenges the behavioral associations with men and women so that real women may be allowed *to behave* as men are thought to behave, virile and strong.

Gertrude is clear that being a woman is not *ipso facto* an obstacle to divine union, as is evident in several ways in the same prayer from her fifth exercise. First, she addresses the prayer to a divine attribute, charity, which she personifies as a woman, a "queen." It is the "queen of queens, charity" (*reginarum regina charitas*) that she has the reader invoke in order to acquire characteristics conventionally associated with men; that is, to become "well strengthened [*bene solidata*] . . . with an unconquerable mind [*invincibili mente*]."[16] Second, she uses a feminine noun for the person in the prayer who has been made strong in Christ. As the English translators of her *Exercises* note, "Given the context of repetitions of 'virility' in the prayer, Gertrude seems to intend a pun on *bene solidata*. Instead of 'well strengthened', the phrase could be translated as 'the female/woman soldier' (from *solidatus* which means

---

[15] Such an idea is witnessed in the early Christian tradition, particularly in eschatological speculations, that "woman" will be resurrected in the body as "man," or as sexless. On this, see Megan K. DeFranza, *Sex Difference in Christian Theology: Male, Female, and Intersex in the Image of God* (Grand Rapids, MI: Eerdmans, 2015), 239–89.

[16] Gertrude, *Exercises* 5.386, 393 (CF 49:87; SCh 127:186).

'soldier, mercenary')."[17] Furthermore, in the conclusion of the prayer, Gertrude envisions the annihilation of traits conventionally associated with women in this newly made, "manly," "woman" to lead to a female, "bridal" kind of divine union: "I may, by virtue of a virile soul and mind [*animi menteque virili*], attain to that kind of love which leads to the bridal-couch [*thalamum cubiculi*] of the interior bed-chamber of perfect union with you."[18] The kind of soul (and body) that Gertrude envisions for "woman" as (re-)conceptualized or even (re-)invented in the *memoria Dei* is still a woman in the body. But she is no longer limited in her Godward progress by the associations of women with sensuality and weakness.

Even when Gertrude writes a prayer for the death of self, using the feminine voice, later in Exercise five, it is the traits associated with women that she describes as hindrances (*impedimenta*) to the religious life, like the archetypal temptation to sin (*tentamenta*)— not being a woman, per se. In the petitions she describes these associations as "hindrances" and identifies them as the things to be annihilated in the death of self. For instance, Gertrude composes the prayer, "O Wisdom, most outstanding virtue of divine majesty, if only your efficacy prevailed over me, an unworthy woman. If only, with the breath of your mouth, you were to blow upon and annihilate in me, small as I am, all hindrances to your will and gracious purpose, that through you I might conquer all temptations, and through you overcome all hindrances, that in greatness of love, dying to myself, I might live in you."[19] In the climactic conclusion of this prayer, the female *persona* is entirely possessed by the divine attribute Wisdom, personified as a woman. By remembering how all obstacles to divine union died with Christ in his crucifixion, Gertrude has readers annihilate the restrictions of sinfulness associated with women. She thus teaches how women can be transformed in Christ, through the power of

[17] Gertrude, *Exercises* (CF 49:87, n. 81).
[18] Gertrude, *Exercises* 5.396–99 (CF 49:87; SCh 127:186), with my emendations to the translation.
[19] Gertrude, *Exercises* 7.232–38 (CF 49:130; SCh 127:274).

his resurrection, to live a new life of virtue, freed from such hindrances, in Wisdom.

In a related case, later in the *Spiritual Exercises* Gertrude shifts her authorial voice, and therefore the voice of her readers as well, to the masculine perspective. She makes this significant change in the seventh and final exercise, an "Exercise of Making Amends for Sins and of Preparing for Death."[20] In composing the prayer, Gertrude provides the reader a female *persona* to invoke "Peace," in a prayer written in the first-person perspective. But then, as the prayer continues, she assigns the reader a male *persona*: the prayer asks Jesus to say words that refer to the reader in the third person, using the masculine pronoun *eum* (him). Finally, the prayer shifts back to the first person, applying words of a masculine gender (i.e., *miserorum* [miserable] and *desperatum* [hopeless]) to the reader:

> O my Peace [*Pax*], most dulcet Jesus, how long will you be silent? How long will you be secretive? How long will you say nothing? Ah, rather speak for me now, saying a word in charity: "I will redeem him [*eum*]." Surely, you are the refuge of all those who are miserable [*miserorum*]. You pass by no one without a greeting. You have never left unreconciled anyone who has taken refuge in you. Ah, do not pass me by without charity, miserable [*miserum*] and hopeless [*desperatum*] as I am.[21]

One of the English translators of the *Exercises*, Gertrud Jaron Lewis, interprets this change in gender perspective as abrupt and inadvertent. Her interpretation is based on the fact that the nuns in the choir at Helfta used masculine nouns and pronouns to refer

---

[20] Gertrude, *Exercises* (CF 49:122, n. 1).
[21] Gertrude, *Exercises* 7.52–158 (CF 49:127; SCh 127:268, 270) (with my emendations): *O pax mea Iesu dulcissime, quosque siles? quousque dissimulas? quousque taces? Eia vel nunc pro me loquere, verbum in charitate dicens: Ego redimam eum. Tu quippe es omnium miserorum refugium. Tu neminem praeteris insalutatem. Tu nunquam aliquem ad te confugientum dimisisti irreconciliatum. Eia ne pertranseas sine charitate me miserum et desperatum.*

to themselves when they chanted the Divine Office:[22] "Gertrud thus includes adjustments for which the liturgy did not provide. There are two places where Gertrud, in fact, relapses into this generally adopted male *persona*. In Chapter Seven she abruptly and perhaps inadvertently shifts to the masculine gender in speaking about herself (cf. 155 and 158); and one time (VII, 684) she prays that 'brotherly charity' may be increased in her. These two passages let us appreciate all the more Gertrud's conscious effort throughout to maintain the feminine perspective."[23]

But perhaps in these cases Gertrude's gender shift is deliberate. Indeed, in the context of the exercise's theme of death, coupled with Gertrude's rhetorical strategy in the passages from Exercise five considered above, it seems Gertrude is using the gender shift as a conscious linguistic tool to call for the final and absolute death of typically restrictive behaviors associated with women. While speaking in the male *persona* in this prayer, readers no longer have to renounce the traits of sensuality, weakness, irrationality as they do in the passage from Exercise five. Having progressed this far, readers have effectively sloughed off the "hindrances" to the religious life that are specific to women.

Here again, Gertrude's thought is underpinned with her belief that the memory of God transcends time and entails a transformative encounter with Christ, the Mediator, between already and not yet. The encounter with the divine Mediator in performing the *memoria Dei* is what allows women on their journey toward divine union to transcend the cultural conventions of gendered behavior. This state, in which the restrictive associations with women have been annihilated, reflects the "not yet" eschatological reality "already" in the female *persona*, so much so that she adopts a male *persona*.

---

[22] Gertrude, *Exercises* (CF 49:127, n. 18)

[23] Lewis, "Introduction," in Gertrude, *Exercises* (CF 49:5–6). Lewis notes another gender shift in Exercise seven when Gertrude includes in a long litany a prayer for "brotherly charity" (Gertrude, *Exercises* 7.684 (CF 49:145; SCh 127:306). This shift appears to be less a conscious linguistic tool than the passage discussed above, as Gertrude's language here comes from the Rule of Saint Benedict (RB 72.8).

Yet even in this state, when her readers have adopted the male *persona*, Gertrude insists that they have *not yet* achieved a fully integrated *persona*. Indeed, the male *persona* Gertrude has her readers adopt momentarily is "miserable [*miserum*] and hopeless [*desperatum*]"; he cries out to the feminine personification of divine peace (*Pax*) for a redeemed identity: "O my Peace [*Pax*] . . . speak for me now, saying a word in charity: 'I will redeem him [*eum*].'"[24]

Then, as the passage continues, Gertrude quickly shifts back into composing prayers in the feminine voice. From this point on until the conclusion of the *Spiritual Exercises*, she has her readers (both actual men and women) use a woman's voice in making their prayers. In this way in particular, Gertrude seems to be dismantling male and female associations. She replaces the traits associated with women with those associated with men because sensuality, weakness, and irrationality are hindrances to the religious life, while virility and rationality are necessary for it. Gertrude's shift from the feminine to the masculine voice are thus important features of her meticulously constructed text.

As Gertrude painstakingly built a memory store for her readers by associating select tropes from the biblical, liturgical, and monastic traditions in order to argue that the *memoria Dei*, like the Eucharist, transcends time and entails a direct encounter with Christ, the Mediator between the *then* and *now*, humanity and divinity, this rhetorical strategy provides a hermeneutical key to her treatment of gender in the *Exercises*. She uses her theory that the *memoria Dei*, like the Eucharist, transcends time as a springboard to refigure the traditional conceptualization of woman. Therefore, in a move similar to her construction of a tension between the mediated and unmediated vision of God, which corresponds to the already and not yet, she builds a tension between typical associations with men and women in her text. She collapses the tension between the mediated/unmediated sight of God, within a eucharistic context, and she subverts the male/female dichotomy in the memory of God.

---

[24] Gertrude, *Exercises* 7.52–158 (CF 49:127; SCh 127:268, 270), with my emendation.

Gendered Images of God and Self
in Gertrude's Writings

Just as Gertrude constructed her *Exercises* to teach women and
men alike how weakness and irrationality can be transcended in
keeping the memory of God, she also avoided male/female dichotomies in her images of God. Anna Harrison and Caroline
Walker Bynum note, "Gertrude associates with God characteristics the dominant culture often dichotomized as male and female
(justice versus mercy, honor and reason versus intimacy and emo-
tionality, and so forth). What is striking about her usage, however,
is her attribution of all such qualities to God without, apparently,
any strong sense that they are dichotomous. Her God is angry
and severe, yet nurturing and supportive; he both demands repa-
ration and elevates the lowliest sinner."[25] Even when Gertrude
compares God to a mother, she does not reinforce the false opposites of male/female categories; she either transcends or subverts them.

Two examples from the *Herald* illustrate Gertrude's approach
to male/female categories in her God imagery. The first occurs
when she writes of God's promise to be present with her at the
time of her death, comparing God's "paternal care" to that of "a
consoling mother": "I will hide you under my paternal care, as a

---

[25] Anna Harrison and Caroline Walker Bynum, "Gertrude, Gender, and the
Composition of the *Herald of Divine Love*," in *Frieheit des Herzens: Mystik bei
Gertrud von Helfta*, ed. Michael Bangert, Mystik und Mediävistik 2 (Münster:
Lit, 2004), 67. See also Caroline Walker Bynum, *Jesus as Mother: Studies in the
Spirituality of the High Middle Ages* (Berkeley: University of California Press,
1982), 189–90; Grace Jantzen, *Power, Gender, and Christian Mysticism* (Cambridge: Cambridge University Press, 1995), 298–99. In a related discussion of
the way Gertrude's female language for God extends beyond anthropomor-
phisms and stereotypes, Lewis writes, "Auch sind die bei Gertrud verwen-
deten Epitheta für Gott, wie z.B. *bonitas, caritas, dilectio, misericordia, pax,
pietas, veritas*, wie die moisten abstraketen Begriffe im Lateinischen, Feminina,
woraus sich ergibt, daß in ihrer Prosa von Gott großenteils im Kontext weib-
licher Vorstellungen die Rede ist" ("Das Gottes- und Menschenbild im Werk
einer mittelalterlichen Mystikerin: Uberlegungen zu Gertrud Von Helfta
[1256–1302]," in *Gottes Nahe: Religiöse Erfahrung in Mystik Und Offenbarung*,
ed. Paul Imhof [Wurzburg: Echter, 1990], 64).

mother would cover and caress her beloved child when terrified by fear of shipwreck. And as the mother would rejoice in the joy of her child when they had reached land in safety, so will I rejoice in your joy when you are safe in paradise."[26] In the second passage, which lacks a "paternal" motherhood, God as mother is stern, even scaring her children, although she also kisses them and draws them to her breast: "I . . . am like a mother who has a little boy whom she loves so dearly that she wants him to be with her all the time; when the boy wants to run off to his friends because of a secret game, she sometimes puts scarecrows or something terrifying in certain areas so that the frightened boy runs back to her bosom. . . . Just as a kindly mother is accustomed to kiss fondly anything that troubles her delicate child, so I desire to soothe away by the blandishments of loving whispers all your troubles and contrarieties."[27]

Depictions of God as mother were commonplace in patristic and medieval spiritual writings.[28] Authors often expounded the maternal metaphors found in the Bible[29] to describe the divine union. Although the imagery offers an alternative to the dominant and reified theme of the male God Father, unlike Gertrude's usage, it was often hampered by dichotomous gendered categories.[30] For instance, the Benedictine Anselm of Canterbury expands the biblical imagery of God as mother hen[31] in his "Prayer to St. Paul": "Are you not the mother who, like a hen, gathers her chickens

---

[26] Gertrude, *Herald* 5.25.3 (SCh 331:206, 208). My translation.

[27] Gertrude, *Herald* 3.63.1–2 (CF 63:177–78; SCh 143:250, 252). For other passages where Gertrude describes God as a mother who both tests and consoles her children, see Gertrude, *Herald* 3.71.2 (CF 63:198; SCh 143:288, 290).

[28] For an overview of patristic images of God as mother, see Marsha L. Dutton, " 'When I Was a Child': Spiritual Infancy and God's Maternity in Augustine's Confessiones," *Collectanea Augustiniana*, ed. Joseph C. Schnaubelt and Frederick Van Fleteren (New York: Lang, 1990), 113–17. For an overview of medieval images of God's as mother, see Bynum, *Jesus as Mother*, 110–69.

[29] E.g., Isa 49:1; 49:15; and 66:11-13; Eccl 24:24-26; Matt 23:37; Luke 13:34.

[30] Bynum, *Jesus as Mother*, 110–69, especially 131. See also Grace Jantzen, *Power, Gender, and Christian Mysticism*, 297–98.

[31] Matt 23:37; Luke 13:34.

under her wings? . . . For if you had not been in labor, you could
not have borne death; and if you had not died, you would not
have brought forth. Mother . . . warm your chicken, give life to
your dead man, justify your sinner. Let your terrified one be con-
soled by you; and in your whole and unceasing grace let him be
refashioned by you." As the prayer continues, Anselm distinguishes Jesus as mother from Jesus as father with culturally determined gender characteristics: "we, born to die, may be reborn
to life. Fathers . . . by result, mothers by affection; fathers by
authority, mothers by kindness; fathers by protection, mothers by
compassion."[32]

Anselm's comparison of God to a mother seemed to have influenced Cistercian monks like Bernard of Clairvaux, Aelred of
Rievaulx, Guerric of Igny, Isaac of Stella, Adam of Perseigne,
Helinand of Froidmont, and William of Saint-Thierry (who was
a Benedictine and became a Cistercian late in life).[33] For instance,
both Bernard and William borrowed the image to expound the
breast imagery in the Song of Songs; they depict Christ as a mother
who nurses the individual human soul. William says, for example,
"it is your breast, O eternal Wisdom, that nourishes the holy infancy of your little ones. . . . Since that everlasting blessed union
and the kiss of eternity are denied the Bride on account of her
human condition and weakness, she turns to your bosom; and
not attaining to that mouth of yours, she puts her mouth to your
breasts instead."[34] On the surface there appears to be a kind of
fluidity of male/female roles in this prayer. Indeed, William de-

[32] Anselm, *The Prayers and Meditations of St. Anselm*, trans. Benedicta Ward
(Hardmondsworth, Middlesex, UK: Penguin, 1973), 153–56. On this prayer
and its gender dichotomies, see Bynum, *Jesus as Mother*, 113–14. Augustine's
imagery of God as mother also uses these conventional associations with
women's behavior. For example, see the description of his use of the metaphor in his *Confessions* in Dutton, " 'When I Was a Child,' " 117–19.

[33] Bynum provides several examples of their maternal imagery in Bynum,
Jesus as Mother, 112–25.

[34] William de St. Thierry, *Sur le Cantique*, chap. 38, pp. 122–24; Mother
Columba Hart, trans., *The Works of William of St. Thierry 2: Exposition on the
Song of Songs*, CF 6 (Spencer, MA: Cistercian Publications, 1970), 30; quoted
in Bynum, *Jesus as Mother*, 119.

scribes Christ, the man, as a mother with breasts, and the monk, who is also male, as a Bride. Furthermore, in a seeming reversal of traditional sex roles, the union between the soul described as a female Bride who kisses the breasts of Christ, appears to be homoerotic. Yet as Jean Leclercq and others have emphasized, the breasts of the Bridegroom in Bernard's and other Cistercian commentary on the Song of Songs play up the maternal rather than the erotic metaphor.[35] Most germane to this discussion, William associates the female Bride (i.e., the human soul, or humankind in general) with weakness.

In contrast, when Gertrude compares Jesus to a mother, she draws from biological characteristics (i.e., breastfeeding) rather than culturally determined characteristics (i.e., weakness and inferiority).[36] Her strategy is consistent with that of the prayers in her *Exercises*. In her visions, Gertrude often sees herself drinking spiritual sustenance from the heart of Jesus through the wound in his side, as if suckling milk from his maternal breast. Her religious sisters relate such an instance, wherein Gertrude "with the utmost constancy, leant on the bosom of her beloved with such great pressure and constant adherence that it seemed to her that the force of all creation would not be strong enough to shift her even a little from that resting-place where she was rejoicing to drink in, from the side of the Lord's body, life-giving savor, sweetness far surpassing balsam."[37] Here, in describing Jesus, Gertrude uses nursing imagery, which is biologically tied

---

[35] Jean Leclercq, *Monks and Love in Twelfth-Century France: Psycho-Historical Essays* (Oxford: Clarendon Press, 1979), 27–61; Bynum, *Jesus as Mother*, 146–48.

[36] Rosalyn Voaden, "All Girls Together: Community, Gender, and Vision at Helfta," in *Medieval Women and Their Communities*, ed. Diane Watt (Toronto: University of Toronto Press, 1997), 74. For an index of Gertrude's comparisons of Jesus to a mother, see Bynum, *Jesus as Mother*, nn. 47–48, 190.

[37] Gertrude, *Herald* 3.4.1 (CF 63:34; SCh 143:24). For other passages where Gertrude feeds spiritually from Jesus' breasts, see Gertrude, *Herald* 2.16.1 (CF 35:139; SCh 139:290); *Herald* 3.42.1 (CF 63:139–40; SCh 143:192, 194). Here Gertrude seems to have in mind the biblical image of John who drinks wisdom from Jesus' breast (John 13:23, 25). Therefore, this is another case in which Gertrude translates the male anecdote of a biblical image to a female one.

to women, but she does not engage in the dominant culture's association of women with intellectual and moral inferiority.

In another passage, Gertrude tells of her contracting a "pink scar" from the "life-giving" wound in Jesus' side, after she received eucharistic communion one day. Medieval depictions of Christ's bleeding wound often resembled a womb at which to find safety and union.[38] Gertrude's description of her experience may be a development of this womb imagery. She recalls that when she swallowed the sacred host, it seemed to pass through her and then emerge from the wound in Jesus' side to cover her own freshly contracted wound like a bandage. In the account, Jesus himself explains this to her: "See how this host unites you to me in such a way that it covers up your scar from one side and my wound from the other, and becomes a dressing for both of us."[39] The wound is the site of incorporation for Gertrude's body with Christ's. Through receiving the Host, she enters his wound and becomes joined to and also like him in her body. Again, she uses women's biological imagery—in this case fertility, security, and incorporation—rather than behavioral associations to develop her God imagery.

The images Gertrude sketches of God and self, like the prayers she constructs in her *Spiritual Exercises*, teach her readers that spiritual progress is equally accessible to all persons, men and women. On the basis of her belief that reception of the eucharistic Host is the paramount opportunity for union with Christ's humanity and divinity in the here and now, and thus for subverting such male/female dichotomies, she is a strong advocate for frequent communion.

Gertrude pleads for daily communion, which clergymen enjoyed, but the average lay person and nun did not.[40] In addition, she complains of how some priests take advantage of their privilege by receiving the Host mindlessly, out of routine obligation.[41] Within this context, she understands her apostolate of frequent

[38] See Bynum, *Jesus as Mother*, 122.
[39] Gertrude, *Herald* 3.18.27 (CF 63:81; SCh 143:104).
[40] Rubin, *Corpus Christi*, 84–85, 149.
[41] Gertrude, *Herald* 3.36.1 (CF 63:128; SCh 143:136).

communion as a priestly mission. She often sees herself in her visions with priestly accoutrements, and she authorizes her claim with her eucharistic view that union with Christ's humanity and divinity, achieved by receiving the Host, frees the human person (at least in the spiritual life) from male/female dichotomies. Thus Gertrude is able to act as a priest in her visions, thereby modeling the way her conception of men and women subverts the ecclesial roles aligned with them.

Gertrude's Visionary Priesthood

Gertrude's visionary reports are replete with priestly trappings. In them, she describes herself taking on ecclesial roles reserved for clergymen. For example, she describes herself as a preacher who heralds the Gospel message with an inherent force,[42] a judge who rightfully distinguishes between worthy and unworthy recipients of the Eucharist and between consecrated and unconsecrated Hosts,[43] and a spiritual counselor who effectively announces God's forgiveness of sins to her sisters when no ordained priest can be found to administer the sacrament of reconciliation.[44] Moreover, Gertrude testifies that on multiple occasions she received from God the priestly power of binding and loosing. Book One of the *Herald*, for instance, relates an occasion when God gives

---

[42] Gertrude, *Herald* 1.12.1 (CF 35:78; SCh 139:186).

[43] See Gertrude, *Herald* 3.13.1 (CF 63:54; SCh 143:54).

[44] When an absent confessor prevents her sisters from receiving the sacrament, Gertrude preaches the message of forgiveness to them; later she has a vision of her own effectiveness in administering grace, seeing those to whom she had preached sitting closest to Christ's altar in heaven. See Gertrude, *Herald* 4.7.1–4 (CF 85:49–51; SCh 255:98–104). For comment on and further discussion of this vision, see Bynum, *Jesus as Mother*, 204–5. In addition, on several occasions in her visions, Gertrude bypassed the role of priest, by relying on Christ instead. Once, Christ directly celebrated the Mass for her (Gertrude, *Herald* 3.8.1 [CF 63:40–41; SCh 143:32–34]). He also renewed within her all seven sacraments at once (Gertrude, *Herald* 3.60.1 [CF 63:174; SCh 143:244, 246]). This renewal would have included ordination, as it is, of course, one of the seven sacraments. For comment on and further discussion of Gertrude's priestly activities see Bynum, *Jesus as Mother*, 196–209.

her the keys to the kingdom that were once given to Saint Peter.[45] In the visionary scene, God asks Gertrude,

> "Does not the Church's faith rest universally on the promise I once made to Peter alone when I said: 'Whatever you shall bind on earth shall be bound also in heaven'? And does not the Church firmly believe that this has come about to the present day through all the ministers of the Church? Therefore why do you not believe with equal faith that I am able and willing to do anything, prompted by love, which I promise you with my divine mouth?" And touching her tongue he said: "There! I have put my words in your mouth, and I confirm in my truth every single word that you might speak to anyone on my behalf, at the prompting of my Spirit. And if you make a promise to anyone on earth on behalf of my goodness, it will be held in heaven as a promise that has been irrevocably validated."[46]

Gertrude certainly understands her priestly vocation as divinely ordained. An account from Book Four of the *Herald* recounts her receiving the call from God while reflecting on John 20:22 during the Easter octave one year. When meditating on the Holy Spirit's breathing on the disciples, she prays that she might receive the same anointing. She understands from Jesus that she must search his side and hands, as the disciples did in John 20:27. That is, she understands that she should reflect on his Sacred Heart, particularly on his bestowing of limitless, unmerited grace upon humankind despite the fact that humans are unworthy of it. While meditating on his hands, she recalls the works of the thirty-three years of his incarnation, particularly his passion and death. She next understands that Jesus wants everyone to participate in his salvific work, in accordance with the Scripture: *As the living Father has sent me, I also send you.*[47] As the passage continues, it applies the calling of the apostles to the priesthood—verbatim—to Gertrude herself: "Then the Lord breathed on her and

[45] Matt 16:19.
[46] Gertrude, *Herald* 1.14.4 (CF 35:83; SCh 139:198).
[47] John 20:21.

gave her, too, the Holy Spirit, saying, *Receive the Holy Spirit: whose sins you shall forgive, they are forgiven them.*"[48]

As the *Herald* relates it, Gertrude then questioned God as to whether she could really receive this power of binding and loosing, since it is reserved to the office (*officium*) of the priesthood: "At this she said, 'Lord, how can this be, since this power to bind and loose is given to priests alone?' The Lord replied, 'Anyone whose case you have judged to be innocent, discerning through my Spirit, will certainly be reckoned guiltless in my sight, and anyone whose case you have determined to be guilty shall appear answerable in my sight: for I shall speak through your mouth.' "[49] For Gertrude, obtaining this gift was nothing new, since God had given it to her several times before.[50] So in this experience of receiving the gift again, as it is reported in Book Four, Gertrude asks, "Since your courtesy, most merciful God, has very often sanctified me with this same gift, what do I gain from your granting me the same thing once again?" The response she receives is significant. God makes a direct analogy between the gift he repeatedly bestows on her soul to the offices of deacon and priest that he bestows upon the same individual in the sacrament of ordination. "The Lord replied, 'When someone is ordained as deacon and later as priest, he does not lose the office of deacon in this way but acquires greater honor from the priesthood. So too when a soul is given some gift a second time, the reiteration certainly establishes it more firmly, and through this her accumulation of blessedness is increased.' "[51]

The relationship of Gertrude's visionary priesthood (*sacerdotium*) and the office (*officium*) is repeated later in Book Four of the *Herald*. It occurs in a passage that describes a visionary encounter

[48] John 20:22-23. Gertrude, *Herald* 4.32.1 (CF 85:159–60; SCh 255:278, 280).

[49] Gertrude, *Herald* 4.321 (CF 85:159–60; SCh 255:280).

[50] Similarly, time and again in her visions, Gertrude is assured that she will not misjudge anyone and that God will speak through her. See, e.g., *Herald* 1.1.3 (CF 35:40; SCh 139:122, 124); *Herald* 1.14.4–5 (CF 35:83–85; SCh 139:198, 200).

[51] Gertrude, *Herald* 4.32.1 (CF 85:159–60; SCh 255:280). See also Gertrud Jaron Lewis, "God and the Human Being in the Writings of Gertrud of Helfta," *Vox Benedicta* 8 (1991): 310.

Gertrude has with Saint Peter, who is dressed in papal attire: "After this, while she was praising and extolling blessed Peter during Mass for his special privileges and, among others, that he had heard the Lord say, *Whatsoever you shall bind*,[52] and so on, that same apostle appeared to her in papal glory, dressed in sacred vestments. Stretching out his hand above her, he blessed her to carry out in her soul all the work of salvation that he had ever been able to do in any soul from the power bestowed on him by those words."[53]

Of course, Gertrude never actually occupied the office of ordained priest in the social order. But in that same visionary scene with Peter dressed as pope she shows how she understands herself to fulfill this priestly mission to the "work of salvation." It is the feast day of Saints Peter and Paul, and when she is about to receive communion, she sees both of the apostles standing beside her, one on the right and the other on the left. Then, before she receives the Host, Jesus embraces her with both his arms, saying, "Look! I too conducted you with the same arms with which I receive you; but I preferred to carry this out through my apostles, so that from this your devotion toward them would be increased." After she receives communion and is praying, she sees herself as queen, seated beside Jesus, who appeared to her as a king. Peter and Paul appeared to be kneeling before both of them as princes, "as if they were knights receiving their recompense from their lord and lady. For the saints' reward seemed to have been increased by the virtue of her communion."[54] In this way, the account claims that Gertrude is extending and building upon the apostles' work through her own eucharistic communion and devotion.

At this point it becomes clear that Gertrude's disregard for male/female dichotomies is consistent with her confident image of herself as priest. At the same time, she practices her priestly identity entirely within the interior realm. She is therefore not arguing for dismantling the social order and roles associated tra-

---

[52] Matt 16:19.
[53] Gertrude, *Herald* 4.44.2 (CF 85:202; SCh 255:342).
[54] Gertrude, *Herald* 4.44.2 (CF 85:202; SCh 255:342).

ditionally with nuns and priests. Indeed, her priestly activities may be understood as a means to sublimate and thereby even reinforce her social situation as a cloistered woman.

Hildegard of Bingen too addresses the issue of women and the priestly office in Part Two of her *Scivias*, Vision 6. There she recounts her vision of Ecclesia personified as a woman, who stands before Christ crucified. Ecclesia holds a chalice in which she collects the blood pouring out from Christ's side before offering the chalice at the altar.[55] As scholars have noted, in this scene Hildegard develops a traditional parallel between Ecclesia and Mary.[56] Like Mary, Hildegard's Ecclesia stands at the feet of Christ on the cross. Especially significant for this comparison to Gertrude is that Hildegard's Marian Ecclesia takes on priestly actions: she holds a chalice and ministers at the altar.

In that same vision, despite the fact that *Ecclesia* is grammatically feminine, Hildegard reaffirms the exclusion of the priestly office to men. In fact, she engages traditional sex role imagery to make her theological argument: "A woman conceives a child not by herself but through a man, as the ground is plowed not only by itself but by a farmer. Therefore, just as the earth cannot plow itself, a woman must not be a priest and do the work of consecrating the body and blood of My Son."[57] In short, because women cannot conceive children without the contribution of men, they cannot be priests.

---

[55] Hildegard of Bingen, *Scivias*, ed. Adelgundis Führkötter and Angela Carlevaris, CCCM 48 (Turnhout: Brepols, 1978), plate 15. As Anne Clark notes, this manuscript, sometimes referred to as the Rupertsberg *Scivias*, was probably created under Hildegard's direction. It is from Wiesbaden, Hessiche Landesbibliothek MS 1, but has been missing since 1945. The CCCM edition is taken from twentieth-century facsimile of the manuscript (Anne L. Clark, "The Priesthood of the Virgin Mary: Gender Trouble in the Twelfth Century," *Journal of Feminist Studies in Religion* 18, no. 1 [Spring 2002]: 12, n. 26).

[56] Clark, "The Priesthood of the Virgin Mary," 12–17; Barbara Newman, *Sister of Wisdom: St. Hildegard's Theology of the Feminine* (Berkeley: University of California Press, 1987), 188–95.

[57] Hildegard, *Scivias* 2.6.76; Hildegard of Bingen, *Scivias*, trans. Columba Hart and Jane Bishop (New York: Paulist Press, 1990), 278.

Interestingly enough, in the same vision, Hildegard repeatedly undercuts her theological rationale by holding up Mary as a model for priests. In one such instance, Hildegard discusses Mary's faithfully invoking God in her responses to the words announced to her by the angel; in a similar way, she says, the priest should invoke God to confect his body in the Eucharist. Of course, according to the doctrine of the Virgin birth, biological reproduction was disrupted: the male reproductive role was surpassed in the case of the conception of the body of the Incarnate Christ in the womb of the Virgin Mary. For this reason, Hildegard understands that women who are professed virgins, not lay women who engage in sexual intercourse, are associated with the priesthood of the Virgin Mary. Anne Clark explains, "Hildegard seems to distinguish between the social position and concomitant authority vested in a publicly recognized office and the religious identity of the priesthood. Just as virginity offers women the possibility of a life at least in some ways outside the *social* subordination to men, so the priesthood offered by virginity also functions outside the social order and is thus not linked with *office*."[58]

In comparison, Gertrude's understanding of priestly authority is not based on traditionally conceived roles for men and women, but rather on her subversion of these roles. For this reason, Gertrude says nothing about restricting such interior priestly authority to professed virgins, as does Hildegard.[59] Indeed, for Gertrude it is not virginity that offers women freedom from social prescriptions like the subordination to men, but rather the Eucharist. For this reason, she believes that anyone—male or female, professed virgin or laity—may "have" the authority of the priesthood. While this position does not subvert the social context, Gertrude's claims seem to be more audacious than Hildegard's.

[58] Clark, "The Priesthood of the Virgin Mary," 17.
[59] On Gertrude's Marian devotion and theology, see Ella Johnson, "Reproducing Motherhood: Images of Mary and Maternity in the Writings of Gertrud the Great of Helfta," *Magistra* 18, no. 1 (2012): 3–23. This article suggests a reading different from that in Anne L. Clark, "An Uneasy Triangle: Jesus, Mary, and Gertrude of Helfta," *Maria: A Journal of Marian Studies* 1 (2000): 37–56.

Gertrude's Eucharistic Theory in Service of her Priestly Identity

Gertrude's sense of priesthood, including her gift of binding and loosing, is profoundly characteristic of her eucharistic understanding that reception of the Host entails a direct encounter with Christ, the Mediator between the *then* and *now*, humanity and divinity. This perspective is particularly evident in another passage from the *Herald* that recounts a vision of her soul, appearing to her as if had been rooted in the form of a tree in the wound in Christ's side. After she received communion that day, she understood her rootedness in Christ to symbolize that she was being "penetrated by the power of the divine and human natures together." She then saw that the tree of her soul was bearing copious fruit, which seemed to exude potent liquor. And praying that this liquor would benefit the souls in heaven, on earth, and in purgatory, she saw that, "Part, flowing onto those in heaven, piled up their joy; part, flowing into purgatory, lessened their pains; part, flowing to the earth, increased sweetness of grace for the righteous and bitterness of penitence for sinners."[60] Verifying the efficacy of her gift of binding and of loosing, later, in the same chapter of the *Herald*, Christ tells Gertrude, "In the reception of the sacrament I shall draw you towards me in such a way that you will draw with you all to whomsoever the fragrance of your desires extends."[61] Gertrude's priestly mission of binding and loosing souls is thus based on her belief that the Eucharist *is* Christ, who is both fully human and fully divine.

Gertrude asserts her belief explicitly in Book Two of the *Herald*, asserting that the "fullness of the divine dwells bodily" (*habitat corporaliter omnis plenitudo divinitatis*) in the sacred wafer.[62] Moreover, she teaches that because Christ's two natures are conjoined and their corresponding properties communicate with one another, human persons encounter both properties when they receive the Eucharist. Indeed, Book Three of the *Herald* reports that

[60] Gertrude, *Herald* 3.18.6 (CF 63:72–73; SCh 143:86).
[61] Gertrude, *Herald* 3.18.25 (CF 63:80; SCh 143:102).
[62] Gertrude, *Herald* 2.7.1 (CF 35:119–20; SCh 139:260).

Christ once asked Gertrude, "Does not the catholic faith hold that anyone who receives communion on a single occasion, to him I give myself for his salvation with all the benefits contained in the treasuries of my divine and human natures alike? And the more often, however, a person has received communion, the more greatly the accumulation of his blessedness is increased and multiplied."[63]

Gertrude is here engaging with the doctrine of the hypostatic union of Christ's two natures and the related notion of *communicatio idiomatum*—that is, while Christ's divine attributes are communicated to his humanity, his human properties are communicated to his divinity.[64] On the basis of this principle, Gertrude teaches that when someone eats the sacred communion wafer, that person becomes united to Christ's *humanitas* in the body, and, through this bodily union, also becomes spiritually united to his *divinitas*.

As Gertrude sees it, there is a parallel between Christ's two natures and the body-soul composite of every human being, male or female. Christ's humanity mediates the Logos to the soul of the embodied human person: *Verbum caro factum est.*[65] In a passage from the *Spiritual Exercises*, she praises God for the opportunity for her soul to be joined with the Word: "O love, [*amor*] the fruition [*fruitio*] of you is that worthiest coupling [*copulatio*] of your Word and the soul which is brought about by perfect union with

[63] Gertrude, *Herald* 3.54.2 (CF 63:164; SCh 143:234).

[64] The principle was widely used in early patristic Christology, but it was endorsed more specifically in the formulation of the Councils of Ephesus (431 CE) and Chalcedon (451 CE) in response to the Nestorian controversy. The Councils concluded that because of the union in the incarnation, which is rooted in the one person of Jesus Christ, what is said of this one person in regard to one of his natures can also be said of that same person in regard to the other nature. For example, it is theologically permissible to say that the Son of God was crucified and that the Son of Man came down from heaven. The unity of the subject of Jesus Christ permits a distinction, but not a separation. For a summary of the *communicatio idiomatum* treated in the context of the Nestorian controversy, see J. N. D. Kelly, *Early Christian Doctrines* (London: Adam and Charles Black, 1977), 310–17. On the doctrine generally, see *The Oxford Dictionary of the Christian Church*, ed. F. L. Cross and E. A. Livingstone, 2nd ed. (Oxford: Oxford University Press, 1974, 1983), 321–22.

[65] John 1:14.

God. To use [*uti*] you is to become intertwined [*intricari*] in God. To enjoy [*frui*] you is to be one with God. You are the peace which surpasses all understanding and [you are] the road [*iter*] by which one comes to the inner chamber [*thalamum*]."[66] For Gertrude, the "coupling" of the Word with the human soul is made possible by way of becoming "intertwined" with Christ's humanity, which she identifies as the "road" (*iter*) to the "inner chamber" (*thalamum*).

Particularly noteworthy here is Gertrude's appropriation of Augustine's rhetorical pair (*frui/uti*), from his teaching on divine love in *On Christian Doctrine*. In many places throughout the first book he employs the pair as a binary to distinguish between the way one should "enjoy" (*frui*) God for God's own sake and should "use" (*uti*) all other things as means toward one's enjoyment of God.[67] Of particular note is the passage that Gertrude seems to have in mind in the passage above, because it also uses road (*iter*) imagery. Augustine writes: "So in this mortal life we are like travelers away from our Lord: if we wish to return to the homeland where we can be happy we must use this world [*utendum est hoc mundo*], not enjoy it [*non fruendum*], in order to discern 'the invisible attributes of God, which are understood through what has been made' or, in other words, to ascertain what is eternal and spiritual from corporeal and temporal things."[68] Later, still in book

[66] *O amor, tui fruitio est verbi et animae dignantissima copulatio, quam efficit perfecta dei unio. Te uti, est deo intricari. Te frui, est cum deo unum effici. Tu es illa pax quae exsuperat omnem sensum, et illic iter quo pervenitur ad thalamum* (Gertrude, *Exercises* 5.130–34 (CF 49:78; SCh 127:166). Translator's gloss.

[67] For secondary scholarship on the notion, see Oliver O'Donovan, "'Usus' and 'Fruitio' in Augustine, 'De Doctrina Christiana I,'" *The Journal of Theological Studies*, New Series 33, no. 2 (1982): 361–97; Helmut David Baer, "The Fruit of Charity: Using the Neighbor in 'De Doctrina Christiana,'" *The Journal of Religious Ethics* 24, no. 1 (1996): 47–64. Baer shows that the term "use" (*uti*) does not have an exploitative or utilitarian connotation; instead it means that one should refer the love of all other things toward God, whom one should alone "enjoy" (*frui*).

[68] *sic in hujus mortalitatis vita peregrinantes a Domino (II Cor. V, 6), si redire in patriam volumus ubi beati esse possimus, utendum est hoc mundo, non fruendum; ut invisibilia Dei, per ea quae facta sunt intellecta conspiciantur (Rom. I, 20), hoc est ut de corporalibus temporalibusque rebus aeterna et spiritualia capiamus* (Augustine, De doc 1.4.4, ed. and trans. R. P. H. Green, Oxford Early Christian Texts, ed. Henry Chadwick [Oxford: Clarendon Press, 1995], 16–17; PL 34:21).

one, Augustine is explicit about identifying Jesus Christ as the road (*iter*): "In fact Christ, who chose to offer himself not only as a possession for those who come to their journey's end but also a road for those who come to the beginning of the ways, chose to become flesh."[69] Significantly, in this context Augustine's *uti/frui* binary appears to change into a dialectic. Through Christ, he says, enjoyment may be experienced to some degree in this life: "To enlighten us and enable us, the whole temporal dispensation was set up by divine providence for our salvation. We must make use of this, not with a permanent love and enjoyment of it, but with a transient love and enjoyment of our journey, or of our conveyances . . . or any other expedients whatsoever [*non quasi mansoria quadam dilectione et delectatione sed transitoria potius tamquam viae*], so that we love the means of transport only because of our destination."[70]

Later, when reading Augustine in the twelfth century, Peter Lombard is puzzled by this contradiction. In his *Sentences*, Book 1, he notes that Augustine is clear in *On Christian Doctrine* about the meaning of the two terms: "To enjoy is to adhere in love to some thing for its own sake; but to use is to apply whatever comes into one's hand in order to obtain that which is to be enjoyed."[71] From this the Lombard understands that, "even in this life we may come to adhere to God."[72] But he notes that the same

[69] *Ille quippe qui non solum pervenientibus possessionem, sed etiam viam se voluit praebere venientibus ad principium viarum, voluit carnem assumere* (Augustine, De doc 1.34.38.81 [Chadwick ed., 46–47; PL 34:33]).

[70] *Hoc ergo ut nossemus atque possemus facta est tota pro nostra salute per divinam providentiam dispensatio temporalis, qua debemus uti non quasi mansoria quadam dilectione et delectatione sed transitoria potius tamquam viae, tamquam vehiculorum vel aliorum quorumlibet instrumentorum, aut si quid congruentius dici potest, ut ea quibus ferimur propter illud ad quod ferimur diligamus* (Augustine, De doc 1.35.39.85 [Chadwick ed., 48–49; PL 34:34]). Augustine is using the words *dilectione* and *delectatione* rather than *frui*; yet this discussion is in the immediate context of the preceding lines of his distinction between *frui* and *uti*.

[71] Augustine, De doc 1.1.2, as quoted in Peter Lombard, *The Sentences, Book 1: The Mystery of the Trinity*, trans. Giulio Silano, Medieval Sources in Translation 42 (Toronto: Pontifical Institute of Mediaeval Studies, 2007), 1.2.3, p. 6.

[72] Peter Lombard, *The Sentences, Book 1: The Mystery of the Trinity*, 1.3.1, p. 7.

Augustine, in *On the Trinity*, Book 10, seems to say that "in this life we do not enjoy, but only use, since we rejoice in hope." The Lombard quotes Augustine on this point: "To use is to place something in the power of the will; but to enjoy is to use with the joy, no longer of hope, but of the thing itself. And so everyone who enjoys also uses, because he places something in the power of the will with delight as the end. But not everyone who uses also enjoys, if he has desired the thing which he places in the power of the will not for its own sake, but for the sake of something else."[73] The Lombard comes to determine this apparent contradiction to mean "that we enjoy both here and in the future, but there we will do so properly, perfectly, and fully, because there we shall see clearly that which we enjoy. But here, while we walk in hope, we do indeed enjoy, but not so fully."[74]

The Lombard notes that Augustine is clear that human beings and the angels both enjoy and use things in this life, because they are placed between the "two other types of things."[75] He quotes Augustine's explanation from *On Christian Doctrine*: "The angels are already happy in the enjoyment [*fruentes*] of him whom we also desire to enjoy [*frui desideramus*]; and the more we enjoy [*fruimur*] him already in this life, even if through a glass darkly, the more tolerably do we endure our pilgrimages, and the more ardently do we desire to come to its end."[76] In other words, there is a kind of transient enjoyment on the road of loving God in this life, because of the destination, which is a fuller love. Thus, the Lombard determines, "It may also be said that one who already enjoys in this life not only has the joy of hope, but also of the thing

---

[73] Peter Lombard, *The Sentences, Book 1: The Mystery of the Trinity*, 1.3.1, p. 7; quoting Augustine, Trin 10.10.13.

[74] Peter Lombard, *The Sentences, Book 1: The Mystery of the Trinity*, 1.3.2, p. 7.

[75] Peter Lombard, *The Sentences, Book 1: The Mystery of the Trinity*, 1.1.2, p. 6. Here the Lombard is referring to Augustine's De doc 1.3.3.

[76] Peter Lombard, *The Sentences, Book 1: The Mystery of the Trinity*, 1.3.2, p. 8. He is here quoting Augustine, De doc 1.30.31: *Illo enim fruentes etiam ipsi beati sunt, quo et nos frui desideramus; et quantum in hac vita fruimur vel per speculum vel in aenigmate, tanto eam peregrinationem et tolerabilius sustinemus et ardentius finire cupimus.*

itself, because he already delights in that which he loves, and so he already has the thing itself to a certain degree."[77] Peter Lombard's determination of this apparent contradiction in Augustine's meaning of using and enjoyment helps to peel back the multiple layers underneath the seemingly simple surface of Gertrude's words: "To use [*uti*] you is to become intertwined [*intricari*] in God. To enjoy [*frui*] you is to be one with God." She seems to be noticing the same apparent contradiction in Augustine that the Lombard did, because her analysis resembles his in the *Sentences*. Indeed, like the Lombard, Gertrude gives priority to "enjoyment [*fruition*]," which she too defines in terms of degrees, as "that worthiest coupling of your Word and the soul." Moreover, like Augustine before her, she is explicit about identifying Jesus Christ as the road (*iter*) to enjoyment: "You are the peace which surpasses all understanding and [you are] the road [*iter*] by which one comes to the inner chamber [*thalamum*]." In addition, she seems to be using the *uti/frui* pair to make a distinction between Christ's two natures—that is, Christ's humanity is what one "uses" in order to enjoy the more perfect union with his divinity. In her words, "to become intertwined in God" (i.e., to "use" his humanity) is the "road [*iter*] by which one comes to the inner chamber" (i.e., to "enjoy" his divinity).

Thus Peter Lombard's discussion clarifies that Gertrude is not interested in the apparent conflict between *uti* and *frui*, but only in the way the two work together. It is consistent with her continuous effort to emphasize the interplay between Christ's humanity and divinity that she seizes upon and exploits this spot in Augustine's discussion of *uti* and *frui*. Moreover, she refers to the dialectic relationship he develops rather than the binary distinction because she has no need to distinguish between degrees of enjoyment in the difference between divine union in this life and the next, because they are the same. When the human person becomes intertwined with Jesus' humanity in receiving the eucharistic Host, he or she becomes united to his divinity as well. Gertrude thus creatively subverts her time's common polarity between male=divinity and female=humanity with impeccably orthodox eucharistic theology.

It becomes clear, then, that Gertrude's eucharistic understanding and its use of the "communication of properties" principle subvert the dualities of human/divine and body/soul and thereby challenge the conventional association of Christ's humanity with femaleness and his divinity with maleness. For Gertrude, union with Christ's divinity by way of union with his humanity in the Eucharist is available to every human person, with no exceptions made for men or women, or clergy and laity.

Gertrude understands Christ's salvific mediation at Mass as carried out through the double role Christ occupies as both High Priest and Host. The *Herald* relates Gertrude's seeing Jesus' self-sacrifice during the Mass: "at the elevation of the saving Host, the Lord Jesus, seemed to offer himself with every blessedness of his divine and his human natures in the form of the sacramental Host."[78] What is therefore critical for Gertrude in declaring her parallel role as salvific mediator is her union with Christ in each of these roles. Throughout the *Herald* Gertrude asserts not only her union with Christ in the Host, but also her union with Christ the High Priest by envisioning herself as priest and minister at the altar.

Gertrude often describes her devotions at Mass as paralleling the actions of the priestly celebrant. For example, she prays for the souls of the departed during the priest's elevation of the Host, when according to thirteenth-century rubrics of the Mass while holding the Host over the chalice the priest was directed to offer prayers and thanks for those on earth, the beatified in heaven, and the suffering in purgatory.[79] Gertrude also adopted in her

---

[78] Gertrude, *Herald* 4.48.5 (CF 85:216; SCh 255:364); Claire Taylor Jones, "*Hostia jubilationis*: Psalm Citation, Eucharistic Prayer, and Mystical Union in Gertrude of Helfta's *Exercitia spiritualia*," *Speculum* 89, no. 4 (October 2014): 1036.

[79] Miri Rubin, *Corpus Christi*, 51. On the priest's actions accompanying the consecration and the *Memento* of the dead at the Liturgy of the Eucharist, see Josef Jungmann, *The Mass of the Roman Rite: Its Origins and Development (Missarum Sollemnia)*, trans. F. A. Brunner, 2 vols. (New York: Benzinger, 1951, 1955), vol. 2.

eucharistic devotion the popular notion of "vicarious communion," in which the priest was understood to receive the sacrament for the laity.[80] In fact, the *Herald* relates that at every reception of the Host, Gertrude celebrated the fraction and distribution rites alongside those of the priest. She did this, the work says, by chewing up the Host in as many pieces as she could so that she could then receive each piece vicariously for a different purgatorial penitent:

> Whenever at the reception of the sacrament she longed that the Lord would grant her as many souls from purgatory as the number of parts into which the Host was broken in her mouth, and consequently tried to break it up into very many parts, the Lord said to her, "That you may understand that the effects of my mercy are more than all my works and that there is no one who can exhaust the abyss of my loving-kindness, look, I grant that by the ransom of this life-giving sacrament you shall receive much more than you venture to pray for."[81]

Christ guarantees the efficacy of Gertrude's salvific mediation, because it is in union with his own, which is present in the "life-giving sacrament."

In other visionary scenes, Gertrude exercises her priesthood by making a total oblation of self, in union with Christ's sacrifice in the Mass. She articulates this desire in the *Herald* by telling God, "if it were possible, I would divide my heart into so many pieces that from it I could share with everyone the virtuous intention of obeying you according to the supreme delight of your divine heart."[82] In addition, in the sixth of her *Spiritual Exercises*, her prayer reads, "O, when will I burn up the marrow of my soul on your altar and, in this holy fire that continuously burns there, inflame my heart and immolate myself totally as a sacrifice of

---

[80] See Jungmann, *The Mass of the Roman Rite*, 2:364–65. On the doctrine of vicarious communion and the practice of women in particular, see Bynum, *Holy Feast and Holy Fast*, 56–57, 227–37.

[81] Gertrude, *Herald* 3.18.26 (CF 63:80–81; SCh 143:102).

[82] Gertrude, *Herald* 4.21.1 (CF 85:109; SCh 255:200).

praise to you [*totam in hostiam laudis tibi immolabo*]?"[83] Later in the
same exercise, she prays to God "that together with the angels,
all the parts of my body may render you a vociferant sacrifice
[*hostiam vociferationis*]."[84] Remarking on such uses of *hostia* in this
exercise, Claire Taylor Jones points out that Gertrude is exploiting
the ambiguity of the term: "Although the Latin word means sacrifice or offering in a very general sense, it also carries the more
specific sense of Communion wafer, the Host."[85] Indeed, as Jones
notes, the prayers Gertrude prescribes for her readers in this exercise are intended to be performed while they receive communion.
Gertrude thus urges her readers "to offer up sacrifices [*hostiae*] of
praise" within "the liturgical context of Eucharistic celebration in
order to transform the performance of the ceremony itself into
the sacrifice it effects."[86]

Gertrude here enjoins others to engage in her priestly ministry
of eucharistic devotion. She holds fast to her teaching that anyone
who receives the Host—male or female, lay or clergy—can be
physically incorporated into Christ's humanity and thus be joined
spiritually to his divinity. In a passage from Book Three of the
Herald, Gertrude is clear that the priestly role of vicarious communion is not just available to her—or to clergymen—but to anyone who receives the Host with proper devotion: "when a person
eats, by which the whole body is strengthened in every individual
member, nevertheless only the mouth delights in the taste of the
food. In the same way, when a special grace is granted to those
who have been chosen, out of God's unrestrained loving-kindness
merit also increases for all members [of the Church] and especially
for those belonging to the same community, with the exception
of those who deprive themselves of it through envy and ill-will."[87]

[83] Gertrude, *Exercises* 6.75–76 (CF 49:96; SCh 127:206). See also Gertrude,
Exercises 6.511–14 (CF 49:111–12; SCh 127:236–38); Jones, "*Hostia jubilationis*,"
1034, n. 111.
[84] Gertrude, *Exercises* 6.316–17 (CF 49:104; SCh 127:222).
[85] Jones, "*Hostia jubilationis*," 1032.
[86] Jones, "*Hostia jubilationis*," 1032.
[87] Gertrude, *Herald* 3.17.3 (CF 63:68; SCh 143:78) (Lewis's emendation). See
also Gertrude, *Herald* 3.18.8 (CF 63:74; SCh 143:88).

When viewed in light of its thirteenth-century context, Gertrude's reasoning here is remarkably similar to that of Berthold of Regensburg (d. 1272) when he advocated withholding the chalice from the laity, by declaring that when the priest receives both species, he "nourishes us all," because he is the mouth, and we are the body.[88] Of course, Berthold's use of the analogy as a justification for withholding the cup is sharpening the priest/clergy divide, whereas Gertrude's is transcending it.

Gertrude links her religious identity as priest to the office (*officium*), while at the same time she transcends it. She sees herself with the accoutrements of the office. Yet what is essential for her is not the public role of priest; instead she stresses union with Christ's salvific mediation in the Mass. In her visions of self in the *Herald* and also her instructions for others in the *Spiritual Exercises*, she teaches that anyone—lay and ordained, male and female—may achieve close union with God in his role as both High Priest and Host at Mass, by way of receiving eucharistic communion. Gertrude does not take this opportunity lightly, because it carries with it the power to act as a co-redeemer. Thus she desires, as Christ does, that everyone who receives the Host might do so with the intention of salvific mediation.

---

[88] Caroline Walker Bynum, *Wonderful Blood: Theology and Practice in Late Medieval Northern Germany and Beyond* (Philadelphia, PA: University of Pennsylvania Press, 2007), 93. Berthold's discussion of "vicarious communion" is related to the eucharistic doctrine of concomitance. As scholastic theologians focused increasingly on the precise definition and exact mode of Christ's "real" presence in the bread and wine, beginning in the eucharistic debates of the eleventh century, the doctrine of concomitance was developed to explain how the whole Christ (*totus Christus*) is present in each of the two elements on the altar and in every piece of the fragmented Host (James Megivern, *Concomitance and Communion: A Study in Eucharistic Doctrine and Practice*, Studia Friburgensia, n.s. 33 [Fribourg, Switzerland: University Press, 1963]). In fact, theologians like Thomas Aquinas used the doctrine to justify withholding the cup from the laity to explain that the communicating priest receives both species (Aquinas, ST 3, q. 80, a. 12, reply obj 3, 59:84–85); Bynum, *Wonderful Blood*, 93, 299, n. 39. Gertrude's notion that each fragment of the Host that she chews is co-redemptive also participates in this doctrine of concomitance.

Conclusion

The idea expressed in Hildegard's words that "woman signifies humanity" led some medieval women to develop a desire to participate in Christ's salvation of all humankind.[89] As Barbara Newman has shown, medieval women occasionally sought to substitute their suffering to relieve the penalties incurred by the sins of others. To satisfy the debt of sin's punishments, she writes, "the most common currency of women was their pain: tears wrung from their heart, prayers poured like blood from wounded spirits, fever and chills, hunger and sickness and savage blows to the flesh."[90] They wanted all persons to be redeemed, those in this life, in purgatory, and even those they believed were condemned to hell.

Gertrude is thus not alone as a medieval woman reimagining deeply rooted institutions in the structure of Christian thought to extend women's religious possibilities. But she does not exactly fit into this picture of medieval women's spirituality. Of course, her writings and devotions are physical, eucharistic, and Christocentric. And her purgatorial piety shows that she too craved the salvation of others. But she dismantles female/male and human/divine dichotomies. Her assimilation with Christ and co-redemptive work are based on her belief that human persons, both women and men, encounter both Christ's humanity and his divinity in eucharistic communion. This understanding allows her to subvert traditional topoi of women's inadequacy in the spiritual life and audaciously to claim a sense of herself as priestly, with the capacity for binding and loosing.

Gertrude's claim of being able to loose purgatorial penitents is supported by her eucharistic understanding, which consistently engages the principle of *communicatio idiomatum*. Her claim of participatory union with both Christ's divinity and his humanity

[89] Harrison and Bynum, "Gertrude, Gender and the Composition of the *Herald of Divine Love*," 73–74.

[90] Barbara Newman, "On the Threshold of the Dead: Purgatory, Hell, and Religious Women," in *From Virile Woman to WomanChrist: Studies in Medieval Religion and Literature* (Philadelphia: University of Pennsylvania Press, 1995), 119; see also 120–22.

by way of her eucharistic communion with him allows her to transcend the conventional association of Christ's humanity with women.

Given Gertrude's membership in a strong female community that valued women's learning, that context may suggest that she appears not to have internalized the idea of women as "less than." In addition, the high level of education she received at Helfta allowed her to engage with theological doctrines like *communicatio idiomatum* to support her claims of spiritual authority. But of course Gertrude was not the only medieval woman who lived in a monastic community of women with intellectual resources at her fingertips. The question is how greatly she developed her own innovative way or built upon previous iterations broadening acceptable standards for feminine piety and authority. The issue arises regarding gender conventions employed by her female contemporaries, especially those conventions that engaged eucharistic devotion and thought.

CHAPTER SEVEN

Gertrude in Context:
A Challenge to Difference Fixed
into Dichotomy

The tendency to harden difference into hierarchical dichotomy is a perennial problem.[1] Of course, in theology certain oppositions are essential (e.g., that between God and creation). The problem is not these real and necessary oppositions, but how difference has been distorted under patriarchal philosophy and theology. For example, Plato is a protagonist in the narrative of pitting the body against the soul and mind, while Aristotle is a key suspect for the contrasting of men, light, and unity with women, darkness, and plurality.

Gertrude the Great of Helfta disrupts these fixed dichotomies between soul and body. She teaches about the concomitance of the spiritual and physical senses as well as about the integrative function of the Eucharist. She teaches a more harmonious relationship between the activity of the corporeal senses and the invisible, immaterial knowledge of the divine than is generally evident in the reception history (*Wirkungsgeschichte*) of that subject impacted by Platonic and Aristotelian thought—particularly, in the case of Gertrude's sources, of the influential works of Origen, Augustine,

---

[1] See Michelle Voss-Roberts, *Dualities: A Theology of Difference* (Louisville, KY: Westminster John Knox Press, 2010), xvii; Elaine Graham, "Gender, Personhood and Theology," *Scottish Journal of Theology* 48, no. 3 (1995): 356; Gillian McCulloch, *The Deconstruction of Dualism in Theology* (Milton Keynes, UK: Paternoster Press, 2002), 1–2.

and Bernard. For Gertrude, corporeal sensory experience is the basis for divine knowledge: bodily sensation in the Liturgy can and does cross the domains that separate the human and the divine. Furthermore, because dichotomies between body and soul (e.g., human/divine, matter/spirit, irrational/rational) were traditionally paired with female/male dichotomies, Gertrude's understanding of the Eucharist addresses the associations with women and men of her time.[2] She braids language of taste and wisdom, humanity and divinity, and physicality and rationality to construct a concept of woman that is united to God through the body and soul—particularly in making contact with God by tasting the Eucharist. For this reason, Gertrude has no scruples about describing herself in her visions as engaging in actions reserved for the ordained priesthood. In her visions, she makes it clear that anyone—male or female, professed virgin or lay—may exercise the authority of the priesthood.

Gertrude breaks down all of these dichotomies—particularly those between body and soul, humanity and divinity, female and male—in articulating her teaching on the Eucharist. She shows God to cross the boundaries of space and time by being present to Christians physically in the sacred Host, in the here and now. This is her central belief. Her transformation of fixed dichotomies comes directly from her belief in the Eucharist. Because she knows that key principles in the tradition support her belief, she laces her writings with them, using select theological doctrines and monastic and liturgical tropes to augment the mnemonic efficacy of her teaching. Ultimately, Gertrude's disruption of dichotomies

---

[2] For other medieval women and men writers who subverted such dichotomies in their writings, see Elizabeth L'Estrange and Alison More, "Representing Medieval Genders and Sexualities in Europe: Construction, Transformation, and Subversion, 600–1530," in *Representing Medieval Genders and Sexualities in Europe: Construction, Transformation, and Subversion, 600–1530* (New York and London: Routledge, 2011), 1–13; Sharon Farmer and Carol Braun Pasternack, eds., *Gender and Difference in the Middle Ages*, Medieval Cultures 32 (Minneapolis, MN: University of Minnesota Press, 2003).

is the fruit of her evangelical impulse to provide a vivid call to every human person to achieve divine union in the here and now. Scholarship on medieval women's religious writing in the last few decades has revealed that women used various structures of Christian thought to manipulate dichotomies—especially those of gender.[3] Caroline Walker Bynum and those following her, like Barbara Newman, have led the way in this work, showing medieval women's creativity and agency in constructing the idea of the female body as the locus of religious and societal possibilities over and against societal norms. Yet Gertrude the Great complicates this narrative. Her disruption of male/female dichotomies is less a strategy to legitimate her religious authority than an effect of her self-presentation, which reflects her firm belief in her Christian identity and work as an apostolate of frequent communion.

Disrupting Male/Female Dichotomies: Gertrude and her Women Contemporaries

Carolyn Walker Bynum and others following her have pointed to the way that medieval women writers, like nuns Catherine of Siena, Catherine of Genoa, and Beatrice of Nazareth, as well as Beguines Hadewijch of Brabant, Marguerite Porete, and Mechthild of Magdeburg, claimed the ancient association of women with flesh by aligning themselves with the humanity of Christ in order to legitimate their association with divinity, and thereby their

[3] Caroline Walker Bynum, *Holy Feast and Holy Fast: The Religious Significance of Food to Medieval Women* (Berkeley: University of California Press, 1988); Barbara Newman, *From Virile Woman to WomanChrist: Studies in Medieval Religion and Literature* (Philadelphia: University of Pennsylvania Press, 1995); Linda Lomperis and Sarah Stanbury, eds., *Feminist Approaches to the Body in Medieval Literature*, New Cultural Studies (Philadelphia, PA: University of Pennsylvania Press, 1993); Ulrike Wiethaus, *Maps of Flesh and Light: The Religious Experience of Medieval Women Mystics*, 1st ed. (Syracuse, NY: Syracuse University Press, 1993); Grace Jantzen, *Power, Gender, and Christian Mysticism*; Ingrid Bennewitz and Ingrid Kasten, eds., *Genderdiskurse und Körperbilder im Mittelalter: Eine Bilanzierung nach Butler und Laquer* (Münster: Lit, 2002); Sarah Kay and Miri Rubin, eds., *Framing Medieval Bodies* (Manchester: Manchester University Press, 1996).

religious and literary authority. They tended to draw from the traditional notion of the "female as physical" to claim they were especially redeemed "by a Christ who was supremely physical, because supremely human."[4]

Literary historian Barbara Newman has named this kind of gender construction the "womanChrist" model. She explains that the model is not named in writings and takes many forms: "It is not a succinct ideology so much as an experimental praxis, diversely and sporadically theorized: the possibility that woman, qua woman, could imitate Christ with particularly feminine inflections and thus achieve a high-ranking religious status in the realm of the spirit."[5] Newman distinguishes this gender approach common to medieval women's writing from a previous one, the "virile woman" model or *virago* ideal found in patristic and desert fathers' writing, which calls women to learn to live by the traits associated with men, and thereby claims the potential for Christian women to surpass their brothers in holiness.[6] For example, Newman demonstrates that Hildegard of Bingen, writing in the twelfth-century, ignored the "virile woman *topos*" and exploited the "womanChrist" model: "Instead of seeing herself as masculine, she developed a paradoxical self-image combining two different versions of the feminine: the 'weak woman' (whom God had chosen to shame strong men) and the exalted virgin. Hildegard's ideal of feminine chastity united *virginitas* with *viriditas*, the gra-

---

[4] Caroline Walker Bynum, *Fragmentation and Redemption: Essays on Gender and the Human Body in Medieval Religion* (New York: Zone Books, 1992), 147.

[5] Newman, *From Virile Woman to WomanChrist*, 3.

[6] Newman, *From Virile Woman to WomanChrist*, 3. Newman illustrates the transition "from virile woman to womanChrist" in gender ideals appropriated in female religious-life writing from the early twelfth century to the early sixteenth century. On virile womanhood in the early Middle Ages, see Elizabeth A. Castelli, " 'I Will Make Mary Male': Pieties of the Body and Gender Transformation of Christian Women in Late Antiquity," in *Body Guards: The Cultural Politics of Gender Ambiguity*, ed. Julia Epstein and Kristina Straub (New York: Routledge, 1991), 29–49; Jo Ann McNamara, "The *Herrenfrage*: The Restructuring of the Gender System, 1050–1150," in *Medieval Masculinities: Regarding Men in the Middle Ages*, ed. Clare A. Lees (Minneapolis: University of Minnesota Press, 1994), 3–30.

cious fertility that bloomed in both flesh and spirit. Far from remaining abstract and bloodless, this idea was embodied in the
Virgin Mary and each individual virgin, but also in diverse in-
stantiations of the cosmic Ecclesia, the divine figures of Wisdom
and Charity."[7]

In addition, Newman classifies the purgatorial piety of medieval women, which was commonplace in writings by and about
them, as a version of the womanChrist model: "Through purgatorial piety, women could offer their prayers, tears, illnesses
and ascetic feats for the salvation of those they loved: daughter
for parent, widow for husband, sister for religious sister. Such
offerings were invisible to transform the pain of their lives, self-
inflicted or otherwise, into free and constructive acts of love. The
holy woman who mastered this alchemy of pain became a co-
redeemer with Christ."[8] Newman provides examples of Lutgard
of Aywières offering a seven-year fast for the dead, Alice of
Shaerbeke her leprosy, Margery of Kempe her tears, Christina the
Astonishing her bizarre physical pantomimes, Christine of
Stommeln her torments from demons, and Madre Juana de la
Cruz her fevers.[9]

Women's prerogative to co-redeem is emphasized in Beguine
literature from the thirteenth century as a distinctive feature of
their spirituality.[10] Moreover, as Newman notes, even men who
were hagiographers and spiritual directors of devout women
recommended intercessory prayers for the dead: "Such prayer
constituted a safe, invisible, contemplative mission to work
without violating any gender taboos."[11] One eleventh-century
hagiography—that of Edith of Wilton—describes Christ as granting the saint "the apostolic power of binding and loosing (Mt
16.19, 18.18)." Goscelin of Saint-Bertin, Edith's hagiographer, describes her use of the power as in her post-mortem existence: "And

[7] Newman, *From Virile Woman to WomanChrist*, 6–7.
[8] Barbara Newman, "Introduction," in Newman, *From Virile Woman to WomanChrist*, 11–12.
[9] Newman, *From Virile Woman to WomanChrist*, 120–22.
[10] Newman, *From Virile Woman to WomanChrist*, 112.
[11] Newman, *From Virile Woman to WomanChrist*, 111.

so now, having been taken up into the grace of Christ, she enjoys the apostolic power of binding and loosing, and releases the suppliants bound with iron and restrains the guilty without iron; she stands forth as an alumna of the apostles, their daughter, worshiper and close imitator."[12] Of course understanding a woman as having this apostolic power was uncommon. But attributing her with the power after her death did not challenge the gender restrictions in actual ecclesial roles.

Viewed in this context, Gertrude's understanding of being a woman oscillates between the "womanChrist" and the "virile woman" topoi. Her devotions and writings, centered on the incarnation, Eucharist, and Sacred Heart, enhance the association between flesh and being a woman. In addition, the female *persona* Gertrude crafts within her writings, particularly in the *Exercitia*, builds upon the kind of gender-specific religious path for women claimed by the "womanChrist" model.[13] Like Hildegard's "exalted virgin," for example, Gertrude's concept of woman embodies the divine images of Sapientia, Ecclesia, and Caritas.

At the same time, Gertrude witnesses to features of the virile woman *topos*. She encourages women to aspire to characteristics typically associated with men, like rationality and virility, because she views conventionally defined feminine irrationality as a hindrance to the religious life, and the conventionally defined masculine trait of rationality as an aid.

Yet these gender constructions do not operate within Gertrude's works as a heuristic for dealing with the problem of female religious authority, as the contemporary narrative of medieval women's writings might suggest. Gertrude deploys images of rationality in writing prayers in the feminine perspective, because

---

[12] The *Vita of Edith*, in Stephanie Hollis, ed., *Writing the Wilton Women: Goscelin's Legend of Edith and* Liber confortatorius (Turnhout: Brepols, 2004), 34.

[13] Gertrude's writings affirm the possibility that woman *qua* woman could attain a particularly direct body-soul union with Christ in eucharistic communion and thereby participate in and represent Christ's body here on earth. See Ella Johnson, "Bodily Language in the Spiritual Exercises of Gertrud the Great of Helfta," *Magistra* 14, no. 1 (2008): 79–107.

she understands herself as a rational woman with spiritual authority. She has a scholarly intellect, writes in Latin, studies the male scholastic tradition, and encourages all—against widespread and crippling doubt and scruples—to receive the Eucharist. Yet Gertrude's understanding of her apostolate to frequent communion is complicated. By encouraging participation in the liturgy, Gertrude is supporting the church's hierarchy and emphasis on the priest's sacerdotal powers. While she envisions herself as a priest, her sacerdotal powers are reserved to the interior realm—to her mystical visions, within an enclosure. Her priesthood, therefore, has no real societal implications for women. But this contradiction between principle and reality is not Gertrude's concern. She does not attempt to make an indirect or subtle claim against the ban on women's ordination. It is as if she sees herself as a genderless priest. She presents herself as engaging in the spiritual activities she sees as critical to the priesthood: being a preacher and teacher, a mediator between God and humankind, a taster and toucher of God, and a binder and looser of souls.[14]

Gertrude does not use gender strategies or the subversion of dichotomies in order to support her authority as a woman. Her primary focus is not on gender constructions, but on the Eucharist. While her writings transform dichotomies and include ideas liberating for women, these should be read as fruits of her instructions on the Eucharist. Both women and men unite with Christ by receiving the sacred Host, because Christ is present there, in his humanity and divinity, to the human person, in body and soul, regardless of gender.

That Gertrude does not quite fit the scholarly narrative of medieval women's treatment of gendered conventions reaffirms the point made well by French feminists, that "women" is not a homogenous and stable group. They are different from men and also different from each other. Individual female authors had different reasons for writing the different ways they did, no doubt

---

[14] Caroline Walker Bynum, *Jesus as Mother: Studies in the Spirituality of the High Middle Ages* (Berkeley: University of California Press, 1982), 258. Bynum notes here that Gertrude's support of the priesthood and her interior claiming of its powers need not be read as inconsistent.

depending on differences in their individual personalities, affinities, predilections, life experiences, sexual identities, and socio-economic, geographic, racial, cultural, and historical contexts. These differences shape their writings in individual and pivotal ways. Gertrude's understanding of being a woman should therefore be read as a variegated thread in the elaborate and dense web of medieval women's religious experience and writing.

It is also important to note that Gertrude was not as pressed to establish her literary and religious authority as were so many of her female contemporaries. Her authority was already bolstered by the fact that she wrote in Latin and could therefore critically engage the authoritative writings of the tradition. She also lived in a well-established women's monastery for nearly all of her life. She therefore carried some literary authority simply by her association with that house. But as Bynum has noted, the house also offered her a female-friendly socialization, which certainly contributed to her confident self-image.[15] Indeed, later Anna Harrsion and Bynum assert that ultimately Gertrude's notion of *humanitas*, which appears throughout her writing, is not gendered: "Gertrude writes of herself not as female but as human. If we look at her understanding of authorship and her sense of authorization, it seems true . . . that the sex of the author is beside the point. Nothing Gertrude says about her inadequacy or her power is gendered female."[16]

Gertrude's most audacious priestly claim—that of binding and loosing—provides a site for further examination of her disregard of male/female dichotomies. It also serves to reveal that Gertrude is both similar to and different from her female contemporaries, and that her context contributed to her singularity. The claim to bind and loose also appears in other extant literature from Helfta at her time, that of Mechthild of Hackeborn and Mechthild of Magdeburg. But these women articulated their theological self-

---

[15] Bynum, *Jesus as Mother*, 184–85, 252–55.

[16] Anna Harrison and Caroline Walker Bynum, "Gertrude, Gender, and the Composition of the *Herald of Divine Love*," in *Frieheit des Herzens: Mystik bei Gertrud von Helfta*, ed. Michael Bangert, Mystik und Mediävistik (Münster: Lit, 2004), 75.

understanding differently, perhaps because of the difference in their life circumstances. The Helfta literature presents a helpful comparative case for the effect of socio-cultural influences on the images of self and God used by medieval writers. While Mechthild of Hackeborn and Gertrude of Helfta, who had entered the cloister as child-oblates, knew nothing other than the liturgical and intellectual woman-centered community that Abbess Gertrude worked to provide, Mechthild of Magdeburg experienced the scathing effects of living within a misogynistic culture for most of her life.

The Helfta Nuns: A Case for Comparison

Mechthild of Magdeburg's literary context is marked by her experience of isolation, alienation, and persecution, living as a Beguine in the city of Magdeburg, in contrast to Gertrude's and the other Mechthild's cozy environment of women's learning, literary collaboration, and communal worship in the house at Helfta.[17] For example, while Gertrude is lauded within her community as an apostle of frequent communion,[18] Mechthild of Magdeburg laments that as a Beguine, opportunities for communal celebrations of the liturgy are quite rare: "Oh, Lord, now I am extremely destitute in my sickly body and am so miserable in my soul which is so lacking in spiritual order that no one recites the hours of the office in my presence and no one celebrates holy mass

---

[17] A synod held in Magdeburg in 1261 threatened Beguines with excommunication if they disobeyed their parish priests (Ernest W. McDonnell, *The Beguines and Beghards in Medieval Culture, with Special Emphasis on the Belgian Scene* [New York: Octagon Books, 1969], 508). For comparisons Mechthild makes between her sufferings as a Beguine and those of Christ, see Mechthild of Magdeburg, *The Flowing Light of the Godhead*, trans. Frank Tobin (New York/Mahwah, NJ: Paulist Press, 1998), 54; 117–19 (hereafter FL); Hans Neumann and Gisela Vollmann-Profe, eds., *Mechthild Von Magdeburg, "Das Fliessende Licht Der Gottheit"* (Munich: Artemis-Verlag, 1990, 1993) 1.29; 3.10 (hereafter Licht); Saskia Murk-Jansen, *Brides in the Desert: The Spirituality of the Beguines* (Maryknoll, NY: Orbis Books, 1998), 109–10.

[18] Gertrude, *Herald* 1.10.3 (CF 35:67; SCh 139:166).

for me!"[19] Mechthild is not safe, as is Gertrude, and cries out, "I constantly notice with anguish the stench to that dead mongrel, my body; and others of my enemies are always assailing me; and I, Lord, when I consider the matter, have no idea how things shall turn out for me in the end."[20] Indeed, Mechthild writes that her experiential and participatory union with Christ's humanity is based in suffering:

> Truth was cross with me.
> Fear scolded me.
> Shame scourged me.
> Sorrow condemned me.
> . . . Mighty God received me.
> His pure humanity united itself to me.[21]

She writes that she is incorporated into Christ through her pain and yearns to subsume others' pain into their participatory union: "To the extent that we suffer poverty, humiliation, rejection, and pain here we are like the true Son of God, who in complete forbearance endured all his adversity and suffering."[22] Rather than uniting to God through consoling liturgical visions and experiences like the other two Helfta authors, Mechthild extols participatory union with God through pain.

This union with God through suffering is the foundation of Mechthild's literary authority. Her claim is most clear in a third-person account in which she asserts, "She is pierced in the side . . . from her heart flows forth many a holy teaching."[23] In another, first-person, account she describes the intermingling of her blood with Christ's: "Lord, your blood and mine are one, un-

---

[19] Mechthild, *Flowing Light*, 3.5 (FL 111; Licht 83). As Bynum points out, Beguines submitted to the utmost earthly suffering and purification, which included the likelihood of being cut off even from routine ministerial care and the sacraments (Bynum, *Jesus as Mother*, 231, n. 214).

[20] Mechthild, *Flowing Light* 3.5 (FL 112; Licht 83).

[21] Mechthild, *Flowing Light* 3.15 (FL 122; Licht 95).

[22] Mechthild, *Flowing Light* 6.32 (FL 258; Licht 240).

[23] Mechthild, *Flowing Light* 3.10 (FL 118; Licht 90).

tainted. / Your love and mine are one, inseparable."[24] Additionally, she reports God's declaration about her book, the *Flowing Light*: "I hereby send this book as a messenger to all religious people, both the good and the bad. . . . Truly, I say to you . . . in this book my heart's blood is written, which I shall shed again in the last times."[25]

Like Gertrude and Mechthild of Hackeborn, Mechthild of Magdeburg uses the heart as a synecdoche for the whole person. In fact, many scholars believe it is Mechthild of Magdeburg who introduced to the Helfta nuns the devotion of the Sacred Heart for which they are known.[26] All three of the Helfta writers use the metaphor of exchanging hearts to convey their participatory union with Christ.[27] On the basis of this union, all three women claim their own blood as eucharistic and therefore co-redemptive. Where the women differ is in regards to their terms of incorporation in Christ's humanity. Gertrude and Mechthild of Hackeborn claim their participation in Christ's eucharistic body and blood simply by way of receiving the sacred Host, whereas Mechtild of Magdeburg claims hers by referring to the most gruesome aspects of Christ's humanness—i.e., his bloody crucifixion and death—

---

[24] Mechthild, *Flowing Light* 2.25 (FL 96; Licht 67).

[25] Mechthild, *Flowing Light* 5.34 (FL 217; Licht 195). See also *Flowing Light* 1.1; 4.3; 6.43 (FL 39, 144, 267; Licht 6, 114–15, 251).

[26] Sabine Spitzlei, *Erfahrungsram Herz: Zur Mystik des Zisterzienserinnenklosters Helfta im 13. Jahrhundert* (Stuttgart-Bad Canstatt: Frommann-Holzboog, 1991); Sabine B. Marquardt-Spitzlei, "O Gott meines Herzens: Das Herz als Erfahrungsraum Gottes in den 'Exercitia spiritualia,' in *Aufbruch zu neuer Gottesrede: Die Mystik der Gertrude von Helfta*, ed. Siegfried Ringler (Ostfildern: Matthias Grünewald Verlag, 2008), 46–60; Cyprian Vaggagini, "La Dévotion au Sacré Coeur chez Sainte Mechthilde et Sainte Gertrude," in *Cor Jesu* (Rome: Herder, 1959), 29–48; Gabriele Winter, "Die Herz-Jesu-Mystik bei Mechtild von Magdeburg, Mechtild von Hackeborn, und Gertrud von Helfta," *Jahrbuch für Salesianische Studien* 17 (1981): 72–82.

[27] Barbara Newman, "Exchanging Hearts: A Medievalist Looks at Transplant Surgery," *Spiritus* 12, no. 1 (Spring 2012): 1–20; Barbara Newman, "Iam cor meum non sit suum: Exchanging Hearts: From Heloise to Helfta," in E. Ann Matter and Leslie Smith, eds., *From Knowledge to Beatitude: St. Victor, Twelfth-Century Scholars, and Beyond* (Notre Dame, IN: Notre Dame Press, 2013), 281–99.

and the mingling of her own pained, bleeding heart with his. Mechthild of Magdeburg's approach is evident in her poem:

> Now I shall joyfully go to God's table
> And I shall receive that same bloody Lamb
> That willed to be on the cross,
> Bloody, with his holy five wounds untended. . . .
> Lord, what then do we want to say about love
> As we are lying here so close together
> In the bed of my suffering?
> I received you, Lord,
> As you were when you arose from the dead.[28]

In one visionary account, Mechthild of Magdeburg even regards consoling experiences of divine union as less noble than those experiences that entail suffering: "Our Lord held two golden chalices in his hands that were both full of living wine. In his left hand was the red wine of suffering, and in his right hand the white wine of sublime consolation. Then our Lord spoke: "Blessed are those who drink this red wine. Although I give both out of divine love, the white wine is nobler in itself; but noblest of all are those who drink both the white and the red."[29] In another visionary account, Mechthild sees the virgin "who is Christianity" and describes her as drinking and distributing this "red wine of suffering": "The virgin stood on two feet. The one is the bond, the other is the loosening of the holy power. She carries in her right hand a chalice filled with red wine, which she drinks alone in untold bliss." When Mechthild asked her why she carries the chalice in her right hand, the virgin replies, "I am . . . supposed to give away his blood with my right hand, just as Christ is turned to his Father into glory."[30] For Mechthild, the red wine of the "virgin who is Christianity"—i.e., the church—is nobler because it shares directly in Christ's pain. She teaches that the blood of virgins and martyrs, spilled through innocent suffering, will be

---

[28] Mechthild, *Flowing Light* 6.21 (FL 294; Licht 232).
[29] Mechthild, *Flowing Light* 2.7 (FL 77; Licht 46).
[30] Mechthild, *Flowing Light* 4.3 (FL 145; Licht 115).

weighed together with Christ's blood on the redemptive scale of justice.[31]

Mechthild conceives her pain and suffering as the means to her participation in the church's power of binding and loosing. Mechthild describes her imitation of this virgin, Ecclesia, who has the powers of binding and loosing, by offering the red wine of her heart to the souls in purgatory; referring to "the poor souls who are tormented in purgatory," Mechthild declares, "To them, I must give my heart's blood to drink."[32]

In perhaps the most powerful occasion of Mechthild exercising her power to bind and loose, she reports, "I went to God's table in a noble throng. . . . Then I said: '. . . Now, Lord, I desire your praise and not my advantage that today your glorious body might come as a consolation to the poor souls. You are truly mine. Now, Lord, you shall be today a ransom for those imprisoned.'" Because of her participation with Christ's blood in both her pain and in the Eucharist, on this occasion Mechthild next valiantly ushers Christ into purgatory; once there, she persuades him to deliver suffering souls. She recounts in the third person, "Then she received such power that with his strength she led him, and they came to as grim a place as ever was seen by human eye—a horrifying bath, a mixture of fire and pitch, of muck, smoke, and stench. . . . The souls were lying in it like toads in filth. . . . Our Lord said: 'It was right for you to bring me here, I shall not let them go unremembered.'" On that day, Mechthild declares that 70,000 souls were released from purgatory.[33]

Mechthild believed she had the priestly power to bind and loose, but she understood the power to come from her efficacious union with the *humanitas* of Christ. Unlike Gertrude, she does not view her power in relationship to the sacerdotal office. Also unlike Gertrude, Mechthild understands *humanitas* as associated with being a woman. Mechthild's union with Christ is always experiential, aligning the pain of her embodied experience to the flesh

---

[31] Mechthild, *Flowing Light* 5.3 (FL 181; Licht 155).
[32] Mechthild, *Flowing Light* 5.8 (FL 187; Licht 162).
[33] Mechthild, *Flowing Light* 3.15 (FL 122; Licht 95).

of Christ, and Mechthild identifies this way of being united to God as "the noblest of all." Because of the association of women with flesh, participating in Christ's pain is an opportunity presented to women especially. She writes of herself as a "poor maid," and as a "despised" and "weak" woman.[34] Furthermore, Mechthild directly states that she is following the model of the church, figured as the virgin Ecclesia, in binding and loosing souls, rather than that of clergymen. Mechthild's self-descriptions do not include priestly imagery like those of the other two Helfta women. Mechthild is aware that she is unlearned and lacks authoritative status, and that this condition is a liability. She cries out to God, "Ah, Lord, if I were a learned religious man, / . . . You would receive everlasting honor from it [her book]."[35] She also bewails the persecution her writing brought upon her: "Alas, dear Lord . . . how long shall I stand here on the earth of my flesh like a stick or a target that people run, hurl and shoot at, having long ago sullied my honor with cunning and malice?"[36] In order to finish her book in the midst of such backlash, she fled to Helfta to write in safety.

At the same time, Mechthild is much more outspoken than Gertrude and Mechthild of Hackeborn in her critique of the state of the contemporary church and, especially, its clerics. She does not mince words when it comes to describing in vivid detail the state of sinful souls, often those of local priests and bishops, whom she sees in Purgatory.[37] Furthermore, Mechthild's narrations frequently usurp the moral and teaching authority of clergymen: underlying the accounts are her own lessons on how to avoid a similar fate.[38] For example, in one passage, she recounts her sight

[34] See Mechthild, *Flowing Light* 2.26; 6.1; 7.47–48; 7.64 (FL 96–98, 227, 316; 334; Licht 68–70, 204–5, 293, 309).

[35] Mechthild, *Flowing Light* 2.26 (FL 96; Licht 68).

[36] Mechthild, *Flowing Light* 6.38 (FL 264; Licht 248).

[37] On Mechthild's sharp clerical criticisms, see Marianne Heimbach, *"Der ungelehrte Mund" als Antorität: mystische Erfahrung als Quelle kirklich-prophetischer Rede im Werk Mechthilds von Magdeburg* (Stuttgart-Bad Cannstatt: Frommann-Holzboog, 1989), 152–57.

[38] Sara Poor shows that in addressing clergymen Mechthild activated their power to preach for her own written proclamation of the Word (Sara S. Poor,

of a deceased member of the Dominican Order who was facing the just penalty of his earthly sin by reading from an eerie kind of book: "All the words were screaming at him with all the books that he had ever read chiming in. He said: 'In my life on earth I was too fond of ideas, words, and deeds.' "[39] In another vignette, Mechthild relates seeing priests' souls enduring nightmarish punishments for their transgressions: "These were the souls of wretched priests who in this world floated in greedy desires and burned in damned lust that so utterly blinds them that they are unable to love anything good."[40]

Mechthild warns against power as a temptation and danger to the spiritual life.[41] While femaleness might be a liability in the world's eyes, maleness and the priesthood, if given to the temptations of arrogance and earthly honor, are liabilities in God's eyes. Precisely because Mechthild lacks maleness and clerical authority, she has religious authority. Her femaleness is a sign of her freedom from power and her ability to be united to the debased, humble, and suffering Christ.[42]

Mechthild of Hackeborn, on the other hand, treats gender similarly to Gertrude. This Mechthild seldom expresses her union with God in terms of participatory suffering, opting instead for liturgical imagery of incorporation.[43] For example, after receiving the Host on one occasion, she reports that Christ said to her, "Now I give myself to your soul, with all the goodness that I myself and all I can give. You are in me and I in you. You will never be separated from me."[44]

In addition, like Gertrude, Mechthild of Hackeborn often includes priestly accoutrements in her eucharistic visions of herself.

Mechthild of Magdeburg and Her Book: Gender and the Making of Textual Authority, Middle Ages Series [Philadelphia: University of Pennsylvania Press, 2004], 33–37).

[39] Mechthild, *Flowing Light* 3.17 (FL 125; Licht 98).

[40] Mechthild, *Flowing Light* 5.14 (FL 191–92; Licht 167).

[41] Mechthild, *Flowing Light* 6.1 (FL 223–27; Licht 200–206).

[42] Bynum, *Jesus as Mother*, 241–42.

[43] Mechthild of Hackeborn makes at least one reference to offering her involuntary suffering for the souls of the dead: *Liber* 2.36 (BSG 142; LSG 185).

[44] Mechthild, *Liber* 1.13 (BSG 63; LSG 41).

During one Mass, she saw Christ give "her his divine heart in the likeness of a wonderfully decorated golden goblet, saying, 'Through my divine heart you shall always praise me. Go and offer the living cup of my heart to all the saints, so they can be happily intoxicated with it." Mechthild then approached the angels, patriarchs and prophets, apostles, martyrs, confessors, virgins, and saints, offering all of them the cup. "After she had made the rounds of the whole celestial palace, Mechthild returned to the Lord. He received the goblet and placed it in the Soul's own heart, and thus she was blissfully united to God."[45]

As is true for Gertrude, so too for Mechthild of Hackeborn, efficacious purgatorial piety is a fruit of her eucharistic union, not of her suffering. The *Book of Special Grace* recounts that, "She also saw purgatory, where there were as many kinds of punishments as there are vices to which souls had been subject in this life. . . . But after she had poured out her prayers for them, the Lord delivered a great multitude."[46] On another occasion, when Mechthild experienced intimate union with God, "she desired that all creatures in heaven and earth should be made sharers in the grace of God.[47] And, taking the Lord's hand, she made such a great cross that it seemed to fill heaven and earth. From this the host of heaven received greater joy, the guilty pardon, the sorrowful comfort, and the righteous, strength and perseverance, while souls in purgatory were granted absolution and relief of their pains."[48]

Indeed, Mechthild describes much of her purgatorial piety as Gertrude does, with priestly imagery. For example, in one vision at Mass, during the octave of Easter, Mechthild had a vision of Christ's heart with a wound through which she entered like a door. He told her, "Come in and walk the length and breadth of my divine heart. The length is the eternity of my goodness; the breadth, the love and desire I have had from eternity for your salvation. Walk the length and the breadth—claim what is your own. For

---

[45] Mechthild, *Liber* 1.1 (BSG 40; LSG 10).
[46] Mechthild, *Liber* 5.20 (BSG 197; LSG 350).
[47] See 2 Pet 1:4.
[48] Mechthild, *Liber* 2.35 (BSG 142; LSG 182–83).

every good thing you find in my heart is truly yours." Then, in a gesture very similar to what Gertrude recorded as having experienced (as discussed in chapter six above), Christ "breathed on her [Mechthild], saying *Receive my Holy Spirit*."[49] As the biblical account refers to Christ's calling of the apostles to the priesthood with the words *whose sins you shall forgive, they are forgiven them*,[50] God applies the biblical words to Mechthild herself: she receives the power to bind and loose with the very words that the apostles received. According to the *Book of Special Grace*, after Christ breathed on Mechthild, she was then "filled with the Holy Spirit" and "saw fiery rays streaming from all her limbs, and everyone for whom she had prayed received a ray from her."[51]

Mechthild's hagiography even suggests that she continued her priestly apostolate of binding and loosing in the afterlife. In an account filled again with eucharistic and priestly imagery, the *Book of Special Grace* reports that Gertrude of Helfta received a vision at Mass in which she saw the deceased Mechthild "carrying baskets full of pyxes and offering them to souls in the different places of punishment. Each soul cheerfully took a pyx and, as soon as it was opened, that soul was delivered from all punishments and stationed in a dwelling place of delightful rest."[52]

Like Gertrude, Mechthild of Hackeborn understands her authority to bind and loose as based in her union with Christ's humanity in the Eucharist. But for them this *humanitas* is not necessarily the prerogative for all women because of being women. Rather than developing the association of female with flesh, they seem to ignore it. They evince this approach most clearly in adorning their co-redemptive powers with priestly trappings. The two nuns who lived at Helfta for nearly all their

<hr/>

[49] John 20:22. Mechthild, *Liber* 1.19 (BSG 83; LSG 68).
[50] John 20:22-23.
[51] Mechthild, *Liber* 1.19 (BSG 83; LSG 68). Some of Mechtild's co-redemptive claims are based on her duties as Cantress at Helfta. See Ella Johnson, "The Nightingale of Christ's Redemption Song: Mechthild of Hackeborn's Musical Apostolate," in *Music, Theology, and Justice*, ed. Michael O'Connor, Hyun-Ah Kim, and Christina Labriola (Lanham, MD: Lexington Books, 2017), 181–96.
[52] Mechthild, *Liber* 7.14 (BSG 237; LSG 408–9).

lives were even comfortable appropriating biblical words addressed to the apostles,[53] typically reserved in their day to clergymen. Even in this case, they appear to feel no need to qualify their femaleness, because they do not see it as a disqualification. Of course, they are restricted by gendered societal norms from actually acting as priests in society. But in their literary authority they seem to have the sense that their gender is not an issue. Having received a premier education within the Helfta cloister, they knew they were on the same intellectual footing as men. Unlike Mechthild of Magdeburg, who wrote in the vernacular, Gertrude and Mechthild of Hackeborn wrote in Latin and quoted freely from the writings of Origen, Augustine, Gregory the Great, Bernard of Clairvaux, Thomas Aquinas, Albert the Great, and the Victorines.[54] Of course Mechthild of Magdeburg's writing is just as replete with theological insights as Gertrude's and the other Mechthild's, but the latter two women are not so pressed to insist on the background of their teaching because they are women.

In the final analysis, like other women of her time, Gertrude stresses her incorporation into the *humanitas* of Christ as the basis of her religious authority. But her sense of *humanitas* is not gendered. She deploys gendered imagery and conventions from time to time in her writing, but as the comparison with Mechthild of Magdeburg and Mechthild of Hackeborn shows, she is not so inclined as other women in her day to reconcile her being female with her religious and literary authority, because of her socialization at Helfta. Not even in her self-presentation as a priest, including having the capacity to bind and loose souls, does she feel the need to defend the fact that she is a woman claiming to engage in actions both the society and church reserved to men. Gertrude's

---

[53] John 20:22-23.

[54] Theresa A. Halligan, "The Community at Helfta. Its Spirituality and Celebrated Members," in *The Booke of Gostlye Grace of Mechtild of Hackeborn* (Toronto: Pontifical Institute of Mediaeval Studies, 1979), 34–35. See also Miriam Schmitt, "Gertrud of Helfta: Her Monastic Milieu (1256–1301) and Her Spirituality," in *Cistercian Monastic Women: Hidden Springs*, Medieval Religious Women, CS 113 (Kalamazoo, MI: Cistercian Publications, 1995), 476.

writings thus provide further shading and contouring to our contemporary understandings of both medieval purgatorial piety and women's numerous and varied constructions of gender. Based on the ground-breaking work of Patricia Hill Collins on intersectionality, recent multiracial and postcolonial feminist theories show how a variety of inequalities have been constructed within class, race, religious status, gender, and sexual orientation, and have interlocked with and affected one another.[55] In particular, scholars have shown how gender categories have been constructed within other categories of difference (e.g., social status, religious, or ethnic difference).[56] Medievalist Sharon Farmer has shown how variations within these categories of difference, particularly social and religious status, have resulted in not one stereotype of maleness and one of femaleness, but several.[57] This work suggests that Gertrude's socialization and religious authority at Helfta may have contributed to her innovative gender constructions. Perhaps Gertrude was not as concerned as her contemporaries about proving her female authority because it was never challenged in a real way. In her day-to-day life, Gertrude lived in an environment in which she was sought out for spiritual counsel because of her wisdom, intellect, and mystical visions. While she never held an official position at the monastery at Helfta, she was even from childhood distinguished within the

[55] See for example Patricia Hill Collins, *Black Feminist Thought: Knowledge, Consciousness, and the Politics of Empowerment*, 2nd ed. (New York: Routledge, 2000). See also Cherríe Moraga and Gloria Anzaldúa, eds., *This Bridge Called My Back: Writings by Radical Women of Color* (Watertown, MA: Persephone Press, 1981); Maxine Baca Zinn and Bonnie Thornton Dill, "Theorizing Difference from Multiracial Feminism," *Feminist Studies* 22 (1996): 321–31.

[56] Sharon Farmer, "The Beggar's Body: Intersections of Gender and Social Status in High Medieval Paris," in *Monks and Nuns, Saints and Outcasts: Religion in Medieval Society: Essays in Honor of Lester K. Little*, ed. Sharon Farmer and Barbara H. Rosenwein (Ithaca, NY: Cornell University Press, 2000), 153.

[57] Farmer, "The Beggar's Body"; Sharon Farmer, "Introduction" in *Gender and Difference in the Middle Ages*, eds. Sharon Farmer and Carol Braun Pasternack, Medieval Cultures 32 (Minneapolis, MN: The University of Minnesota Press, 2003), ix–xxvii.

community for her keen intellect.[58] She did not understand her femaleness as a liability for her rationality, because the environment within which she lived did not make it one.

Gertrude makes a substantial contribution to the tradition of eucharistic theology and theological anthropology through her main teaching: that the human person, regardless of gender, as a body-soul composite, encounters both Christ's humanity and divinity in eucharistic communion. Yet what is most important about this eucharistic understanding of Gertrude is her challenge to the age-old human tendency to harden difference into dichotomy. By writing her religious beliefs so articulately and by believing so confidently in who she was, she ignores and therefore challenges the hierarchies and polarizing trends of holding up soul and mind over against body, divinity over against humanity, theologians over against mystics, men over against women. Gertrude the Great of Helfta thus offers contemporary theologians a way forward in overcoming the dichotomies that have been made out of difference—something central to the claim of Christianity, which celebrates the divine becoming human.

---

[58] Gertrude, *Herald* 1.1.2 (CF 35:38; SCh 139:120).

Bibliography

Works by Gertrude the Great of Helfta

The Exercises of Saint Gertrude. Trans. Columba Hart. Westminster, MD: Newman, 1956.

The Herald of Divine Love. Trans. and ed. Margaret Winkworth. New York: Paulist Press, 1993.

The Herald of God's Loving Kindness, Books One and Two. Trans. Alexandra Barratt. CF 35. Kalamazoo, MI: Cistercian Publications, 1991.

The Herald of God's Loving Kindness, Book Three. Trans. Alexandra Barratt. CF 63. Kalamazoo, MI: Cistercian Publications, 1999.

The Herald of God's Loving Kindness, Book Four. Trans. Alexandra Barratt. CF 85. Collegeville, MN: Cistercian Publications, 2018.

Insinuationes divinae pietatis seu vita et revelationes S. Gertrudis virginis et abbatissae ordinis S. Benedicti, vol. 1. Trans. Nicholas Canteleu. Paris: Léonard, 1662.

The Life and Revelations of Saint Gertrude: Virgin and Abbess, of the Order of St. Benedict. Trans. M. Frances Clare Cusack. 2nd ed. London: Burns and Oates, 1876.

Oeuvres spirituelles I: Les Exercices. Trans. Jacques Hourlier and Albert Schmitt. SCh 127. Paris: Les Éditions du Cerf, 1967.

Oeuvres spirituelles II: Le Héraut, Livres I et II. Trans. Pierre Doyère. SCh 139. Paris: Les Éditions du Cerf, 1968.

Oeuvres spirituelles III: Le Héraut, Livre III. Trans. Pierre Doyère. SCh 143. Paris: Les Éditions du Cerf, 1968.

Oeuvres spirituelles IV: Le Héraut, Livre IV. Trans. Jean-Marie Clément, the Nuns of Wisques, and Bernard de Vregille. SCh 255. Paris: Les Éditions du Cerf, 1978.

Oeuvres spirituelles V: Le Héraut, Livre V. Trans. Jean-Marie Clément, the Nuns of Wisques, and Bernard de Vregille. SCh 331. Paris: Les Éditions du Cerf, 1986.

Sanctae Gertrudis Magnae, virginis ordinis sanctae Benedicti, Legatus divinae pietatis, accedunt ejusdem Exercitia spiritualia, vol. 1 of Revelationes Gertrudianae ac Mechtildianae. Ed. Louis Paquelin. Paris: Oudin, 1877.

Spiritual Exercises. Trans. Gertrud Jaron Lewis and Jack Lewis. CF 49. Kalamazoo, MI: Cistercian Publications, 1989.

Other Primary Sources from Helfta

Mechthild of Hackeborn, *The Book of Special Grace*. Trans. Barbara Newman. New York/Mahwah, NJ: Paulist Press, 2018.

————. *The Booke of Gostlye Grace of Mechtild of Hackeborn*. Ed. Theresa A. Halligan. Toronto: Pontifical Institute of Mediaeval Studies, 1979.

————. *Le Livre de la Grâce Spéciale: Révélations de Sainte Mechtilde, Vierge de l'Ordre de saint-Benoit*. Trans. the Nuns of Wisques, from the Latin edition of Solesmes. Tours: A. Mame, 1921.

————. "Letters from Mechthild of Hackeborn to a Friend, a Laywoman in the World Taken from the 'Book of Special Grace' Book IV, Chapter 59." In *Vox Mystica: Essays on Medieval Mysticism in Honor of Professor Valerie M. Lagorio*, edited by Anne Clark Bartlett, et al. Cambridge: D. S. Brewer, 1995. 173–76.

————. *Liber Specialis Gratiae*. Ed. the Monks of Solesmes (Louis Paquelin). *Revelationes Gertrudianae ac Mechtildianae*, vol. 2. Paris: Oudin, 1877.

Mechthild of Magdeburg. *"Das Fliessende Licht Der Gottheit."* Ed. Hans Neumann and Gisela Vollmann-Profe. Munich: Artemis-Verlag, 1990, 1993.

————. *The Flowing Light of the Godhead*. Trans. Frank Tobin. New York/Mahwah, NJ: Paulist Press, 1998.

Other Primary Sources

Anselm. *The Prayers and Meditations of St. Anselm*. Trans. Benedicta Ward. Harmondsworth, Middlesex, UK: Penguin, 1973.

Aristotle. "On Sense and Sensible Objects." In *On the Soul. Parva naturalia*. Cambridge, MA: Harvard University Press, 1957. 205–83.

Augustine. *The City of God*. Trans. Marcus Dods. New York: Modern Library, 1950.

———. *Confessions*. Trans. Henry Chadwick. Oxford: Oxford University Press, 1991.

———. *De Doctrina Christiana*. Ed. and trans. R. P. H. Green. Oxford Early Christian Texts. Ed. Henry Chadwick. Oxford: Clarendon Press, 1995.

———. *Eighty-Three Different Questions*. Trans. David L. Mosher. The Fathers of the Church, vol. 70. Washington, DC: The Catholic University of America Press, 2002.

———. *The Trinity*. Trans. Stephen McKenna. Fathers of the Church. Washington, DC: Catholic University of America Press, 1963.

Bernard of Clairvaux. *On the Song of Songs I*. Trans. Kilian J. Walsh. CF 4. Kalamazoo, MI: Cistercian Publications, 1976.

———. *On the Song of Songs II*. Trans. Kilian J. Walsh. CF 7. Kalamazoo, MI: Cistercian Publications, 1976.

———. *On the Song of Songs III*. Trans. Kilian J. Walsh and Irene M. Edmonds. CF 31. Kalamazoo, MI: Cistercian Publications, 1979.

———. Sancti Bernardi Opera. Ed. Jean Leclercq, et al. Rome: Editiones Cistercienses, 1957–1977 (SBOp).

———. *Selected Works*. Trans. G. R. Evans. Classics of Western Spirituality Series. New York: Paulist Press, 1987.

———. *Sermones super Cantica canticorum*. SBOp 1–2.

Biblia Vulgata iuxta Vulgatam Clementinam nova editio. Ed. Alberto Colunga and Laurentio Turrado. Biblioteca de Autores Cristianos, 14. Madrid: La Editorial Catolica, 1985.

Hildegard of Bingen. *Liber divinorum operum*. PL 197:885.

———. *Scivias*. Ed. Adelgundis Führkötter and Angela Carlevaris. Corpus Christianorum, Continuatio Mediaevalis 48. Turnhout, Belgium: Brepols, 1978.

Le pontifical romano-germanique du dixième siècle I: Le texte 1. Città del Vaticano: Biblioteca Apostolica Vaticana, 1963.

Lombard, Peter. *The Sentences. Book 1: The Mystery of the Trinity*. Trans. Giulio Silano. Mediaeval Sources in Translation, 42. Toronto: Pontifical Institute of Mediaeval Studies, 2007.

Origen. *The Commentary of Origen on St. John's Gospel*, vol. 1. Ed. A. E. Brooke. Cambridge: Cambridge University Press, 1896.

———. *Contra Celsum*. Trans. Henry Chadwick. Cambridge: Cambridge University Press, 1953.

———. *On First Principles*. Trans. G. W. Butterworth. Gloucester, MA: Peter Smith, 1973.

———. *Origen*. Trans. A. S. Worrall. Ed. Henri Crouzel. San Francisco: Harper and Row, 1989.

———. *The Song of Songs: Commentary and Homilies*. Trans. R. P. Lawson. Ancient Christian Writers, 26. New York: Paulist Press, 1957.

Richard of Saint Victor. *Les douze patriarches, ou, Beniamin minor. Texte critique et traduction*. Ed. Jean Châtillon and Monique Duchet-Suchaux. SCh 419. Paris: Les Éditions du Cerf, 1997.

The Rule of Saint Benedict in English. Ed. Timothy Fry. Collegeville, MN: Liturgical Press, 1982.

"The Vita of Edith." In *Writing the Wilton Women: Goscelin's Legend of Edith and Liber confortatorius*. Trans. and ed. Michael Wright and Kathleen Loncar. Turnhout: Brepols, 2004. 23–67.

William of Saint-Thierry. *Exposition on the Song of Songs* (trans. of "Sur le Cantique"). The Works of William of St. Thierry, 2. Trans. Mother Columba Hart. CF 6. Spencer, MA: Cistercian Publications, 1970.

———. *Meditations*. Trans. Sister Penelope. CF 3. Kalamazoo, MI: Cistercian Publications, 1977.

———. *Oraisons méditatives*. Trans. Jacques Hourlier. SCh 324. Paris: Les Éditions du Cerf, 1985.

William of Saint-Thierry, Arnold of Bonneval, and Geoffrey of Auxerre. *The First Life of Bernard of Clairvaux*. Trans. Hilary Costello. CF 76. Collegeville, MN: Cistercian Publications, 2015.

———. *St. Bernard of Clairvaux: The Story of his Life as recorded in the Vita Prima Bernardi by certain of his contemporaries, William of St. Thierry, Arnold of Bonnevaux, Geoffrey and Philip of Clairvaux, and Odo of Deuil*. Trans. Geoffrey Webb and Adrian Walker. Westminster, MD: Newman Press, 1960.

———. *Vita prima Bernardi*. PL 185:225–416.

Secondary Sources

Allen, Prudence. *The Concept of Woman: Volume II: The Early Humanist Reformation, 1250–1500.* Grand Rapids, MI: Wm B. Eerdmans Publishing, 2002.

Andersen, Elizabeth A. "Mechthild von Magdeburg: Her Creativity and Her Audience." In *Women, the Book and the Godly,* edited by Lesley Smith and Jane H. M. Taylor. Cambridge: D. S. Brewer, 1995. 77–88.

———. *The Voices of Mechthild of Magdeburg.* Oxford and New York: Peter Lang, 2000.

Anderson, Luke. "The Rhetorical Epistemology in Saint Bernard's Super Cantica." In *Bernardus Magister: Papers Presented at the Nonacentenary Celebration of the Birth of Saint Bernard of Clairvaux, Kalamazoo, Michigan, Sponsored by the Institute of Cistercian Studies, Western Michigan University, 10–13 May 1990,* edited by John R. Sommerfeldt. CS 135. Spencer, MA: Cistercian Publications, 1992. 95–128.

Ankermann, Maren. "Der 'Legatus divinae pietatis'–Gestaltete Mystik?" In *Freiheit des Herzens: Mystik bei Gertrud von Helfta,* edited by Michael Bangert. Mystik und Mediävistik. Münster: Lit, 2004. 37–56.

———. *Gertrud die Grosse von Helfta: eine Studie zum Spannungsverhältnis von religiöser Erfahrung und literarischer Gestaltung in mystischen Werken.* Göppingen: Kümmerle Verlag, 1997.

Appleby, David F. "The Priority of Sight according to Peter the Venerable." *Mediaeval Studies* 60 (1998): 123–57.

Astell, Ann W. " 'Hidden Manna': Bernard of Clairvaux, Gertrude of Helfta, and the Monastic Art of Humility." In *Eating Beauty: the Eucharist and the Spiritual Arts of the Middle Ages.* Ithaca, NY: Cornell University Press, 2006. 62–98.

Baer, Helmut David. "The Fruit of Charity: Using the Neighbor in De Doctrina Christiana." *The Journal of Religious Ethics* 24, no. 1 (1996): 47–64.

Bangert, Michael. *Demut in Freiheit: Studien zur geistlichen Lehre im Werk Gertruds von Helfta.* Studien zur systematischen und spirituellen Theologie, 21. Würzburg: Echter, 1997.

———. "Die sozio-kulturelle Situation des Klosters St. Maria in Helfta." In *"Vor dir steht die leere Schale meiner Sehnsucht": Die Mystik der Frauen von Helfta,* edited by Michael Bangert and Hildegund Keul. Leipzig: Benno, 1998. 29–47.

————. "A Mystic Pursues Narrative Theology: Biblical Speculation and Contemporary Imagery in Gertrude of Helfta." *Magistra* 2, no. 2 (Winter 1996): 3–20.

Barratt, Alexandra. "Infancy and Education in the Writings of Gertrud the Great of Helfta." *Magistra* 6, no. 2 (Winter 2000): 17–30.

Bennet, Renée. "The Song of Wisdom in Bernard's Sermones Super Cantica Canticorum," CSQ 30, no. 2 (1995): 147–78.

Bennewitz, Ingrid, and Ingrid Kasten, eds. *Genderdiskurse und Körperbilder im Mittelalter: eine Bilanzierung nach Butler und Laquer.* Münster: Lit, 2002.

Berman, Constance H. *The Cistercian Evolution: The Invention of a Religious Order in Twelfth-Century Europe.* Philadelphia: University of Pennsylvania Press, 2000.

————. "Were there Twelfth-Century Cistercian Nuns?" *Church History: Studies in Christianity and Culture* 68, no. 4 (December 1999): 824–64.

Biernoff, Suzannah. *Sight and Embodiment in the Middle Ages.* Basingstoke, UK: Palgrave Macmillan, 2002.

Blamires, Alcuin. "Paradox in the Medieval Gender Doctrine of Head and Body." In *Medieval Theology and the Natural Body*, edited by Peter Biller and A. J. Minnis. York Studies in Medieval Theology. York: York Medieval Press, 1997. 13–29.

Bostock, D. G. "Quality and Corporeity in Origen." In *Origeniana Secunda*, edited by Henri Quacquarelli Crouzel. Rome: Edizioni dell'Ateneo, 1980. 323–37.

Boyle, Leonard E. "Popular Piety in the Middle Ages: What is Popular?" *Florilegium: Carleton University Annual Papers on Classical Antiquity and the Middle Ages* 4 (1982): 184–93.

Bredero, Adriaan H. *Christendom and Christianity in the Middle Ages.* Grand Rapids, MI: Wm. B. Eerdmans Publishing, 1994.

Brown, Peter. *The Body and Society: Men, Women, and Sexual Renunciation in Early Christianity.* Twentieth-Anniversary ed. New York: Columbia University Press, 2008.

Bullough, Vern L. "Medieval, Medical and Scientific Views of Women." *Viator* 4 (1973): 485–501.

Bynum, Caroline Walker. ". . . And Women His Humanity: Female Imagery in the Religious Writing of the Later Middle Ages." In *Gender and Religion: On the Complexity of Symbols,* edited by Caroline Walker Bynum, Steven Harrell, and Paula Richman. Boston, MA: Beacon Press, 1986. 257–88.

———. "The Blood of Christ in the Later Middle Ages." *Church History* 71, no. 4 (2002): 685–714.

———. *Fragmentation and Redemption: Essays on Gender and the Human Body in Medieval Religion.* New York: Zone Books, 1992.

———. *Holy Feast and Holy Fast: The Religious Significance of Food to Medieval Women.* Berkeley: University of California Press, 1987.

———. *Jesus as Mother: Studies in the Spirituality of the High Middle Ages.* Berkeley: University of California Press, 1982.

———. *The Resurrection of the Body in Western Christianity, 200–1336.* New York: Columbia University Press, 1995.

———. "Women Mystics and Eucharistic Devotion in the Thirteenth Century." *Women's Studies* 11 (1984): 179–214.

———. "Women Mystics in the Thirteenth Century: The Case of the Nuns of Helfta." In *Jesus as Mother: Studies in the Spirituality of the High Middle Ages.* Berkeley: University of California Press, 1982. 186–209.

———. *Wonderful Blood: Theology and Practice in Late Medieval Northern Germany and Beyond.* Philadelphia: University of Pennsylvania Press, 2007.

Cadden, Joan. *Meanings of Sex Difference in the Middle Ages: Medicine, Science, and Culture.* Cambridge, UK: Cambridge University Press, 1993.

Canévet, Mariette. "Sens spirituel," In *Dictionnaire de spiritualité ascétique et mystique, doctrine et histoire,* edited by Marcel Viller, et al. Paris: Beauchesne, 1937. 15:598–619.

Caron, Ann Marie. "Mechthild of Hackeborn, Prophet of Divine Praise: To Sing God's Praise, To Live God's Song." CSQ 36, no. 2 (2001): 145–61.

Carruthers, Mary. *The Book of Memory: A Study of Memory in Medieval Culture.* 2nd ed. Cambridge Studies in Medieval Literature, 70. Cambridge, UK: Cambridge University Press, 2008.

———. *The Craft of Thought: Meditation, Rhetoric, and the Making of Images, 400–1200.* Cambridge Studies in Medieval Literature, 70. Cambridge, UK: Cambridge University Press, 2000.

Carruthers, Mary, and Jan M. Ziolkowski, eds. *The Medieval Craft of Memory: An Anthology of Texts and Pictures*. Philadelphia, PA: University of Pennsylvania Press, 2002.

Casey, Michael. "Gertrud of Helfta and Bernard of Clairvaux: A Reappraisal." *Tjurunga* 35 (1988): 3–23.

———. *A Thirst for God: Spiritual Desire in Bernard of Clairvaux's Sermons on the Song of Songs*. CS 77. Kalamazoo, MI: Cistercian Publications, 1988.

Castelli, Elizabeth A. " 'I Will Make Mary Male': Pieties of the Body and Gender Transformation of Christian Women in Late Antiquity." In *Body Guards: The Cultural Politics of Gender Ambiguity*, edited by Julia Epstein and Kristina Straub. New York: Routledge, 1991. 29–49.

Cavadini, John C. "The Sweetness of the Word: Salvation and Rhetoric in Augustine's *De doctrina christiana*." In De doctrina christiana: *A Classic of Western Culture*, edited by Duane W. H. Arnold and Pamela Bright. Notre Dame: University of Notre Dame Press, 1995. 164–81.

Cawley, Martinus. "The Ancient Usages as 'Cantorial Science.' " CSQ 34, no. 1 (1999): 3–18.

Chen, Sheryl Frances. "Bernard's Prayer Before the Crucifix that Embraced Him: Cistercians and Devotion to the Wounds of Christ." CSQ 29, no. 1 (1994): 47–51.

Cherewatuk, Karen, and Ulrike Wiethaus, eds. *Dear Sister: Medieval Women and the Epistolary Genre*. Philadelphia: University of Pennsylvania Press, 1993.

Chidester, David. *Word and Light: Seeing, Hearing, and Religious Discourse*. Champaign-Urbana: University of Illinois Press, 1991.

Clark, Anne L. "The Priesthood of the Virgin Mary: Gender Trouble in the Twelfth Century." *Journal of Feminist Studies in Religion* 18, no. 1 (Spring 2002): 5–24.

———. "An Uneasy Triangle: Jesus, Mary, and Gertrude of Helfta." *Maria: A Journal of Marian Studies* 1 (2000): 37–56.

Clemons, Cheryl. "The Relationship between Devotion to the Eucharist and Devotion to the Humanity of Jesus in the Writings of St. Gertrude of Helfta." Ph.D. dissertation. Catholic University of America, 1996.

Coleman, Janet. *Ancient and Medieval Memories: Studies in the Reconstruction of the Past.* Cambridge: Cambridge University Press, 1992.

Collins, Patricia Hill. *Black Feminist Thought: Knowledge, Consciousness, and the Politics of Empowerment.* 2nd ed. New York: Routledge, 2000.

Coolman, Boyd Taylor. *Knowing God by Experience: The Spiritual Senses in the Theology of William of Auxerre.* Washington, DC: Catholic University of America Press, 2004.

DeFranza, Megan K. *Sex Difference in Christian Theology: Male, Female, and Intersex in the Image of God.* Grand Rapids, MI: Wm. B. Eerdmans Publishing, 2015.

Degler-Spengler, Brigitte. "The Incorporation of Cistercian Nuns into the Order in the Twelfth and Thirteenth Century." In *Hidden Springs: Cistercian Monastic Women*, vol. 1, edited by John Nichols and Lillian Thomas Shank. Medieval Religious Women Series. CS 113. Kalamazoo, MI: Cistercian Publications, 1995. 85–135.

Dewart, Joanne E. McWilliam. *Death and Resurrection.* Wilmington, DL: Michael Glazier, 1986.

Dickens, Andrea Janelle. "Unus Spiritus cum Deo: Six Medieval Cistercian Christologies." Ph.D. dissertation. University of Virginia, 2005.

Dolan, Gilbert. *St. Gertrude the Great.* London: Sands, 1913.

Dombi, Markus. "Waren die hll. Gertrud und Mechtild Benedikterinnen oder Cistercienserinnen?" *Cistercienser-Chronik* 25 (1913): 257–68.

Doyère, Pierre. "Sainte Gertrude et les sens spirituels." *Revue d'ascétique et de mystique* 144 (1960): 429–46.

Dumoutet, Edoaurd. *Le Christ selon la chair et la vie liturgique au Moyen-Âge.* Paris: Beauchesne, 1932.

Dutton, Marsha L. "A Case for Canonization: The Argument of the *Vita Prima Sancti Bernardi.*" CSQ 52, no. 2 (2017): 131–60.

———. "The Cistercian Source: Aelred, Bonaventure, and Ignatius." In *Goad and Nail: Studies in Medieval Cistercian History, X*, edited by E. Rozanne Elder. CS 84. Kalamazoo, MI: Cistercian Publications, 1985. 151–78.

———. "Eat, Drink, and Be Merry: The Eucharistic Spirituality of the Cistercian Fathers." In *Erudition at God's Service: Studies in Medieval Cistercian History, XI*, edited by John R. Sommerfeldt. CS 98. Kalamazoo, MI: Cistercian Publications, 1987. 1–31.

————. "Intimacy and Imitation: The Humanity of Christ in Cistercian Spirituality." In *Erudition at God's Service: Studies in Medieval Cistercian History, XI,* edited by John R. Sommerfeldt. CS 98. Kalamazoo, MI: Cistercian Publications, 1987. 33–70.

————. "'When I Was a Child': Spiritual Infancy and God's Maternity in Augustine's Confessiones." In *Collectanea Augustiniana.* Ed. Joseph C. Schnaubelt and Frederick Van Fleteren. New York: Lang, 1990. 113–40.

Eckenstein, Lina. *Women under Monasticism: Chapters on Saint-Lore and Convent Life between A.D. 500 and A.D. 1500.* Reprint ed. New York, NY: Russell and Russell, 1963.

Eggemann, Ina. "Betende Theologie: Beten und Beten-Lehren als Ort theologischer Erkenntnis im Exerzitienbuch Gertruds von Helfta." In *Aufbruch zu neuer Gottesrede: Die Mystik der Gertrud von Helfta,* edited by Siegfried Ringler. Ostfildern: Matthias Grünewald, 2008. 153–66.

Eliass, Claudia. *Die Frau ist die Quelle der Weisheit: Weibliches Selbstverständnis in der Frauenmystik des 12. und 13. Jahrhunderts.* Frauen in Geschichte und Gesellschaft, Band 28. Pfaffenweiler: Centaurus-Verlangsgesellschaft, 1995.

Evans, G. R. *Bernard of Clairvaux.* Great Medieval Thinkers Series. New York: Oxford University Press, 2000.

Everson, Stephen. *Aristotle on Perception.* Oxford: Clarendon Press, 1997.

Farmer, Sharon. "The Beggar's Body: Intersections of Gender and Social Status in High Medieval Paris." In *Monks and Nuns, Saints and Outcasts,* edited by Sharon Farmer and Barbara H. Rosenwein. Religion in Medieval Society: Essays in Honor of Lester K. Little. Ithaca, NY: Cornell University Press, 2000. 153–71.

————. "Introduction." In *Gender and Difference in the Middle Ages,* edited by Sharon Farmer and Carol Braun Pasternack. Medieval Cultures, 32. Minneapolis, MN: Minneapolis Press, 2003. ix–xxvii.

Farmer, Sharon, and Carol Braun Pasternack, eds. *Gender and Difference in the Middle Ages.* Medieval Cultures, 32. Minneapolis, MN: Minneapolis Press, 2003.

Finnegan, Mary Jeremy. "Idiom of Women Mystics." *Mystics Quarterly* 13 (1987): 65–72.

————. "'Similitudes' in the Writings of Saint Gertrude of Helfta." *Mediaeval Studies* 19 (1957): 48–54.

———. *The Women of Helfta: Scholars and Mystics.* Athens: University of Georgia Press, 1991.

Fiorenza, Elisabeth Schüssler. *Bread Not Stone: The Challenge of Feminist Biblical Interpretation.* Boston: Beacon Press, 1984.

Fischer, Karl-Hubert. *Zwischen Minne und Gott: Die geistesgeschichtlichen Voraussetzungen des deutschen Minnesangs mit besonderer Berücksichtigung der Frömmigkeitsgeschichte.* Frankfurt am Main; New York: Peter Lang, 1985.

Forman, Mary. "Gertrud of Helfta's 'Herald of Divine Love': Revelations through *Lectio Divina.*" *Magistra* 3, no. 2 (Winter 1997): 3–27.

Fortin, E. L. "Saint Augustin et la doctrine néo-platonicienne de l'âme." In *Augustinus Magister,* vol. 3. Paris: Études augustiniennes, 1954. 371–80.

Fredriksen, Paula. "Beyond the Body/Soul Dichotomy: Augustine on Paul against the Manichees and the Pelagians." *Recherches augustiniennes* 23 (1988): 87–114.

Freed, John B. "Urban Development and the 'Cura monialium' in Thirteenth-Century Germany." *Viator* 3 (1972): 311–27.

Freeman, Elizabeth. "Nuns." In *The Cambridge Companion to the Cistercian Order,* edited by Mette Birkedal Bruun. Cambridge: Cambridge University Press, 2013. 100–11.

Fulton, Rachel. "'Taste and See that the Lord is Sweet' (Ps. 33:9): The Flavor of God in the Monastic West." *Journal of Religion* 86, no. 2 (2006): 169–204.

Geary, Patrick J. *Phantoms of Remembrance: Memory and Oblivion at the End of the First Millennium.* Princeton, NJ: Princeton University Press, 1994.

Gilson, Étienne. *The Mystical Theology of St. Bernard.* Trans. A. H. C. Downes. New York: Sheed and Ward, 1940.

Gosebrink, Hildegard. "In der Sinne Achtsamkeit—Leib und Sinne in Gertruds 'Exercitia spiritualia.'" In *Aufbruch neuer Gottesrede: Die Mystik der Gertrud von Helfta,* edited by Siegfried Ringler. Ostfildern: Grünewald, 2008. 76–92.

Grimes, Laura Marie. "Bedeutung der Liturgie im Werk Gertrudes von Helfta." In *"Vor dir steht die leere Schale meiner Sehnsucht": Die Mystik der Frauen von Helfta,* edited by Michael Bangert and Hildegund Keul. Leipzig: Benno, 1998. 68–80.

224 *This Is My Body*

———. "Theology as Conversation: Gertrude of Helfta and her Sisters as Readers of Augustine." Ph.D. dissertation. University of Notre Dame, 2004.

———. "Writing as Birth: The Composition of Gertrud of Helfta's *Herald of God's Loving Kindness*." CSQ 42, no. 3 (2007): 329–45.

Grössler, Hermann. "Die Blütezheit des Kloster Helfta bei Eisleben." *Jahres-Bericht über das Königliche Gymnasium zu Eisleben von Ostern 1886 bis Ostern 1887.* Eisleben: Programm des kaiserlich Königliche academischen Gymnasiums, 1887. 1–38.

Haas, Alois Maria. "Mechthilds von Magdeburg dichterische heimlichkeit." In *Gotes und der werlde hulde: Literatur im Mittelalter und Neuzeit. Festschrift für Heinz Rupp zum 70. Geburtstag,* edited by Rüdiger Schnell. Bern/Stuttgart: Francke, 1989. 206–23.

Hale, Rosemary Drage. " 'Taste and See, for God is Sweet': Sensory Perception and Memory in Medieval Christian Mystical Experience." In *Vox Mystica: Essays on Medieval Mysticism in Honor of Professor Valerie M. Lagorio,* edited by Anne Clark Bartlett, et al. Cambridge: D. S. Brewer, 1995. 3–14.

Halligan, Teresa. "The Community at Helfta. Its Spirituality and Celebrated Members." In *The Booke of Gostlye Grace of Mechtild of Hackeborn.* Toronto: Pontifical Institute of Mediaeval Studies, 1979.

Hamburger, Jeffrey S. "Speculations on Speculation: Vision and Perception in the Theory and Practice of Mystical Devotion." In *Deutsche mystik im abendlandischen Zusammenhang: Neu erschlossene Texte, neue methodische Ansätze, neue theoretische Konzepte. Kolloquium Kloster Fischingen 1998,* edited by Walter Haug and Wolfram Schneider-Lastin. Tübingen: Max Niemeyer Verlag, 2000. 353–408.

———. *The Visual and the Visionary: Art and Female Spirituality in Late Medieval Germany.* New York: Zone Books, 1998.

Harl, Marguerite. *Origène et la fonction révélatrice du verbe incarné.* Paris: Éditions du Seuil, 1958.

Harper, John. *The Forms and Orders of Western Liturgy: From the Tenth to the Eighteenth Century.* Oxford: Clarendon Press, 1991.

Harris, Jennifer A. "The Fate of Place in the Twelfth Century: Creation, Restoration, and Body in the Writing of Bernard of Clairvaux." *Viator* 30, no. 2 (2008): 119–41.

Harrison, Anna. "I Am Wholly Your Own: Liturgical Piety and Community Among the Nuns of Helfta." *Church History* 78, no. 3 (2009): 549–83.

————. "Oh! What Treasure is in this Book?" Writing, Reading, and Community at the Monastery of Helfta," *Viator* 39, no. 1 (2008): 75–106.

————. "Sense of Community Among the Nuns at Helfta." Ph.D. dissertation. Columbia University, 2007.

Harrison, Anna, and Caroline Walker Bynum. "Gertrude, Gender, and the Composition of the Herald of Divine Love." In *Frieheit des Herzens: Mystik bei Gertrud von Helfta*, edited by Michael Bangert. Mystik und Mediävistik 2. Münster: Lit, 2004. 57–76.

Harrison, Carol. "Spiritual Senses." In *Augustine through the Ages*, edited by Allan Fitzgerald. Grand Rapids, MI: Wm. B. Eerdmans Publishing, 1999. 767–68.

Harvey, Susan Ashbrook. *Scenting Salvation: Ancient Christianity and the Olfactory Imagination. Transformation of the Classical Heritage*, 42. Berkeley: University of California Press, 2006.

Heimbach, Marianne. *"Der ungelehrte Mund" als Autorität: mystische Erfahrung als Quelle kirchlich-prophetischer Rede im Werk Mechthilds von Magdeburg*. Stuttgart-Bad Cannstatt: Frommann-Holzboog, 1989.

Hennessey, Lawrence R. "A Philosophical Issue in Origen's Eschatology: The Three Senses of Incorporeality." In *Origeniana Quinta: Papers of the 5th International Origen Congress, Boston College, 14–18 August 1989*, edited by Robert Daly. Leuven: Peeters Press, 1992. 373–80.

Hollywood, Amy M. *The Soul as Virgin Wife: Mechthild of Magdeburg, Marguerite Porete, and Meister Eckhart*. Notre Dame: University of Notre Dame Press, 1995.

Holsinger, Bruce W. *Music, Body, and Desire in Medieval Culture: Hildegard of Bingen to Chaucer*. Stanford, CA: Stanford University Press, 2001.

Hontoir, Camille M. "La dévotion au Saint Sacrement chez les premiers cisterciens (XIIᵉ–XIIIᵉ siècles)." In *Studia Eucharista. DCC anni a condito festo Sanctissimi Corporis Christ 1246–1946*, edited by Stephanus Axters. Antwerp: De Nederlandsche Boekhandel, 1946. 144–47.

Ivánka, Endre von. "L'union à Dieu: La structure de l'âme selon S. Bernard." In *Saint Bernard Théologien*, edited by Jean Leclercq. *Analecta Sacri Ordinis Cisterciensis*. Rome: Editiones cistercienses, 1953. 202–8.

Izbicki, Thomas M. *The Eucharist in Medieval Canon Law*. Cambridge: Cambridge University Press, 2015.

Jacquart, Danielle J., and Claude Alexandre Thomasset, eds. *Sexuality and Medicine in the Middle Ages*. Princeton, NJ: Princeton University Press, 1988.

Jager, Eric. "The Book of the Heart: Reading and Writing the Medieval Subject." *Speculum* 71, no. 1 (January 1996): 1–26.

Jantzen, Grace. *Power, Gender, and Christian Mysticism.* Cambridge: Cambridge University Press, 1995.

Javelet, Robert. "Saint Bonaventure et Richard de Saint Victor," In *Bonaventuriana. Miscellanea in onore di Jacques Guy Bougerol, OFM,* edited by Francisco de Asis Chavero Blanco. Rome: Edizioni Antonianum, 1988. 63–96.

Jensen, Robin M. *Baptismal Imagery in Early Christianity: Ritual, Visual, and Theological Dimensions.* Grand Rapids, MI: Baker Academic, 2012.

Johnson, Ella. "Bodily Language in the Spiritual Exercises of Gertrud the Great of Helfta." *Magistra* 14, no. 1 (2008): 79–107.

———. "'*In mei memoriam facietis*': Remembering Ritual and Refiguring 'Woman' in Gertrud the Great of Helfta's *Spiritualia Exercitia.*" In *Inventing Identities: Re-examining the Use of Memory, Imitation, and Imagination in the Texts of Medieval Religious Women,* edited by Bradley Herzog and Margaret Cotter-Lynch. Basingstoke, UK: Palgrave Macmillan, 2012. 165–86.

———. "Liturgical Opportunities for 'Deep Crying unto Deep': The Rhetorical Function of Now/Then Dualities in Gertrud of Helfta." *Medieval Mystical Theology* 24, no. 1 (2015): 45–58.

———. "The Nightingale of Christ's Redemption Song: Mechthild of Hackeborn's Musical Apostolate." In *Music, Theology, and Justice,* edited by Michael O'Connor, Hyun-Ah Kim, and Christina Labriola. Lanham, MD: Lexington Books, 2017. 181–96.

———. "To Taste (*Sapere*) Wisdom (*Sapientia*): Eucharistic Devotion in the Writings of Gertrude of Helfta." *Viator* 44, no. 2 (2013): 175–99.

Jonas, Hans. "The Nobility of Sight: A Study in the Phenomenology of the Senses." In *Phenomenon of Life: Toward a Philosophical Biology.* Chicago: University of Chicago Press, 1982. 135–56.

Jones, Claire. "*Hostia jubilationis*: Psalm Citation, Eucharistic Prayer and Mystical Union in Gertrude of Helfta's *Exercitia Spiritualia.*" *Speculum* 89, no. 4 (2014): 1005–39.

Jungmann, Josef. *The Mass of the Roman Rite: Its Origins and Development (Missarum Sollemnia).* Trans. F. A. Brunner. 2 vols. New York: Benzinger, 1951, 1955.

Kay, Sarah, and Miri Rubin, eds. *Framing Medieval Bodies.* Manchester: Manchester University Press, 1996.

Kelly, J. N. D. *Early Christian Doctrines*. London: Adam and Charles Black, 1977.

Keul, Hildegund. "Das Sakrament des Wortes: Mystik und Seelsorge in den Brüchen der Zeit." In *Aufbruch zu neuer Gottesrede: Die Mystik der Gertrud von Helfta*, edited by Siegfried Ringler. Ostfildern: Grünewald, 2008. 167–81.

————. "Du bist ein inniger Kuss meines Mundes. Die Sprache der Mystik—eine Sprache der Erotik. Am Beispiel Mechthilds von Magdeburg." In *"Vor dir steht die leere Schale meiner Sehnsucht": Die Mystik der Frauen von Helfta*, edited by Hildegund Keul and Michael Bangert. Leipzig: Benno, 1998. 95–111.

Knowles, David. *The Monastic Order in England: A History of its Development from the Times of St. Dunstan to the Fourth Lateran Council, 940–1216*. 2nd ed. Cambridge: Cambridge University Press, 1963.

————. *The Religious Orders in England*. Cambridge: Cambridge University Press, 1948.

Korger, Matthias E. "Grundprobleme der augustinischen Erkenntnislehre: Erläutert am Beispiel von De Genesi ad litteram XII." *Recherches Augustiniennes* 2 (1962): 33–57.

Kristeva, Julia. "*Ego affectus est*. Bernard of Clairvaux: Affect, Desire, Love." In *Tales of Love*. Trans. Leon S. Roudiez. New York: Columbia University Press, 1987. 151–70.

Kruger, Steven F. *Dreaming in the Middle Ages*. Cambridge Studies in Medieval Literature, 14. Cambridge: Cambridge University Press, 1992.

Krühne, Max, ed. *Urkundenbuch der Klöster der Grafschaft Mansfeld*. Geschichtsquellen der Provinz Sachsen und angrenzender Gebiete, 20. Halle: Otto Hendel, 1888.

Lauwers, Michel, and Walter Simons. *Béguins et Béguines à Tournai au bas Moyen Âge: les communautés béguinales à Tournai du XIIIᵉ au XVᵉ siècle*. Tournai; Louvain-la-Neuve: Archives du chapitre cathédral; Université Catholique de Louvain, 1988.

Leclercq, Jean. "Aux sources des sermons sur les Cantiques." In *Receuil d'études sur saint Bernard et ses écrits*. Rome: Edizioni di storia et letteratura, 1962–1969. 275–319.

————. "De quelques procédés du style biblique du S. Bernard." In *Receuil d'études sur saint Bernard et ses écrits*. Rome: Edizioni di storia et letteratura, 1962. 260–63.

————. "Liturgy and Mental Prayer in the Life of Saint Gertrude." *Sponsa Regis* 32, no. 1 (September 1960): 1–5.

————. *The Love of Learning and the Desire for God: A Study of Monastic Culture*. New York: Fordham University Press, 1982.

————. *Monks and Love in Twelfth-Century France: Psycho-Historical Essays*. Oxford: Clarendon Press, 1979.

————. "Origène au XII siècle." *Irenikon* 24 (1951): 425–39.

————. "Sur le caractère littéraire des sermons de S. Bernard." In *Receuil d'études sur saint Bernard et ses écrits*. Rome: Edizioni di storia et letteratura, 1962. 163–210.

Lester, Anne E. *Creating Cistercian Nuns: The Women's Religious Movement and Its Reform in Thirteenth-Century Champagne*. Ithaca, NY: Cornell University Press, 2011.

L'Estrange, Elizabeth, and Alison More. "Representing Medieval Genders and Sexualities in Europe: Construction, Transformation, and Subversion, 600–1530." In *Representing Medieval Genders and Sexualities in Europe: Construction, Transformation, and Subversion, 600–1530*. New York and London: Routledge, 2011. 1–13.

Lewis, Gertrud Jaron. "Das Gottes- und Menschenbild im Werk einer mittelalterlichen Mystikerin: Uberlegungen zu Gertrud Von Helfta (1256–1302)." In *Gottes Nahe: religiöse Erfahrung in Mystik und Offenbarung*, edited by Paul Imhof. Wurzburg: Echter, 1990. 62–78.

————. "Gertrud of Helfta's *Legatus divinae pietatis* and *ein botte der götlichen miltekeit*: A Comparative Study of Major Themes." In *Mysticism: Medieval and Modern*, edited by Valerie Lagorio. Salzburg: Institut fur Anglistik und Amerikanistik, 1986. 58–71.

————. "God and the Human Being in the Writings of Gertrud of Helfta." *Vox Benedicta* 8 (1991): 297–322.

————. "Introduction," In Gertrud the Great of Helfta, *Spiritual Exercises*. Trans. Gertrud Jaron Lewis and Jack Lewis. CS 49. Kalamazoo, MI: Cistercian Publications, 1989. 1–18.

————. "*Libertas Cordis*: The Concept of Inner Freedom in St. Gertrud the Great of Helfta." CSQ 25, no. 1 (1990): 65–74.

Lewis, Gertrud Jaron, Frank Willaert, and Marie-José Govers. *Bibliographie zur deutschen Frauenmystik des Mittelalters*. Berlin: Erich Schmidt, 1989.

Lloyd, G. E. R. *Polarity and Analogy: Two Types of Argumentation in Early Greek Thought.* Bristol: Bristol Classics, 1987.

Lomperis, Linda, and Sarah Stanbury, eds. *Feminist Approaches to the Body in Medieval Literature.* New Cultural Studies. Philadelphia, PA: University of Pennsylvania Press, 1993.

Luddy, Ailbe J. *St. Gertrude the Great: Illustrious Cistercian Mystic.* Dublin: M. H. Gill and Son, Ltd., 1930.

Ludwig, Paul. "Les sens spirituels chez saint Augustin." *Dieu Vivant* 11 (1948): 81–105.

MacHaffie, Barbara. *Her Story: Women in Christian Tradition.* Minneapolis: Fortress, 2006.

Macy, Gary. *The Theologies of the Eucharist in the Early Scholastic Period: A Study of the Salvific Function of the Sacrament according to the Theologians, c. 1080–c. 1220.* Oxford; New York: Clarendon Press, 1984.

———. *Treasures from the Storeroom: Medieval Religion and the Eucharist.* Collegeville, MN: Liturgical Press, 1999.

Malone, Mary T. *Women & Christianity.* 3 vols. Maryknoll, NY: Orbis Books, 2000.

Markus, R. A. "The Eclipse of a Neo-Platonic Theme: Augustine and Gregory the Great on Visions and Prophecies." In *Neoplatonism and Early Christian Thought: Essays in Honor of A. H. Armstrong,* edited by H. J. Blumenthal. London: Variorum Publications, 1981. 204–11.

Marquardt-Spitzlei, Sabine B. "O Gott meines Herzens: Das Herz als Erfahrungsraum Gottes in den 'Exercitia spiritualia.' " In *Aufbruch zu neuer Gottesrede: Die Mystik der Gertrude von Helfta,* edited by Siegfried Ringler. Ostfildern: Matthias Grünewald Verlag, 2008. 46–60.

Marrou, Henri-Irénée. *The Resurrection and Saint Augustine's Theology of Human Values,* translated by Mary Consolate. Saint Augustine Lecture Series (1966). Villanova, PA: Villanova University, 1966.

Marrou, Henri, and A.-M. Bonnardière. "Le dogme de la résurrection des corps et la théologie des valeurs humaines selon l'enseignement de saint Augustin." *Revue des études augustiniennes* 12, nos. 1–2 (1966): 111–36.

McCulloch, Gillian. *The Deconstruction of Dualism in Theology.* Milton Keynes, UK: Paternoster Press, 2002.

McDonnell, Ernest W. *The Beguines and Beghards in Medieval Culture, with Special Emphasis on the Belgian Scene.* New York: Octagon Books, 1969.

McGinn, Bernard. *The Flowering of Mysticism: Men and Women in the New Mysticism (1200–1350).* New York: Crossroad, 1998.

———. *The Foundations of Mysticism: Origins to the Fifth Century.* New York: Crossroad, 1992.

———. "Freedom, Formation and Reformation: The Anthropological Roots of Saint Bernard's Spiritual Teaching." In *La dottrina della vita spirituale nelle opere di San Bernardo di Clairvaux: Atti del Convegno Internazionale. Rome, 11–15 settembre 1990. Analecta Cisterciensia 46.* Rome: Editiones Cistercienses, 1990. 91–114.

———. *The Growth of Mysticism: Gregory the Great through the Twelfth Century.* New York: Crossroad, 1994.

———. "Sur le caractère littéraire des sermons de S. Bernard." In *Receuil d'études sur saint Bernard et ses écrits.* Rome: Edizioni di storia et letteratura, 1962. 163–210.

McGuire, Brian Patrick. "Purgatory, the Communion of Saints, and Medieval Change." *Viator* 20 (1989): 61–84.

McNamara, Jo Ann. "The Herrenfrage: The Restructuring of the Gender System, 1050–1150." In *Medieval Masculinities: Regarding Men in the Middle Ages,* edited by Clare A. Lees. Minneapolis: University of Minnesota Press, 1994. 3–30.

———. "The Need to Give: Suffering and Female Sanctity in the Middle Ages." In *Images of Sainthood in Medieval Europe,* edited by Renate Blumenfeld-Kosinski and Timea Szell. Ithaca, NY: Cornell University Press, 1991. 199–221.

Michael, R. P. Émil. "Die hl. Mechthild und die hl. Gertrud die Grosse Benedictinerinnen?" *Zeitschrift für katholisches Theologie* 23 (1899): 548–52.

Miles, Margaret Ruth. *Augustine on the Body.* Missoula, MT: Scholars Press, 1979.

———. *Practicing Christianity: Critical Perspectives for an Embodied Spirituality.* New York: Crossroad, 1988.

———. "Vision: The Eye of the Body and the Eye of the Mind in Saint Augustine's *De trinitate* and *Confessions*." *Journal of Religion* 63, no. 2 (1983): 125–42.

Milhaven, John Giles. *Hadewijch and her Sisters: Other Ways of Loving and Knowing*. Albany, NY: State University of New York Press, 1993.

Mitchell, Nathan. *Cult and Controversy: The Worship of the Eucharist Outside Mass*. New York: Pueblo, 1982.

Moraga, Cherríe, and Gloria Anzaldúa, eds. *This Bridge Called My Back: Writings by Radical Women of Color*. Watertown, MA: Persephone Press, 1981.

Mourant, John A. *Augustine on Immortality*. Villanova, PA: Augustinian Institute, Villanova University, 1969.

Mouroux, Jean. "Sur les critères de l'expérience spirituelle d'aprés les Sermons sur le Cantique de Cantiques." In *Saint Bernard Théologien, Analecta Cisterciensia*. Rome: Editiones Cistercienses, 1953. 251–67.

Murk-Jansen, Saskia. *Brides in the Desert: The Spirituality of the Beguines*. Maryknoll, NY: Orbis Books, 1998.

Newman, Barbara. "Exchanging Hearts: A Medievalist Looks at Transplant Surgery." *Spiritus* 12, no. 1 (Spring 2012): 1–20.

———. *From Virile Woman to WomanChrist: Studies in Medieval Religion and Literature*. Middle Ages Series. Philadelphia: University of Pennsylvania Press, 1995.

———. " 'Iam cor meum non sit suum': Exchanging Hearts from Heloise to Helfta." In *From Knowledge to Beatitude: St. Victor, Twelfth-Century Scholars, and Beyond: Essays in Honor of Grover A. Zinn, Jr.*, edited by E. Ann Matter and Lesley Smith. Notre Dame, IN: University of Notre Dame Press, 2013. 281–99.

———. "Love's Arrows: Christ as Cupid in Late Medieval Art and Devotion." In *The Mind's Eye: Art and Theological Argument in the Middle Ages*, edited by Jeffrey F. Hamburger and Anne-Marie Bouché. Princeton: Princeton University Press, 2006. 263–86.

———. *Sister of Wisdom: St. Hildegard's Theology of the Feminine, with a New Preface, Bibliography, and Discography*. Berkeley: University of California Press, 1987.

O'Carroll, Michael. *'Corpus Christi': An Encyclopedia of the Eucharist*. Wilmington, DE: Michael Glazier Books, 1988.

O'Daly, Gerard J. P. *Augustine's Philosophy of Mind*. Berkeley: University of California Press, 1987.

232   *This Is My Body*

O'Donovan, Oliver. " 'Usus' and 'Fruitio' in Augustine, 'De Doctrina Christiana I.' " *The Journal of Theological Studies*. New Series. 33, no. 2 (1982): 361–97.

Oliviera, Bernardo. "Aspects of Love of Neighbor in the Spiritual Doctrine of St. Bernard (1)." CSQ 26, no. 2 (1991): 107–19.

Olphe-Galliard, M. "Les sens spirituels dans l'histoire de la spiritualité." In *Nos sens et Dieu, Études carmélitaines*. Bruges: Desclée De Brouwer, 1954. 179–93.

The Oxford Dictionary of the Christian Church. Ed. F. L. Cross and E. A. Livingstone. 2nd ed. Oxford: Oxford University Press, 1974.

Pastor, Ludwig von. *The History of the Popes*. Trans. E. F. Peeler. St. Louis: Herder, 1949.

Penco, Gregorio. "La dottrina dei sensi spirituali in Gregorio Magno." *Benedictina* 17 (1970): 161–201.

Pépìn, J. "Une nouvelle source de Saint Augustin: le zētēma de Porphyre sur l'union de l'âme et du corps." *Revue des études anciennes* 66 (1964): 53–107.

Peters, Ursula. *Religiöse Erfahrung als literarisches Faktum: zur Vorgeschichte und Genese frauenmystischer Texte des 13. und 14. Jahrhunderts*. Tübingen: Niemeyer, 1988.

Pickstock, Catherine. *After Writing: On the Liturgical Consummation of Philosophy*. Oxford: Blackwell Publishers, 1998.

Pike, Nelson. *Mystic Union: An Essay in the Phenomenology of Mysticism*. Cornell Studies in the Philosophy of Religion. Ithaca, NY: Cornell University Press, 1992.

Pontenay de Fontette, Micheline de. *Les religieuses à l'âge classique du droit canon*. Paris: J. Vrin, 1967.

Poor, Sara S. *Mechthild of Magdeburg and her Book: Gender and the Making of Textual Authority*. Middle Ages Series. Philadelphia: University of Pennsylvania Press, 2004.

Posset, Franz. "*Christi Dulcedo*: The 'Sweetness of Christ' in Western Christian Thought." CSQ 30, no. 3 (1995): 143–78.

Power, David Noel. *The Eucharistic Mystery: Revitalizing the Tradition*. New York: Crossroad, 1993.

Quenardel, Olivier. *La communion eucharistique dans* Le Héraut de L'Amour Divin *de sainte Gertrude d'Helfta: situation, acteurs et mise en scène de la divina pietas*. Turnhout: Brepols, 1997.

Rahner, Karl. "The Doctrine of the Spiritual Senses in the Middle Ages: The Contribution of Bonaventure." In *Experience of the Spirit: Source of Theology.* Theological Investigations, 16. New York: Crossroad, 1979. 109–28.

———. "The 'Spiritual Senses' According to Origen." In *Experience of the Spirit: Source of the Theology.* Theological Investigations, 16. New York: Crossroad, 1979. 81–103.

Rayez, André. "La mystique féminine et l'humanité du Christ." In *Dictionnaire de spiritualité ascétique et mystique, doctrine et histoire,* edited by Marcel Villler, et al. Paris: Beauchesne, 1937.

Ringler, Siegfried. *Viten- und Offenbarungsliteratur in Frauenklöstern des Mittelalters: Quellen und Studien.* Münchener Texte und Untersuchungen zur deutschen Literatur des Mittelalters. Bd. 72. Munich: Artemis Verlag, 1980.

Rubin, Miri. *Corpus Christi: The Eucharist in Late Medieval Culture.* Cambridge: Cambridge University Press, 1991.

Rudy, Gordon. *Mystical Language of Sensation in the Later Middle Ages.* Studies in Medieval History and Culture, 14. New York: Routledge, 2002.

Ruh, Kurt. *Geschichte der abendländischen Mystik.* Munich: Beck, 1990.

Santiso, Maria Teresa Porcile. "Saint Gertrude and the Liturgy." *Liturgy* 26, no. 3 (1992): 53–84.

Schindele, Pia. "Elemente der Benediktinerregel in den Offenbarungen der heiligen Gertrud von Helfta." In *Und sie folgten der Regel St. Benedikts: die Cistercienser und das benediktinische Monchtum: Eine Würdigung des abendländischen Mönchsvaters als Nachlese zum Benediktusjubiläum 1980,* edited by Ambrosius Schneider with Adam Wienand. Cologne: Wienand, 1981. 156–68.

Schmitt, Miriam. "Freed to Run with Expanded Heart: The Writings of Gertrud of Helfta and RB." CSQ 25, no. 3 (1990): 219–32.

———. "Gertrud of Helfta: Her Monastic Milieu (1256–1301) and her Spirituality." In *Cistercian Monastic Women—Hidden Springs.* CS 113. Kalamazoo, MI: Cistercian Publications, 1995. 3:471–96.

Scholl, Edith. "Sweetness of the Lord: Dulcis and Suavis." CSQ 27, no. 4 (1992): 359–66.

———. *Words for the Journey: A Monastic Vocabulary.* MW 21. Collegeville, MN: Cistercian Publications, 2009.

234   *This Is My Body*

Schrader, Franz. "Die Zisterzienserkloster in den mittelalterlichen Diözesen Magdeburg und Halberstadt." *Cîteaux: commentarii cistercienses* 21 (1970): 265–78.

Schwalbe, Johanna. "Musik in der Mystik: Zur Sprache der Musik in den Schriften der hl. Gertrud von Helfta." *Erbe und Auftrag* 71 (1995): 108–24.

Sears, Elizabeth. "Sensory Perception and its Metaphors in the Time of Richard of Fournival." In *Medicine and the Five Senses*, edited by W. F. Bynum and Roy Porter. Cambridge: Cambridge University Press, 1993. 17–39.

Siegel, Rudolph E. *Galen on Sense Perception: His Doctrines, Observations and Experiments on Vision, Hearing, Smell, Taste, Touch and Pain, and their Historical Sources.* Basel: Karger, 1970.

Simons, Walter. *Cities of Ladies: Beguine Communities in the Medieval Low Countries, 1200–1565.* Middle Ages Series. Philadelphia: University of Pennsylvania Press, 2001.

Sommerfeldt, John R. "Bernard on Charismatic Knowledge: The Truth as Gift." CSQ 32, no. 3 (1997): 295–301.

———. "The Intellectual Life According to St. Bernard." *Cîteaux* 25 (1974): 249–56.

———. *The Spiritual Teachings of Bernard of Clairvaux.* CF 125. Kalamazoo, MI: Cistercian Publications, 1991.

Soskice, Janet Martin. "Sight and Vision in Medieval Christian Thought." In *Vision in Context: Historical and Contemporary Perspectives on Sight,* edited by Teresa Brenna and Martin Jay. New York and London: Routledge, 1996. 29–43.

Spitzlei, Sabine. *Erfahrungsraum Herz: Zur Mystik des Zisterzienserinnenklosters Helfta im 13. Jahrhundert.* Stuttgart-Bad Canstatt: Frommann-Holzboog, 1991.

Stephens, Rebecca. "The Word Translated: Incarnation and Carnality in Gertrude the Great." *Magistra* 7, no. 1 (Summer 2001): 67–84.

Stock, Brian. "Experience, Praxis, Work and Planning in Bernard of Clairvaux: Observations on the Sermones in Cantica." In *The Cultural Context of Medieval Learning: Proceedings of the First International Colloquium on Philosophy, Science, and Theology in the Middle Ages, September 1973,* edited by John Emory Murdoch. Boston Studies in the Philosophy of Science, 26. Dordrecht, The Netherlands: D. Reidel, 1973. 219–61.

Sweetman, Robert. "Christine of St. Trond's Preaching Apostolate." *Vox Benedicta* 9 (1992): 67–99.

Thompson, Sally. "The Problem of Cistercian Nuns in the Twelfth and Early Thirteenth Centuries." In *Medieval Women*, edited by Derek Baker. Oxford: Blackwell, 1978. 227–53.

Tobin, Frank J. "Audience, Authorship and Authority in Mechthild von Magdeburg's 'Flowing Light of the Godhead.'" *Mystics Quarterly* 23, no. 1 (March 1997): 8–17.

———. "Hierarchy and Ponerarchy: Mechthild von Magdeburg's Visual Representations of Spiritual Orders." In *Nu lôn' ich iu der gâbe: Festschrift for Francis G. Gentry*, edited by Ernst Ralf Hintz. Göppingen: Kümmerle Verlag, 2003. 241–53.

———. *Mechthild von Magdeburg: A Medieval Mystic in Modern Eyes.* 1st ed. Columbia, SC: Camden House, 1995.

———. "Medieval Thought on Visions and its Resonance in Mechthild von Magdeburg's *Flowing Light of the Godhead*." In *The Mystical Gesture: Essays on Medieval and Early Modern Spiritual Culture in Honor of Mary E. Giles*, edited by Robert Boenig. Burlington, NY, and London: Ashgate, 2000. 41–53.

Tørjesen, Karen Jo. *Hermeneutical Procedure and Theological Structure in Origen's Exegesis.* Patristische Texte und Studien, Bd. 28. Berlin: De Gruyter, 1986.

Vagaggini, Cyprian. "The Example of a Mystic: St. Gertrude and Liturgical Spirituality." In *Theological Dimensions of the Liturgy*. Collegeville, MN: Liturgical Press, 1976. 740–803.

———. "La Dévotion au Sacré Coeur Chez Sainte Mechtilde et Sainte Gertrud." In *Cor Jesu*. Rome: Herder, 1959. 29–48.

Van Engen, John. "The Christian Middle Ages as an Historiographical Problem." *American Historical Review* 91 (1986): 519–52.

Vernet, Felix. "Gertrude la Grande." In *Dictionnaire de theologie catholique*, vol. 6. Paris: Letouzey, 1909–1950.

Voaden, Rosalyn. "All Girls Together: Community, Gender, and Vision at Helfta." In *Medieval Women and Their Communities*, edited by Diane Watt. Toronto: University of Toronto Press, 1997. 72–91.

Von Balthasar, Hans Urs. *The Glory of the Lord: A Theological Aesthetics.* Edited by John Riches. Trans. Andrew Louth and Francis McDonagh. Studies in Theological Style, 2. San Francisco: Ignatius Press, 1982.

Von Balthasar, Hans Urs, ed. *Origen, Spirit and Fire: A Thematic Anthology of His Writings*. Washington, DC: Catholic University of America Press, 1984.

Voss-Roberts, Michelle. *Dualities: A Theology of Difference*. Louisville, KY: Westminster John Knox Press, 2010.

Watson, Gerald. "St. Augustine, the Platonists, and the Resurrection Body: Augustine's Use of a Fragment from Porphyry." *Irish Theological Quarterly* 50 (1983/84): 222–32.

Wengier, Francis J. *The Eucharist-Sacrifice*. Milwaukee, WI: The Bruce Publishing Co., 1955.

Wiethaus, Ulrike. *Maps of Flesh and Light: The Religious Experience of Medieval Women Mystics*. 1st ed. Syracuse, NY: Syracuse University Press, 1993.

———. "Suffering, Love and Transformation in Mechthild of Magdeburg." *Listening* 22 (1987): 139–57.

Winter, Gabriele. "Die Herz-Jesu-Mystik bei Mechthild von Magdeburg, Mechthild von Hackeborn, und Gertrud von Helfta." *Jahrbuch für Salesianische Studien* 17 (1981): 72–82.

Zinn, Maxine Baca, and Bonnie Thornton Dill. "Theorizing Difference from Multiracial Feminism." *Feminist Studies* 22 (1996): 321–31.

Index of Scriptural References

References are cited by page number and, when appropriate, notes in which they appear.

General Index

11; 5–7 and n. 23; 11–14 nn. 44,
48, 49, 56, 58; 16–18 n. 66; 21,
22 and n. 80; 24–56 *passim*, 60
and n. 11; 98, 99, 103 nn. 18–19;
108–10 and nn. 32, 33; 112
n. 35; 114 n. 42; 115 nn. 47, 50;
118 n. 55; 131, 137 n. 5; 149
n. 38; 152–56 and nn. 50, 51,
54, 58, 59; 163, 170 n. 24; 173
n. 35; 177 n. 49; 180 n. 57; 187
n. 76; 192, 193, 198 n. 13; 200,
201–12 *passim*, 213, 214, 217–
26, 228, 231–36
Hildegard of Bingen, xv, xvi, xxi,
19, 20 and n. 72; 109 n. 32; 160
and n. 2; 179 and n. 53; 180,
191, 196, 198, 215, 225, 231
holocaust, 114, 149, 150
honey, 4, 5, 16, 94, 97, 106, 121,
124, 129, 131, 143
Host, xvii n. 9; 11 n. 44; 21, 23,
37–41, 49, 104–6 and n. 21; 108,
114, 116, 117, 119–23 and n. 60;
125–28 and n. 71; 131, 132, 143,
147, 159, 174, 175, 178, 181,
186–90 and n. 86; 194, 199, 203,
207, 208, 226
Hugh of St. Victor, 16, 17, 97
human, xxi and n. 14, 4, 6, 10, 11,
20, 57, 58, 61, 62, 63, 68, 69
n. 46; 70 n. 52; 73, 74, 77, 79,
82 n. 90; 86–88, 91 n. 128; 93
n. 140; 97, 98, 101–5, 107, 109,
111, 112, 114–16, 121–25, 128,
132, 133, 140–44, 146, 147, 150,
151, 154, 156, 158, 172, 173,
175–77 and n. 49; 181, 182, 185,
187, 191, 194–96 and n. 4; 199,
200, 205, 212, 219, 228, 229
humanity (*humanitas*), vii, 64, 68,
73, 75, 78–80, 86, 87, 89, 112

and n. 38; 123, 127, 132, 133,
143, 144, 147, 159–61 and n. 2;
169, 181, 187, 194, 212
humanity (*humanitas*) of Christ,
xx, xxi and n. 14; 19–21, 23, 39
n. 49; 86, 100, 104–8, 114, 128,
129, 136–38 and n. 2; 141, 143,
144, 149 n. 38; 158–61, 174, 175,
182, 183, 186, 187, 189, 191, 192,
195, 199, 202, 203, 205, 209, 212,
218, 220, 222
humility, xvii n. 8; 40, 88 n. 115;
110 n. 33; 217

inner man, *see* man

Johnson, Ella, 47 n. 80; 103 n. 18;
118 n. 55; 138 n. 7; 180 n. 57;
198 n. 13; 209 n. 51; 226
join(s), joined, joining, 19, 21, 29,
30, 53, 79, 105, 107, 108, 132,
174, 182, 189
Jones, Claire Taylor, xvii and n. 8;
11 n. 44; 137 n. 5; 187 n. 76;
189 and nn. 81–83; 226

kiss(es), 37 n. 42; 114, 121, 157, 158,
171–73

Lewis, Gertrud Jaron, ix, xiv, xvii
n. 6; xvii n. 8; 9 and nn. 35, 40;
10 and n. 42; 54 n. 103; 100–104
and nn. 5, 11, 16, 19, 21, 23;
112 n. 38; 131 n. 85; 133 n. 89;
137 n. 5; 162 n. 6; 163 nn. 8–9;
167, 168 n. 22; 177 n. 49; 189
n. 85; 214, 228
light(ed), 4, 15, 18, 66 n. 36, 72, 80,
101, 106, 109–11 and n. 34; 115,
116, 120, 125, 133 n. 89; 141, 146,
152, 156, 193, 195 n. 3; 220, 236